VITAL SIGNS

LITERATURE IN HISTORY

SERIES EDITORS

David Bromwich, James Chandler, and Lionel Gossman

The books in this series study literary works in the
context of the intellectual conditions, social
movements, and patterns of action
in which they took shape.

Other books in the series:

Alexander Welsh, *The Hero of the Waverly Novels*
(revised edition, forthcoming)

David Quint, *Epic and Empire* (forthcoming)

VITAL SIGNS

MEDICAL REALISM IN
NINETEENTH-CENTURY FICTION

Lawrence Rothfield

PRINCETON UNIVERSITY PRESS

PRINCETON, NEW JERSEY

COPYRIGHT © 1992 BY PRINCETON UNIVERSITY PRESS
PUBLISHED BY PRINCETON UNIVERSITY PRESS, 41 WILLIAM STREET,
PRINCETON, NEW JERSEY 08540
IN THE UNITED KINGDOM: PRINCETON UNIVERSITY PRESS, OXFORD

LIBRARY OF CONGRESS CATALOGING-IN-PUBLICATION DATA

ROTHFIELD, LAWRENCE, 1956–
VITAL SIGNS : MEDICAL REALISM IN
NINETEENTH-CENTURY FICTION/LAWRENCE ROTHFIELD.
P.   CM. — (LITERATURE IN HISTORY)
INCLUDES BIBLIOGRAPHICAL REFERENCES AND INDEX
ISBN 0-691-06896-8
1. ENGLISH FICTION—19TH CENTURY—
HISTORY AND CRITICISM.   2. MEDICINE IN LITERATURE.
3. FRENCH FICTION—19TH CENTURY—HISTORY AND CRITICISM.
4. LITERATURE, COMPARATIVE—ENGLISH AND FRENCH.
5. LITERATURE, COMPARATIVE—FRENCH AND ENGLISH.
6. PHYSICIANS IN LITERATURE.   7. REALISM IN LITERATURE.
I. TITLE.   II. SERIES: LITERATURE IN HISTORY (PRINCETON, N.J.).

PR868.M42R68   1992   823′.809356—DC20   91-29831

THIS BOOK HAS BEEN COMPOSED IN LINOTRON BASKERVILLE

PRINCETON UNIVERSITY PRESS BOOKS ARE PRINTED
ON ACID-FREE PAPER, AND MEET THE GUIDELINES FOR
PERMANENCE AND DURABILITY OF THE COMMITTEE ON
PRODUCTION GUIDELINES FOR BOOK LONGEVITY
OF THE COUNCIL ON LIBRARY RESOURCES

PRINTED IN THE UNITED STATES OF AMERICA

1   3   5   7   9   10   8   6   4   2

To My Parents

CONTENTS

ACKNOWLEDGMENTS

DURING THIS BOOK'S long passage into print, I have had a great deal of intellectual, moral, and material support. Edward Said, Lennard Davis, Nancy K. Miller, and Robert Paxton read parts of the book in its original form—as a Columbia University doctoral dissertation—and I am indebted to each of them for encouragement and advice. My dissertation research was supported in part by a fellowship from the Whiting Foundation.

I soon realized that writing the book I had in mind would require a substantial revision and broadening of the scope of my dissertation. In carrying out that latter project, I was not, fortunately, left entirely to my own devices. William Veeder, Ronald Thomas, and the graduate students in the Workshop on Nineteenth-Century Literature offered useful advice at an early stage of my revision. I am grateful as well to George Stocking and Jan Goldstein, who invited me to participate in the Workshop in the History of the Human Sciences (WHHS). The papers presented at the WHHS opened my eyes to the ferment in the interdisciplinary field I was exploring, and I benefited as well from the cameraderie with social scientists and from the discussions of my own work, including an early version of one of the chapters in this book. The same could be said about my stay at the Wesleyan University Center for the Humanities, made possible by a Mellon Foundation Fellowship. I am especially grateful to Richard Ohmann, Michael Sprinker, Thomas Ryckman, Khachig Tololyan, and Henry Abelove for their critical responses to drafts of several chapters in this book.

I owe Jonathan Arac a special debt of gratitude for his intellectual generosity and support for this project at several stages in its development. James Chandler, David Bromwich, and Lionel Gossman, who all read the manuscript for Princeton University Press, made judicious suggestions for revision, almost all of which I adopted. And finally, to my wife, Penelope, I owe—in addition to several hundred hours of babysitting—the deepest debt of all.

PREFACE

THIS BOOK starts from a sense of the inadequacy of critical efforts to define that elusive yet indispensable category of nineteenth-century fiction, "realism." Whether evaluated positively (as it is by Harry Levin and George Levine, as well as by Georg Lukács and Fredric Jameson) or pejoratively (as it is by Roland Barthes and Stephen Heath), *realism* over the last half-century has generally been taken as a synonym for *representation*, that is, as a joining of—or for some critics, a split between—words and things, conventions and reality, signifier and signified, or soul and form. Consequently, arguments about realism have tended to trail off into the sterile question of whether realism goes beyond conventions, forms, or signifiers to represent reality "adequately"; or whether realism is merely the literary expression of a "naïve" philosophical assumption that the words in a realistic novel are transparent to a reality they represent; or whether realism on the contrary is an effort to achieve a fresh, defamiliarized vision of reality by breaking down conventions through parody, dialogization, or the mixing of styles.

To go beyond this impasse without altogether abandoning realism as a category in literary history, we need to rethink the entire issue of realism in terms other than those of a problematic of representation, of the relation between words and things, signifiers and signifieds, conventions and reality. The way to do this, I believe, is to take seriously Bakhtin's assertion that the novel is woven out of discourses (rather than out of signifiers or conventions). If the novel is a texture woven out of discourse, then one ought to be able to describe particular novelistic genres (the realistic novel, the naturalist novel, the sensation novel, the modernist novel, the detective story, and so on) not by their implicit theories of representation—or of the impossibility of achieving representation, as is often said of modernist fiction—but by the kinds of discourses, and the relations between discourses, that predominate in each genre. The result of such a description will be to give a more local precision to the "real" of the realistic novel: a real that can then be aligned to the "real" offered by the specific discourses that novelists like Balzac, Flaubert, and Eliot adapt in distinctive ways.

This book has much in common with what has come to be called the "new historicism" in nineteenth-century studies. Like such critics as D. A. Miller, Mark Seltzer, Jonathan Arac, and Catherine Gallagher, I set out to show how fiction is linked to hitherto overlooked but nonetheless powerfully institutionalized discourses operating within a culture. But I think the new historicist enterprise will remain unachieved so long as certain questions are left conveniently vague. The most important of these is the question of how the relationship between discourse and power should be understood. To both Seltzer and Miller, for example, discourses in the novel seem to exist only as a *pretext* for the power that is exercised through them; both critics tend to subsume the intricacies of criminology or moral management or sociology under the more fundamental phenomenon that Miller calls a "general economy of policing."[1] I argue that this view of power is, if not mistaken, at the very least oversimplified. The problem is not that power actually has nothing to do with discourse (whether in a novel or in a culture), but rather that power is immanent in the particular discourses through which it functions. If a literary phenomenon such as realism emerges from a given cultural situation, we need to interpret it not by treating what goes on in a realistic novel as an allegory of the "general economy" of power, but by identifying the specific discourses that are woven into the novel and tracing them in the culture at large back to their disciplinary precincts, the local sites where they exercise their power. Only by proceeding in this way, I think, can one hope to understand the cultural struggles in which these discourses engage and the role the novel can play in such struggles.

I propose in *Vital Signs* to interpret works of fiction within a cultural context that is first and foremost a discursive one. Such an approach avoids oversimplification, but raises problems of its own. How does one decide which discourses might be reasonable starting points in the case of realistic fiction? In principle, a novel can accommodate anything from scientific jargon and professional argot to street slang and religious cant. Analyzing all, or even a substantial portion, of these discursive threads would be a hopeless task. To trace even a single thread through a series of novels and within the larger culture, on the other hand, would no doubt yield some insight into the texture of realism, even if that thread were only adventitiously woven into the texture. The problem, then, is a pragmatic one: which discourse offers the best *Ansatzpunkt* (to borrow Auerbach's word), the most fruitful point of departure? My choice has been deliberately to restrict this study to a single discourse whose network of relations I want to explore: that of nineteenth-century clinical medicine. As I point out in chapter one, clinical discourse seems attractive for several reasons. First, this medicine's characteristics—its rhetorical rules, its objects of knowledge, its aspirations, and its historical emergence, transformation, displacement, and decline—have been detailed by intellectual and social historians over the last ten years. Clinical medicine is also the professional discipline most visibly striving for recognition as a liberal profession in a period when professional values and aspirations begin to dominate European culture. The result is that clinical discourse becomes saturated with a special kind of quasi-avant-garde cultural (and even political) authority at the very moment when Balzac, Flaubert, and Eliot invent their versions of realism.[2] Finally, clinical discourse is present prima facie in important although often unremarked ways in two novels that are often taken to be paradigms of realism, *Middlemarch* and *Madame Bovary*, and medicine in general has been associated with mimesis by literary theorists going back to Plato (although this association has also largely gone unremarked).

To assert that a given discourse is relevant to a literary form, however, does not tell us anything about how that discourse's status within literature might be described. This constitutes a second methodological problem. In what ways can a discourse enter into and inhabit a literary form? Can we conclude that a novel relies on clinical discourse, for instance, only if the novel explicitly invokes its terminology? Or can a discourse help to shape such formal features as point of view, characterization, description, diegesis, or closure, even in the absence of terminology? I argue that one can define medical discourse as a set of "archaeological" (rather than purely logical) conditions—a set of practical cognitive rules or presuppositions about the structure of the living body (and, by extension, of the self), the nature of symptoms, and the temporal development of disease. The chapter on *Madame Bovary* illustrates, in turn, how completely the novel can appropriate those diagnostic presuppositions with the effect of "medicalizing" the real it represents.

Just as realism is more than the sum of its formal categories or techniques, however, so clinical medicine is more than a set of diagnostic assumptions or therapeutic methods. In both cases, the formal elements operate in history within an overall project to enforce a certain kind of authority. For the clinician, this authority is illustrated by his ability to convince others that a person is more truly defined as hysterical rather than, say, evil or possessed; as an alcoholic rather than a drunk; as obese rather than fat; as suffering from the pathology called homosexuality rather than committing the sin called sodomy. Insofar as novelists use clinical presuppositions, they also exploit this capacity to define the relation of self to body as a medical one. But such epistemologically grounded authority cannot simply be assimilated to the power of the police, because it is itself the object of a continuing struggle, a serious dialogue over what should count as true (or even potentially true) when one speaks about human subjects as embodied. I am making no argument one way or another about whether medicine is a science in the abstract, but I am suggesting instead that the history of medicine's status as a science needs to be elucidated. For within English and French cultures, clinical medicine vies, sometimes anxiously, with both scientifically accredited and nonscientific discourses for the authority to define the problems of life and mind (to borrow Lewes's terms), and this micropolitics of knowledge manifests itself in the novel's discontents as well. I try in my chapter on *Middlemarch* to show what was at stake in such contests.

In the course of identifying precisely what clinical discourse is and analyzing how it is situated within culture and the novel, this book inevitably raises the question: why medicine? Why should this discourse serve as a peculiar clue to the authority of realism in literature? Why did realists not choose legal or religious or moral or biological discourse—utilitarianism, say, or zoology, or methodism? Beyond its discursive techniques and its epistemic orientation, I suggest, clinical medicine also offered Balzac, Flaubert, Eliot, and James an ideology of professional exactitude, an ideology that was extremely useful to novelists when new conditions of the marketplace enabled writers to picture themselves as self-sufficient professionals. My chapter on Balzac stresses this ideological element of the connection between medicine and literature. More generally, I argue that the emergence, development, and decline of realism as an authoritative literary praxis can be tied to the vicissitudes of clinical medicine as an ideal profession.[3] As clinical medicine comes under epistemic attack from other sciences, and as it becomes institutionalized, its attractiveness as a radical model fades. One effect is the development, in the latter part of the century, of quasi-realistic genres such as detective fiction and naturalism. In chapters six and seven, I show how exemplary writers in each of these genres revise the medical perspective's literary status in distinct ways, and with distinctive effects: Zola by substituting Claude Bernard's "experimental medicine"—a thoroughly deterministic physiological model—for that of clinical medicine; Conan Doyle by allocating the realist discourse to the pompous but unimpressive professional voice of Dr. Watson, while transferring all the prestige of truth to Holmes's deductive (and far from healing) methods.

Ultimately, I suggest, the decline of medicine's epistemic and ideological authority—caused by the rise of the "basic" life sciences and the consolidation of medicine as a safe and unexciting bourgeois career—is one of the conditions that make possible the rise of a new kind of literary practice: modernism. Rather than see modernism as an effort somehow to go "beyond representation," my perspective offers a definition of modernism as responding antithetically to the clinical mode of representation characteristic of realism. Modernist texts, I argue, may be understood as efforts to invert the technical, epistemic, or ideological assumptions that writers such as Conrad, Joyce, and Kafka inherit from clinical realism. Those who continue to produce realistic fiction register the compromised status of their own authority either in formal incoherencies (as with Arnold Bennett in *Riceyman Steps*) or by the restricted view of the pathologized world they represent (as with Mann in *The Magic Mountain*). But they may also—as I suggest in a discussion of James's *Wings of the Dove*—redefine the real itself, within which medical techniques continue to operate, as a real that is no longer a matter of the body. James displaces the cognitive object of realism while retaining realism's clinical aims. In so doing he creates a fiction incomprehensible for a history that understands modernism as a reaction against realist representation, even as he abandons the particular signified, the body, at which realism's clinical representation had been directed.

I will be using the terms *realism* and *medicine* with reference to a relatively limited set of British and French novels and medical practices. In principle, however, my argument should be applicable not only to those particular novels and practices but to a much larger number of novels, as well as other kinds of art associated with the phenomenon of "critical realism" from other national traditions both literary and medical. But I was not interested in writing an encyclopedic narrative history of the enmeshing of medicine with European culture. There already exist excellent cultural surveys of medical themes (doctor-patient relationships through the ages, the cultural impact of certain specific diseases such as cholera and plague, illness as metaphor), and in any case a narrative history did not seem an appropriate mode for exploring what interested me most about the topic: the polymorphic nexus of information, ideas, and interests that constitute medicine as an art, a science, and a profession. There still remained, however, the problem of limiting an enormous archive to manageable proportions, and more important, creating some sort of intellectual order within that set of materials.

My starting point has been to limit myself geographically and temporally to the British and French cultural experience of clinical medicine during the nineteenth century. Within this experience I have sought to define medicine as a social as well as an intellectual practice. I have further limited my archival scope by focusing on the interchange between nineteenth-century medicine and the Anglo-French tradition of literary realism. This narrowing inevitably eliminates a large part of the literary, not to mention the cultural, resonance of medicine during this period. Most obvious, I have chosen not to discuss in any detail the rich Russian cultural appropriation of medicine in the work of such writers as Chekhov, Turgenev, Tolstoy, and Dostoevsky, or the equally rich Germanic tradition involving Heine, Goethe, and Mann—not because these literary traditions are unimportant, but because the *medical* traditions of Germany and Russia are in many ways derivative of the British and French experience. In the general process of professionalization that medicine so spectacularly exemplifies, France and Britain unquestionably led the way. Moreover, the dynamics of this process in France and Britain can be seen in "purer" forms than in Germany and Russia, where the uneven development of civil society somewhat obscures the ideological and social distinctiveness of professionalism. Then too, the sheer quality, consistency, and mass of French and British medical—and in particular clinical—work during the first half of the nineteenth century lifts it above that done by German and Russian physicians. The clinical perspective arises first in Paris, organized in large part by the paradigms of pathological anatomy (for the body) and "moral treatment" (for mental illness) that were developed by Bichat, Cabanis, Dupuytren, Broussais, Pinel, and Georget. It spreads rapidly to Britain (through such mediums as phrenological societies and the avant-garde medical journal *The Lancet*), eventually working eastward into Germany and Russia. The history of American medicine during the nineteenth century is so different, both in professional and in intellectual conditions, as to constitute an entirely separate field of inquiry.[4]

After narrowing down the field in this way, I still confronted a large set of realistic novels, not to mention voluminous archives of medical materials. It seemed prudent to begin by focusing on novelists who had declared their own styles to be medical, and to look particularly closely at important novels where medical issues are explicitly broached to some extent. A purely thematic approach to the medical content in these novels would be valuable in itself, opening onto important cultural issues relating to the doctor's social status and professional role as well as the patient's relative subjugation or interpellation through stereotyping (an especially vital concern for feminism, given the preponderance of women who are labeled "sick" in nineteenth-century fiction and culture). But my goal was to define realism as a literary mode beyond any particular content. I was less interested in demonstrating how novels reflect social relations than in showing how (and accounting for why) certain kinds of fiction and certain formations of knowledge may enact similar strategies, construct similar kinds of subjects, exert similar kinds of authority. The presence of doctors and/or patients in *Middlemarch* or *Wings of the Dove* was thus for my purposes a matter of convenience rather than of necessity, helpful insofar as the doctor-patient relationship stands as an emblem for the less manifest and more fundamental relationship between writer and text. Medicine gives a novelist not only a stock of characters but a set of quasi-artistic techniques, including, for example, a specifically symptomatological semiology, and the novelist can use those techniques to represent not only doctors and patients, but other characters and plots within these novels. Not only Emma, but Charles and Rodolphe are pathologically embodied selves in *Madame Bovary*; Lydgate's predicament in *Middlemarch* is not his alone, but also Eliot's, and to some extent also Bulstrode's and Dorothea's and Will's. Moreover, insofar as Balzac, Flaubert, and Eliot can be taken as paradigmatic realists, one should be able to find some of these same techniques at work in other realistic novels where doctors and patients do not appear as such or appear only at the margins of the story.

Not only prudence, however, but also methodological imperatives have determined my decision to concentrate on a few key novels, if only because of the constraints that an archaeological approach places on reading. To disarticulate medical prescriptions from the mixture of discourses inscribed in such novels, I have proceeded deliberately, focusing first on particularities of characterization and description, sifting the text for evidence that a medical technique—a method of diagnosis, a conception of internal structure, a set of nosological terms—has been employed. From this detailed work, in each case, I have tried to reconstruct the precise medical paradigm upon which the novelist in question relies. Only then have I turned from discursive to social context, in order to situate culturally this medical paradigm, by describing the kind and degree of authority each particular medical outlook implies. Having done this, I have ultimately returned to the novels, to ask how the novelist makes use of this medical authority to enhance his or her own literary authority. By taking the long way around I have tried to steer clear of the Scylla and Charybdis that threaten every historicist literary analysis: the dangers of historical inaccuracy in failing to specify the exact kind of techniques, assumptions, and outlook involved in a text; and of historical distortion in forcing a text into an inappropriate context.

VITAL SIGNS

ONE

MEDICINE AND MIMESIS

THE CONTOURS OF A CONFIGURATION

LES LIAISONS DANGEREUSES (1782) ends with a cascade of calamities: the deaths of the libertine Valmont and his virtuous victim, Mme. de Tourvel; Chevalier Danceny's withdrawal into celibacy as a Knight of Malta; and Mlle. de Volanges's incarceration in a convent. Crowning these disasters is the fate of the villainous Mme. de Merteuil, recounted by Mme. de Volanges in the last letter of Laclos's novel:

> Mme. de Merteuil's destiny seems at last accomplished, my dear and excellent friend; and it is such that her worst enemies are divided between the indignation she merits and the pity she inspires. I was indeed right to say that it would perhaps be fortunate for her if she died of her smallpox. She has recovered, it is true, but horribly disfigured; and particularly by the loss of one eye. You may easily imagine that I have not seen her again; but I am told she is positively hideous.
>
> The Marquis de . . . , who never misses the opportunity of saying a spiteful thing, speaking of her yesterday, said that her disease had turned her round and that now her soul is in her face. Unhappily, everyone thought the expression a very true one.[1]

As the comments of Mme. de Volanges and the anonymous Marquis indicate, Merteuil's sudden illness serves a quite restricted literary purpose. In disfiguring her, the smallpox offers Laclos's readers a legible figure of moral, social, and narrative closure, a "very true" representation of Merteuil's evil character that Laclos's narrative from its inception has promised but deferred. One might say, then, that at the moment when illness attaches itself to character, what Barthes has referred to as the "hermeneutic code" of *Les Liaisons* is laid bare. No more meaning remains hidden. The game of plotting and interpreting has come to an end, and the quest for the truth about Merteuil's character is complete, both for the "everyone" referred to by the Marquis and for Laclos's readers.

As for the smallpox itself, considered as a disease with symptoms and stages, causes and consequences, it interests Laclos not at all as a possible occasion for interpretation or further narration. On the contrary, in supplying an unequivocal truth, the smallpox puts an end to interpreting. As the outside of the hermeneutic dimension, Merteuil's illness also lies beyond the dimension of secular, experiential time projected in and through the novel.[2] Disfiguration, the manifestation of that illness, lacks any temporal compass and can thus punctuate but not participate in the dynamic of seduction, liaison, manipulation, and betrayal through which Laclos's characters become realized for themselves and for the novel's readers.

In subordinating illness to his narrative requirements as he does, Laclos is far from unique among seventeenth- and eighteenth-century novelists. The tendency to disjoin illness from the life of character is in fact a prevalent one during the period. This is not to say that early novelists introduce illness into their narratives only to mark the end of a character's development in a moment of blinding, quasi-Oedipal realization. On the contrary, the age swarms with characters—from Sterne's Uncle Toby to Diderot's Rameau's nephew to Goethe's Werther—for whom illness, far from appearing as a sudden stroke of fate, constitutes an abiding state of being, even to the extent that their sickness confers upon them an ongoing, often rather comfortable identity as eccentrics.[3] One might even go so far as to argue that this second literary use of illness is more fundamental, or at least more traditional, in the early novel. After all, the archetypal novelistic hero, Don Quixote, qualifies as such in large part because he suffers from what René Girard calls "ontological sickness."[4]

Such variation in the status of illness in fiction, taken together with the fact that so many writers during this period either actually practiced medicine (like Goldsmith) or were intensely and demonstrably interested in exploring medical issues in their literary work (like Diderot and Goethe), should make one wary of generalizing about the historical relation between medicine and the novel. And yet, just as a general distinction is often made between the representational practices of realism in eighteenth-century versus nineteenth-century novels, so one can also profitably distinguish between the literary status of illness in these two kinds of realistic fiction. Although qualifications and allowances for exceptions must of course be made, it seems generally accurate to say that early realists do not go beyond the two alternatives sketched above. In their fiction, illness tends to appear as either a fundamental ontological predicament or a punctual signal of innate moral inadeqacy. In neither case do novelists adopt what might be called a consistent *medical* view of their characters—that is, a view in which illness would be articulated along with, and as a means of illuminating, the developing life of an embodied self. Illness can register the essential truth about a character in early realism, but that truth does not emerge or evolve as an integrated aspect of narrative temporality. Characters in such novels *are* sick, but do not *become* sick over the time that the novel shapes.

If a medical view of character thus is not a constitutive feature of the first novels, the peculiarly occluded structural presence of illness in fiction of the period nevertheless points to a constitutive assumption of early realism: the notion that the truth about character (whether signaled in Merteuil's disfiguration or given as Quixote's monomania) ultimately is detachable from time and interpretation. This epistemological principle has been recognized as central to eighteenth-century realism at least since *The Rise of the Novel*, in which Ian Watt defines "formal" realism as the dominant literary mode of the first novels. Most readers come away from Watt's book with the sense that early realism's most important feature is its down-to-earth empirical orientation: Defoe, Richardson, and their contemporaries are shown to be striving to render a full report of human experience through the use of details—whether of time, space, or action—that serve to situate the individual in a particular present.[5] But as Watt's choice of the word *formal* rather than *empirical* or *reportorial* implies, this realism's verisimilitude—its assumption about what the truth in life is—does not include any sense of human life's historically concrete dimension. In formal realism, the truth about a character is tied to the details of his or her milieu, and to his or her actions, but neither details nor actions are caught up in an historical dynamic that might compromise or transform their meaning, making them more or less true (or true in a different way) depending on when and where they are represented.

Another way of putting all this is to say that in formal realism, action—whether by characters or by some other agency—does not affect the overall context within which truth is defined. Instead, as Watt shows, the early realistic novel moves from detail and action to the truth about a character by relying upon epistemological principles that find their clearest articulation in the philosophical speculations of Locke. Locke argues that the truthfulness of representations or "particular ideas" is permanently guaranteed by their empirical link to sensation. Thus, between representation and truth there is no problem or quarrel; the only possible danger to truth posed by representation is that posed by false representations, and Locke is confident that by appealing to sensation, even false representations can be unmasked. A character may manipulate representation, may let others take in earnest what he or she does in jest (as in *Moll Flanders*), may masquerade (as in *Les Liaisons*, most notably), but ultimately the truth about characters will manifest itself once and for all, beyond the touch of time, empirically revealed. This epistemological faith that truth can be reduced to a representation—what Michael McKeon has more recently called the "naïve empiricism" of formal realism—underlies and sustains characterization in the work of writers like Defoe, as Watt has demonstrated. To define a character authentically, Defoe describes the particular objects that surround the character, the particular chain of ideas that pass through that character's mind, and the sequential series of actions that involve the character. Each particular yields a truth, a truth as irrevocable as Mme. de Merteuil's lost eye. The result is that, as Georg Lukács puts it, "the contemporary world [in formal realism] is portrayed with unusual plasticity and truth-to-life, but is accepted naïvely as something given: whence and how it has developed have not yet become problems for the writer."[6]

Lukács's formulation ought to be taken with a grain of salt, for, in his eagerness to valorize what he calls the critical realism of the nineteenth century, he (like McKeon) rather too quickly labels formal realism as naïve because of its empiricist assumption that truth is something that could be reported. Moreover, Lukács fails to appreciate the extent to which critical realism—a literary mode developed most profoundly in the work of novelists such as Balzac, Dickens, Flaubert, Eliot, James, Tolstoy, and Mann—shares with formal realism this primary fascination with and belief in the possibility of documentation—what Harry Levin describes as "that willed tendency of art to approximate reality."[7] The will-to-mimesis marks both formal and critical realism, providing a fundamental element of continuity for any transhistorical theory of realism as a unified literary mode. On the other hand, Lukács is surely correct to assert that something in the mimetic project has been transformed between Fielding and Eliot, Defoe and James, Prévost and Flaubert. Compare, for instance, Laclos's concluding description of Merteuil's smallpox to Zola's description, on the last page of *Nana*, of the smallpox that has killed his heroine:

> Nana was left alone, her face upturned in the light from the candle. What lay on the pillow was a charnel-house, a heap of pus and blood, a shovelful of putrid flesh. The pustules had invaded the whole face, so that one pock touched the next. Withered and sunken, they had taken on the greyish colour of mud, and on that shapeless pulp, in which the features had ceased to be discernible, they already looked like mould from the grave. One eye, the left eye, had completely foundered in the bubbling purulence, and the other, which remained half open, looked like a dark, decaying hole. The nose was still suppurating. A large reddish crust starting on one of the cheeks was invading the mouth, twisting it into a terrible grin. And around this grotesque and horrible mask of death, the hair, the

beautiful hair, still blazed like sunlight and flowed in a stream of gold. Venus was decomposing. It was as if the poison she had picked up in the gutters, from the carcases left there by the roadside, that ferment with which she had poisoned a whole people, had now risen to her face and rotted it.[8]

What has changed between Laclos and Zola, most obviously, is the value attached to clinical detail, as if the truth Zola wishes to convey requires an almost microscopic precision about the material conditions of the body. What was for Laclos sufficiently defined by the phrase "disfigured . . . by the loss of an eye" demands from Zola an unblinking attention to the smallest features of that disfigurement. The richness of Zola's description of the diseased body, in turn, corresponds to his far more highly elaborated decoding of the disease's signficance. Zola's smallpox bears not only a moral but a sociological content, the disease referring less to an individual's essence than to the degeneration of an entire society. A deeper penetration into the empirical is accompanied by a dynamic conception of social change.

But it is not only that with Zola, disease is being used more explicitly in order to get at a truth that is now understood as primarily sociological. A structural transformation underlies these differences in the content and significance of disease. It is the very relation between disease and character, as more generally the relation between representation and meaning, that has been revised, that no longer matches a reportorial model as it did in Laclos's novel. Locke's epistemological principles, which could allow one to read Madame de Merteuil's disfiguration so comfortably, do not provide adequate grounds for getting at the truth of Nana's decomposition. For, unlike Merteuil's smallpox, which is said to have "turned her around," directly revealing its essence as her evil, Nana's disease emerges from an interior to a surface. Its possible significance therefore cannot be captured, as the meaning of Mertueil's disease is, in an epigram that moves immediately from the simple fact of disfigurement to the truth about character expressed by that disfigurement. On the contrary, Nana's smallpox must be represented not only in excruciatingly fine detail but in detail that emphasizes the temporality of the disease while reducing Nana's character to mere (or rather, sheer) flesh. And the significance drawn from this almost gratuitously precise detail can be articulated by Zola only indirectly, through metaphors and similes that only strain at being aphoristic. Zola's mimesis, in short, operates under an epistemological mandate different from Locke's.

Zola, of course, is something of an extreme case, and, as I shall go on to suggest, his "naturalism" ought to be differentiated as a distinct offshoot of what I will continue, following Lukács, to call the "critical" realism of Balzac, Flaubert, and Eliot. But the passage from *Nana* does illustrate the sea change that separates "formal" realism from its nineteenth-century cousin. Critics have long recognized the existence of some such discontinuity, and remaining faithful to Levin's credo that "the progress of realism can only be charted by its concurrent relationship to the history of ideas," they have naturally tried to establish a philosophical successor to Locke, some source for the elusive idea of "true" mimesis implicit in critical realism. Hegel, Comte, and Marx, among others, have been cited as providing principles of representation and knowledge adequate to account for the realism of their times, and each of these critical mappings of nineteenth-century epistemologies onto the novel has yielded some valuable insights into the work of particular realists. It ultimately has not proved possible, however, to orient the novelistic practice of writers as diverse as Balzac and Flaubert within any single philosophical system.

Indeed, the persistent failure of the history of ideas to provide an adequate contextual explanation for the phenomenon of critical realism leads one to question whether any such system common to nineteenth-century philosophy and literature actually exists. To raise this as a question is by no means to imply that Hegel, Marx, or Comte are any less concerned than Locke with issues of truth and mimesis. Rather, it is to suggest that the general relationship between philosophy and literary realism changes between Locke's time and Marx's. The rise of the novel occurs during an era when philosophy purports to offer a model of truth-conditions (the hypothesis of a general science of order, a mathesis) upon which truth-telling novels, as well as a number of other forms of knowledge, depend for their authority. Sometime near the end of the eighteenth century, however, a rearrangement—uneven, to be sure, and differently motivated within different national cultures, but forcefully registered by Kant's critiques—occurs within the hierarchy of knowledges. Between the noumenal world of metaphysical philosophy and the phenomenal world of the real, between the world of forms and the empirical world, the sciences are now understood to supervene.[9] These sciences may not provide us with philosophical or absolute knowledge, as Kant points out, but the knowledge they *do* provide, although limited by definition, nevertheless qualifies as true knowledge of the real.

The details of this profound epistemological transformation are of course open to debate, and need not concern us here. For our purposes, the important point is that given the emergence of the sciences as competitors to philosophy in the century following Kant, any account of the intellectual climate of nineteenth-century realism would be likely to benefit from a study of scientific, as opposed to strictly philosophical, notions of truth and principles of representation. How, one might ask to begin with, do the sciences define themselves as truthful representations of reality? And how might one relate scientific and literary ways of representing reality?

Over the past several years, such questions have been posed more frequently and pointedly, as literary critics concerned with realism have begun to focus on the formative role played by scientific theories of knowledge in realistic mimesis. George Levine's *The Realistic Imagination* is among the most important of recent works in the field, and as such exemplifies both the strengths and the limitations of current critical interest in scientific-literary relations. Levine convincingly demonstrates how the scientific controversies raging in Victorian culture dealt with epistemological issues in which such novelists as Mary Shelley, Eliot, and Conrad were also deeply interested. Yet in establishing a link between the scientific and the realistic imaginations, Levine still tends to focus on popularized *philosophical* discussions—albeit often by scientists—rather than on scientific discourse per se. The practical advantages of Levine's approach are manifest: instead of the unruly and often opaque contents of scientific archives, one deals with what are recognizably ideas—ideas, moreover, that circulate in a cultural context shared with novelists. (Many of the arguments Levine brings to our attention take place not in the pages of scientific journals but in such widely read magazines as *Blackwood's* or *Cornhill*.) There is a danger in this approach, however, of what one might call epistemological inaccuracy, insofar as what scientists say or do in a public forum may differ greatly from the actualities of their intellectual procedures as scientists. It is possible, in other words, that pragmatic scientific thinking and writing might entail concepts of truthfulness that scientists can articulate publicly only with difficulty because they speak in language borrowed from (and perhaps contaminated by) the philosophy of their day—or more often, of their fathers' day. In the case of the scientific milieu Levine discusses, for instance, the philosophies of science developed by Kant and Comte clearly provide both a vocabulary and an agenda of issues for scientists writing for the public.

Levine would probably defend his approach by arguing that most novelists in fact got their notions of science precisely from such philosophically refracted accounts available to them in the general culture, rather than from any direct experience of science. Certainly for most novelists it is the popular philosophy of science, rather than scientific discourse itself, that enters into their consciousness and consequently into their fiction. Dickens's notorious defense of the scientificity of spontaneous combustion, or the sensation novelists' reliance

upon concepts like *monomania*, or the social Darwinism of Samuel But-
ler and Hardy—these clearly stem from culturally mediated rather
than discrete scientific sources. Even in these cases, however, I would
argue that we blind ourselves to much of what constitutes the realism
of such novelists if we assume that their culturally received idea of
science accounts for the effect of the real that they achieve in deploying scientific rhetoric. There is no necessary connection between the
theory of realism—the notion of truth-to-life, whether connected to
science or not—invoked by such writers and the truth-effects sustained when these same writers make use of particular scientific lexi-
cons or presuppositions. Dickens's use of what George Lewes identifies as a pseudoscientific notion of spontaneous combustion does not
disqualify him as a realist, although Lewes tries to have him disqualified and Dickens then feels compelled to mount a defense of the truth-
value of his science and its compatibility with his realism. Similarly, a
novelist such as Collins may use popularized psychiatric concepts like
hereditary insanity or *monomania* in a confused way, but these concepts
nonetheless contribute, in ways worth thinking about, to the construction of the novel's sensationalistic reality.[10]

The limitations of seeing realism as rehearsing a popularized philosophy of science are, however, most evident if we turn to that group
of novelists for whom the relationship of realism to science is far more
intimate and rigorous. The novels of Balzac, Flaubert, and George
Eliot do more than incorporate culturally received ideas about science
(in fact, Flaubert and Eliot are overtly hostile to such received ideas);
they deploy coherent scientific vocabularies and authorities as well as
the methods and the specific problematics that are posed through
these vocabularies and authorities. As this book will try to show in
some detail, when a scientific figure such as the pathologist Xavier
Bichat is invoked along with his language of tissues in *Middlemarch* or
Madame Bovary, one ought not to mistake him as a stand-in for Kant or
Tyndall or Lewes, as a mere convenience enabling Flaubert or Eliot to
raise broad issues of free will and determinism in the local domain of
biology. Bichat is the founder of a new science, pathological anatomy,
and his way of seeing life and constructing truth has its own distinctive
complexity, its rarety (to borrow Foucault's word). We risk distorting
not only this complexity but also the complexity of Eliot's or Flaubert's
appropriation of Bichat, and ultimately the complexity of their realism, if we view him only through the lens of nineteenth-century epistemological controversies purveyed by the popularizers and philosophers of science.

It is helpful to distinguish among various types of science, for some
nineteenth-century sciences are more prone than others to accept,

and even participate in, the epistemological distortions of their work by popularizers and philosophers—biology or clinical medicine, for instance, more than mathematics or physics.[11] These latter disciplines, at least in their modern formations, have crossed what Foucault, following Kant, calls a "threshold of formalization" or mathematicization that gives them a certain degree of autonomy from philosophical issues of epistemology and mimesis.[12] For such sciences the questions asked by epistemologists and theorists of representation—what is the relation between representation and thing, sign and referent? how does one move from data to truth?—at a certain point become irrelevant. These sciences establish the truth or falsity of a statement on the basis of its internal consistency (whether logical, architectural, or even aesthetic, as in some contemporary fields of physics). Laws, equations, and theorems in the formalized sciences are not subject to variation in space or time, or if such variations emerge, the formalized sciences take them as part of their object of knowledge.

To say that the formalized sciences are fundamentally nonmimetic does not, of course, mean that they are irrelevant to the novel. Post-Einsteinian physics, for example, offers a constitutive model of structure and event, a vision of relations, that novelists from Pirandello to Borges to Barth have fictionalized with great intensity. But like the sciences they invoke, these fictions focus their attention not on a signified reality but on the generative capacity of their own techniques or logics.[13] Again, such formalized sciences may still furnish a culture, and the novelists within that culture, with analogies, metaphors, or schemas that are allegorically transposed onto social life, as with the principles of entropy or of the conservation of energy. But such borrowings announce themselves in novels as borrowings (or betray themselves as crude ideology) rather than as efforts to directly represent the real, as is.

On the other hand, the nineteenth century abounds in sciences whose procedures have not been formalized, and that thus can offer novelists a model of truth-seeking that is also a model of mimesis. These more dubious sciences include, among others, geography, medicine, biology, psychology, economics, linguistics—what the French call the human sciences. Such disciplines mobilize their techniques, concepts, and metaphors to represent a putatively real object, such as life, territory, disease, or labor, rather than a theoretically constituted object, such as a center of gravity or a magnetic moment. In Kant's words, the objects of these dubious sciences "are existing things which must be given empirically in order to be known, and not a mere representation in myself determined *a priori* according to a principle."[14] Because their objects seem to be *there*, such sciences tend to rely not on "mere representations"—abstract, self-instituted symbols—but on words related to things. As a result, their language, unlike that of the formalized sciences, forms a subset of everyday language in the post-Kantian world.[15]

Doubtless, this lower epistemological profile of the human sciences has facilitated the diffusion of terms, ideas, images, and outlook from such sciences into the general culture and into literature; the problem of translation is nowhere near as great as with the formalized sciences, where symbols and equations must be deciphered to become accessible. But precisely because the positive sciences are so implicated in culture, it is more difficult to distinguish the autonomous principles of representation, the epistemological figures, the precise relationships between words and things that such sciences establish. They are encrusted, as it were, with "quasi-" and "pseudo-" sciences (phrenology, physiognomy, criminology, or eugenics, to name a few) as well as with parasitical cultural formations (including such "-isms" as organicism, determinism, orientalism, or social Darwinism).[16] Given these interesting and complex adjacencies, together with the difficulties that would be involved in disarticulating a scientific discourse from its cultural instanciations, most literary critics understandably have veered away from studying the positive sciences themselves as rhetorical modes or techniques of representation. Thus we have had admirable discussions of how individual scientific terms, as well as the themes and disciplines mentioned above, move through literature, but far fewer discussions of how, say, the philological point of view, its way of representing man as a speaking being, is incorporated in certain novels as the point of view of a character, narrator, or author, or as a theme or even a stylistic imperative. Yet, if the argument I have been developing over the last few pages makes sense, then such a study of the discursive features of positive sciences might prove valuable, particularly for the realistic novel, that genre where the mimetic impulse is most deeply invested by claims to truthfulness.

One positive science, medicine, stands out as an especially attractive candidate for this type of interdiscursive investigation. For of those sciences mentioned above, medicine enjoys by far the closest and most long-standing association with the issues of mimesis and knowledge so crucial to critical conceptions of realism. The classical point of departure for any debate on the epistemic claims of representational literature, of course, is Plato's infamous attack on mimetic poets in book 10 of the *Republic*, and even here at the origin one can already find a comparison being broached between medicine and mimesis. The basic argument Plato pursues will be familiar: according to Socrates, poets provide mere imitations of imitations of true reality, because they create "without knowledge of the truth" (599). What is less often recalled is that Socrates bolsters his accusation against mimetic writers by comparing poetry to the art of medicine. Medical practitioners do indeed "create with knowledge," in pointed contrast to poets: one would only embarrass the poets, scoffs Socrates, if one were to ask them, "if any one of them was a physician and not merely an imitator of a physician's thought, what men any poet, old or new, is reported to have restored to health as Asclepius did . . ." (599c). Socrates then goes on to show how poetry actually is antithetical to medicine, insofar as poetry encourages one to wallow in feelings rather than transcend one's pain through reasoned action. When we are hurt, he asks, is it not better

> to deliberate . . . about what has happened to us, and, as it were in the fall of the dice, to determine the movements of our affairs with reference to the numbers that turn up, in the way that reason indicates would be best, and, instead of stumbling like children, clapping one's hands to the stricken spot and wasting the time in wailing, ever to accustom the soul to devote itself at once to the curing of the hurt and the raising up of what has fallen, banishing threnody by therapy. (604c–d)

Medicine for Plato does precisely what mimesis cannot: it deals with the empirical without abandoning its rational basis and becoming a merely empirical *coup des dés*.

If Plato inaugurates the epistemic debate about mimetic fiction in part by strictly *opposing* medicine and mimesis, Aristotle's perhaps even more influential critical theory of mimesis also relies tangentially on a comparison between medical and fictional practices. For Aristotle, however, therapy and threnody are postulated as essentially identical: mimesis itself constitutes a form of therapy, permitting a purging of our sick feelings through catharsis: "An emotion which strongly affects some souls is present in all to a varying degree, for example pity and fear, and also ecstasy. To this last some people are particularly liable, and we see that under the influence of religious music and songs which drive the soul to frenzy, they calm down as if they had been medically treated and purged."[17] Aristotle's assumption that threnody and therapy are fundamentally the same may seem a secondary matter, but it has important consequences, for it enables him to do something Plato disdains—to postulate and initiate a science of poetics giving conceptual form to what Aristotle accepts as the tacit practical knowledge possessed by writers (just as biology systematizes the practical knowledge of physicians). The medicine-mimesis issue thus cuts to the root of the literary epistemology and poetics we have inherited from the Greeks.

But one need not refer back to the Greeks for warrants to investigate the relation between medicine and mimetic fiction. Within the self-theorizations of nineteenth-century realist fiction and its close cousins, there are ample indications that some sorts of linkages exist. Perhaps the most overt of these indications is found in Zola's manifesto, "The Experimental Novel," which aggressively, dogmatically, and (some would say) crudely pursues an analogy between doctors and writers. Claude Bernard's description of the method of "experimental medicine," Zola insists, matches his own conception of literary method. "It will often be but necessary for me to replace the word 'doctor' by the word 'novelist,'" he claims, "to make my meaning clear and to give it the rigidity of a scientific truth."[18] Zola of course overstates and oversimplifies, and the nature of the medicine he invokes is distinctive, but he is by no means alone among nineteenth-century writers in claiming to treat his characters as a doctor treats his patients. Similar sentiments are expressed (although not in quite so tendentious a form) by a wide range of realists, including Dickens, Chekhov, Balzac, Flaubert, George Eliot, and Henry James. Certainly we ought not to take all these claims at face value; for some writers the analogy may be only superficial, and in any case, any writer's opinion about his or her own work has no more necessary validity than does anyone else's opinion. But given the traditional, prima facie theoretical association of diagnosis with mimesis, therapy with threnody, there would seem ample reason to examine medicine—understood in Plato's general terms as a way to "create with knowledge," and therefore as involving the quasi-poetic elaboration of something like a style, point of view, or mode of representation that conveys truth-value—as a constitutive element of the realistic novel and its allied genres.

TWO

DISARTICULATING *MADAME BOVARY*

FLAUBERT AND THE MEDICALIZATION

OF THE REAL

OVER THE PAST twenty-odd years, semiotics has established itself as a powerful, rigorous, and at times elegant technique for the close reading of literary texts. Until recently, however, literary semioticians tended to remain fixated on the text itself, squandering the promise of Barthes's early cultural criticism and leaving the issue of the relation between literature and society to either the liberal imagination or ideological criticism. In the last several years, however, context has reemerged as a respectable object for semiotic interrogation. Some Marxist academics have appropriated semiotic methods to forge a more formally sophisticated analysis of ideology; Frederic Jameson's *The Political Unconscious* offers the most interesting and successful example of this tendency. Concurrently, semioticians themselves have tried to come to grips with the social implications of texts by elaborating a concept of "intertextuality."

Michel Riffaterre's recent work illustrates this change in emphasis.[1] Following a line of investigation originally suggested by Jonathan Culler, Riffaterre argues that literary texts can best be understood as specific "actualizations" of cultural "presuppositions."[2] Culler's definition of *presupposition*—as "that which must be revealed by another, or by an effort of *dédoublement*: of thinking from the point of view of the other"—is heavily tinged with a Hegelianism that Riffaterre rejects, substituting the more Kantian (or Chomskian) formulation of presuppositions as simply "the implicit conditions of an explicit statement." The advantage of Riffaterre's redefinition is that it guides him to look for sets of conditions rather than for Culler's less easily delimited "point of view." In any given instance, the conditions governing statements will constitute a system, and it is this system of presuppositions that the Riffaterrean student of intertextuality hopes to be able to disengage from the literary text and locate in the sociolect.

In seeking to extend the semiotic project beyond the frontiers of the text itself into its context, Riffaterre is to be commended. But because his methodology for elucidating systems of statements within the sociolect remains rather undeveloped, he runs into major problems when he attempts to realize his theoretical claims in particular interpretations, most tellingly in the reading of *Madame Bovary* that he offers in support of his approach. The only prerequisite Riffaterre stipulates for declaring a set of statements to be a system of presuppositions is that they derive from a "matrix sentence" supplied by the dictionary or some other anonymous source. For *Madame Bovary*, the matrix sentence appears, according to Riffaterre, in the cliché—found in a popular dictionary of Flaubert's time in the entry "Adultery"—that "all evils stem from adultery." As a system, an "encoded ideology," adultery entails a number of subordinate consequences, all of which, as it happens, are played out in the course of Flaubert's narrative. Riffaterre concludes that the adultery system thus "entails the whole fictional text."

Apart from this highly dubious claim to account for *total* textual production in terms of a single system, Riffaterre's approach leaves two questions unanswered. The first question is whether it is accurate to describe the literary performance that takes place in *Madame Bovary* as a straightforward actualization of the system of presuppositions about adultery. Of all writers, Flaubert is probably the most sensitive and resistant to the rehearsal of received ideas; when he does make use of such ideas, it is to struggle *against* their simplistic actualization. Flaubert's entire effort, in fact, seems to have been directed toward showing that literariness had nothing to do with a writer's overt subject, that even the most clichéd subject would do. And as Baudelaire points out in his review of *Madame Bovary*, "the tritest theme of all, worn out by repetition, by being played over and over like a tired barrel-organ," is adultery.[3] Flaubert's is a repetition with a difference, but that kind of artistic difference from ordinary actualization is only vaguely gestured toward by Riffaterre, who dismisses it as an *écart stylistique*.[4] Between dictionary and text, presupposition and actualization, Flaubert (and, one presumes, other artists as well) must be doing something extraordinary, and the nature of this deviation needs to be specified.

This leads us to the second question about Riffaterre's method: how does one find one's way from the text to the dictionary entry containing its most important presuppositions? Riffaterre looks up *adultery* because it seems to be the subject of the novel, but Baudelaire, in the review quoted earlier, argues explicitly that Flaubert is using not adultery but *hysteria* to "serve as the central subject, the true core" of his novel. Unfortunately, instead of going on to interpret *Madame Bovary* within the context of nineteenth-century France's presuppositions about hysteria, Baudelaire chooses to guard the artistic value of

Flaubert's text from historical inspection by arguing that "the Academy of Medicine has not as yet been able to explain the mysterious condition of hysteria" (341). This was not quite true. Nineteenth-century medicine did have an explanation for hysteria, as for other diseases. That explanation, however, was not to be found in a general dictionary. The system of medical presuppositions about hysteria did not exist as an encoded ideology elaborated through a cliché (as in the instance of adultery), but as a subset of a coherent, intellectually formalized scientific discourse.

To grasp the presuppositions of hysteria thus would entail pursuing a discursive rather than a semiotic analysis. A good first move might be to look for an equivalent to the popular dictionary, a repository of medical knowledge. Even if one managed to find some such equivalent and describe the discourse on hysteria, however, one still would have to explain how medical presuppositions about hysteria inform and are actualized in *Madame Bovary*. And given the fact that discourse is so much more complex than Riffaterre's ideological codes, the relation between discourse and fiction is likely to be more complicated than one of simple actualization.

Luckily, these problems are not insuperable in the case of hysteria and *Madame Bovary*, for two reasons. First, a methodology for analyzing discourse already exists and has been used to describe in some detail the presuppositions of nineteenth-century clinical medicine.[5] Second, there was in fact a medical equivalent (at least in the nineteenth century) to the general dictionary—the *Dictionnaire des sciences médicales*. This dictionary provides an entry on hysteria. But it also contains the boiled-down entirety of medical discourse, for which it thus may stand. Flaubert uses the medical dictionary this synecdochal way in *Madame Bovary* to thematize the relation between medical discourse and his fictional universe—or, to use Riffaterre's terminology, between a presuppositional system and the text in which it is actualized. This thematization occurs in the midst of a typically exhaustive catalogue of the contents of Charles Bovary's study, when Flaubert pauses to note the characteristics of Bovary's dictionary: "Volumes of the 'Dictionary of Medical Science,' uncut, but the binding rather the worse for the successive sales through which they had gone, occupied almost alone the six shelves of a pinewood bookcase."[6] If Charles's dictionary may be taken as an icon of nineteenth-century medical discourse, this description exemplifies the strangely double status of that discourse in *Madame Bovary*. On one hand, the medical dictionary (and medical discourse) is shown both to exist and to enjoy cognitive authority; on the other hand, this source of cognitive power is never tapped by any of the central characters in the novel. Instead of being put into practical effect, the set of medical rules and commands symbolized by these volumes is treated only as an object of exchange, successively received and passed from hand to hand. Flaubert's description emphasizes the commodification of the dictionary ("successive sales"), the social indifference to its content ("uncut pages"), and its purely formal wear and tear ("suffering of its binding"), as if to underline the pathos of distance between discursive knowledge and *bêtise*.

All knowledge in Flaubert is like medical knowledge here, simultaneously present and inaccessible, ideas received yet uncomprehended. In *Madame Bovary*, however, the inaccessibility of *medical* knowledge in particular turns out to be crucial, a matter of life and death. When Charles discovers that Emma has taken poison, he turns to the medical dictionary for the first time since it was mentioned early in the novel. Faced with the task of discovering an antidote, "Charles tried to look up his medical dictionary, but could not read it; the lines were jumping before his eyes" (231). Canivet and Homais, Bovary's consultants on the case, are also unqualified to treat Emma properly—the former because his knowledge of internal medicine is scant and the latter because he is a quack. The lack of professional competence at this point is critical: Canivet's prescription of an emetic actually hastens Emma's death, as we learn from Dr. Larivière's "severe lecture" to the surgeon after the event.

Charles's dictionary, then, thematizes the determinate absence of medical knowledge in *Madame Bovary*. This knowledge—a system of presuppositions about illness and death—seems to be precisely what the novel excludes. But the strange and innovative fact about Flaubert's novel is that, if Baudelaire's insight is correct, Emma's life is shaped by medical discourse's assumptions about hysteria, even though her death is caused by the discourse's absence. But what are these assumptions? More generally, what is their systematic form, and how does this discursive formation differ from the *ideological* system of clichéd presuppositions that Riffaterre describes?

Taking the second question first, one broad difference between ideology and discourse is that while ideological presuppositions form a part of a widely shared everyday knowledge, discursive assumptions are esoteric. It is difficult to pin down the location of an ideology, which exists as what Terry Eagleton calls "a consensus of unconscious valuations";[7] discourse, on the other hand, tends to nest within an institutional framework that at once delimits and supports it. A discursive practice will be organized not only textually or lexically (in dictionaries, manuals, handbooks, and encyclopedias), but also technologically and politically. To grasp the extent to which discourse is actualized in a literary text, one must thus look for two kinds of presuppositions: those conceptual presuppositions that constitute the discourse proper, and those institutional presuppositions that attend the discourse.

In the case of medical discourse, a very specific institutional environment—a new intellectual and professional hierarchy, a new disposition of duties and status—emerges during the early years of the nineteenth century. One question then is how, and to what extent, these kinds of rearrangements affect Flaubert's imagination of the world of *Madame Bovary*. Although they may seem merely sociological, I shall try to show that the emerging institutional presuppositions do in fact structure *Madame Bovary* to a great degree, by providing a double template of relations upon which Flaubert elaborates. In the first instance, explicit relations between characters within the text are determined by the disciplinary and institutional constraints of the medical profession at this time. But institutional presuppositions also inform a more fundamental, tacit formal relation in Flaubert's work—that between knowledge and bêtise.

The Uses of Medical Bêtise

The inept Charles Bovary is probably the most egregious example in this novel (and perhaps in any novel) of a character both socially and intellectually determined by the medical institutions of the time. His peculiar mediocrity stems, in fact, from his position within a complex professional hierarchy. Despite his honorific title, Doctor Charles Bovary is not a full-fledged doctor, but an *officier de santé*—a category of medical practitioner created during the early years of the Napoleonic era under the direction of the Ideologue physician and philosopher Cabanis.[8] The revolutionary period was marked by a rapid growth in the number of poorly trained army surgeons (for obvious reasons) and the abolition of the older, theoretically oriented *Facultés*. The latter were replaced, by 1795, by new learned societies like the *Société d'émulation*, which counted Bichat, Cabanis, and Pinel among its members. Under the external pressure of public demands for commissions to screen out quack surgeons, and the internal pressure of a newly emerging institutional structure of medical authority, a general reorganization of the profession occurred. It followed a path leading to greater centralization and technocratic efficiency. Cabanis was in the forefront of this drive toward rationalization. He proposed that because medicine was an industry whose products' value could not be gauged by the public—"what price health?"—the government should ensure the value of treatment by controlling the producers but not the product. Under his plan, access to the profession was to be limited, and less qualified physicians were to be supervised by an elite group of clinicians belonging to the learned societies.

As a result of these reforms, the terms of medical authority shifted as it expanded its jurisdiction. The old and bitter conflict between Parisian Faculté doctors and practical surgeons (a rivalry epitomized in *Madame Bovary* by the old surgeon Canivet's bitter remark about "the fads from Paris" propagated by "these gentlemen from the capital!" [131]) gave way, in 1803, to a new consolidation in the division of duties between experienced clinicians (usually located in large cities) and trained officiers de santé. The latter were certified, as is Charles, by department juries on the basis of a shorter course of study, and were allowed to practice only "simple procedures" in specified and restricted areas of the country. In effect, this was the first nationalized health planning, the first attempt to ensure minimal standards of care through a whole society by the controlled deployment of medical technique. It marked the first penetration by a centrally controlled medical perspective into the areas of everyday life that novelists like Balzac, George Eliot, and Flaubert were attempting to penetrate and oversee as realists.

Charles Bovary is caught up genealogically in the transformation of the medical profession—his father served as an assistant-surgeon-major under Napoleon—so that Charles's choice of career (made by his mother, to be sure) is logical: he is following in his father's footsteps. But the intellectual landscape itself has changed, along with the change in title from surgeon to officer of health. Charles, unlike his father, cannot get by only on the strength of his "devil of an arm for pulling teeth," nor can he confidently espouse the brutal surgical egotism of Canivet, who rejects the advanced medical procedures of "strabismus, chloroform, lithotrity" without having the slightest understanding of them (44, 131).[9] Charles, as an officier de santé, must have the slightest understanding, but that is all. Permitted to treat only "primitive accidents" and "simple indispositions," but required to pass an examination in order to do even that, the officier de santé is a subordinate within the new medical institution.

Above all, he is an intellectual subordinate in the new diagnostic and therapeutic paradigm represented by the medical dictionary. His is an empirically oriented training, a closed circuit of perception and treatment; as Foucault points out, for the officier de santé it is "a question of knowing what to do after seeing; experience was integrated at the level of perception, memory, and repetition, that is, at the level of the example."[10] The words that stun Charles when he begins his studies—*physiology, pharmacy, botany, clinical medicine, therapeutics, hygiene, materia medica*—remain "names of whose etymologies he was ignorant, and that were to him as so many doors to sanctuaries filled with magnificent darkness" (6). Instead of entering into the sacred temple of medicine (whose "godlike" authority is Charles's old master, the clinician Larivière), Charles enters into the profane hovels of the peasantry: "He poked his arm into damp beds, received the tepid spurt of bloodletting in his face, listened to death-rattles, examined basins, turned over a good deal of dirty linen."[11] The senses—sight, sound, touch, and smell—are at work here, but little else.

It should be clear from all this why it would be absurd to expect Charles to grasp the higher mysteries of medicine. His very mode of perception, one grounded in repetition yet linked to a knowledge that transcends such activity, goes with the job created by the medical profession. Charles's mediocrity, in other words, is not useless, but is exactly what is called for: his docile repetition—emblematized by Flaubert very early on in the book by the image of "a mill-horse, who goes round and round with his eyes bandaged, not knowing what work it is grinding out"(7)—*does perform work*. This fact tends to get obscured in deconstructive readings of Flaubert, like those of Tony Tanner and Eugenio Donato, which interpret the repetition and turning in the text as purely degenerative processes that reduce all difference to indifferentiation.[12] Charles's repetition is a regularized professional behavior that is useful both to the profession and to its clients, despite its often destructive and dehumanizing effect on the individual involved in it. He does succeed, for instance, in setting Farmer Rouault's leg, even though he is simply repeating by rote: on arriving at the farm, "Charles awoke with a start, suddenly remembered the broken leg, and tried to call to mind all the fractures he knew." Even his bedside manner is an imitation—"calling to mind the devices of his masters at the bedside of patients, he comforted the sufferer with all sorts of kindly remarks" (11)—and yet he gains Rouault as a patient for official medicine, a small victory for the profession.

The military connotations of the word *victory* are far from inappropriate here, for if Charles, as an officier de santé, is a subordinate within the medical hierarchy, he is by the same token a footsoldier in the campaign to extend medical authority throughout the provinces of France. By the time Charles enters the profession, medicine has reorganized itself internally and has received some official backing for its project of controlling the national health care market. But state support is not absolute, and, especially at the local level, the standard-bearers of official medicine during this period find themselves competing with several other authorities for legitimate control of many of the same aspects of human behavior. More traditionally sanctioned authorities—in particular religious healers and unaccredited folk doctors—as well as the more recently established legal functionaries, all claim some responsibility for the same deviants.[13] The story told by Emma's maid—about a fisherman's daughter whose "fog in the head" was treated by priest, doctor, and customs officer—shows the professional polyvalence of illness (especially mental illness) in the nineteenth century.

Given this crowded field, it is easy to understand why the medical profession during this period propagates a mythical history to support its own claims. In such accounts, as Matthew Ramsey points out, "the contest between the physicians and their rivals sometimes appears as the heroic phase of professionalization, pitting medical enlightenment against popular superstition."[14] For the officier de santé, however, this mythical clarity has little to do with reality at the local level, where lines are not so clearly drawn. To consolidate his own position in the community, a country doctor like Charles is forced to develop a series of alliances, accommodations, and defensive tactics.

In the priest, the country doctor is faced with a rival who, like Abbé Bournisien with Hyppolite in *Madame Bovary*, promises a cure in exchange for vows of prayer and pilgrimage. Having little hope of winning in head-on anticlerical attacks of the kind made by the pharmacist Homais, the country doctor tends instead to accommodate the priest, accepting the notion that, as Bournisien remarks to Emma when she seeks help, Charles "is doctor of the body . . . and I of the soul" (80). The result is a therapeutic regime in which, as Jacques Donzelot has pointed out, priest and doctor "occupied two clearly separate registers"[15] while attending to the same problem of pathology, whether physical, sexual, or mental.[16]

With respect to the other two nonscientific authorities, legal and pseudo-medical, the officier de santé faces a more serious problem. The law, in the form of the medical police, is supposedly allied with him in a joint effort to crush illegal healers. In fact, this program for achieving a professional monopoly remains largely unrealized at the local level: folk healing and charlatanism do not constitute regular targets for the police, despite the official mandate. Thus, the officer of health often finds himself in a dangerous economic struggle for patients against an opponent who tends to operate underground. To make matters worse, there is not that much of a difference in the level of skills possessed by doctors like Charles and quacks like the chemist Homais, even though the officer of health's knowledge is sponsored by official medicine with its more advanced cognitive base. Minimally accredited practitioners and charlatans use many of the same basic therapeutic techniques.[17]

Homais's relation to Charles, of course, graphically illustrates this situation and its hazards for the officier de santé. The apothecary, we learn early in the novel, "had infringed the law of the nineteenth Ventôse, year xi, article 1 [Cabanis was one of the principal architects of this legislation] which forbade all persons not having a diploma to practice medicine" (61). Homais is summoned to Rouen, but instead of being incarcerated he is merely reprimanded. Although the apothecary fears the power of the law ("he saw the depths of dungeons, his family in tears, his shop sold, all the jars dispersed . . . "), Flaubert emphasizes the merely symbolic nature of medicine's legal power by focusing on the trappings of authority: the prosecutor receives Homais "in his private office . . . standing up, ermine on shoulder and cap on head." These signs are without content, however, a fact that Flaubert underlines by adding pointedly that "it was in the morning, before the court opened."

Unfortunately for Dr. Bovary, the apothecary is not deterred for long by the scare he has received. He adapts to the reality of his position and undertakes a guerrilla war against a series of officiers de santé who attempt to occupy his territory in the name of official medicine. In this he is remarkably successful: Charles's predecessor runs away, Charles himself is ruined, and, on the last page of the novel, Flaubert informs us that "since Bovary's death three doctors have succeeded one another in Yonville without any success, so effectively did Homais hasten to eradicate them" (255).

Getting Hyperexcitable: Emma's Hysteria in Medical Context

Because he looks directly to a general-knowledge dictionary for ideological presuppositions, Riffaterre remains blind to these kinds of sociological and institutional determinants of textual situations. His approach remains a quite elegant and rigorous one, thanks to its semiotic insistence that context is another kind of text and its demand that textual presuppositions be studied as linguistic entities locatable in anonymous social texts such as dictionaries. But, as the example of medicine shows, some kinds of presuppositions are embedded in discrete social and institutional procedures, disciplines, and hierarchies. To describe the presuppositions of a discourse, then, one must take account of the kinds of verbal entailments noted by Riffaterre, but one also must address assumptions about power that are irreducible to the sheerly lexical dimension of a dictionary.

But what if the dictionary is of a kind that encapsulates not generally held beliefs but the knowledge of a discipline or profession? What would one find if one followed Riffaterre's directions and Baudelaire's intuition, cut the pages of Charles's *Dictionnaire de Médecine* and turned to the entry on hysteria? One would find there a long article containing the following information:

> The circumstances that most predispose a patient to hysteria are . . . a nervous constitution, her female sex and her age, between twelve and twenty-five or thirty years of age. . . . A majority have from a young age shown a disposition toward convulsive ailments, a melancholic, angry, passionate, impatient character. . . . Exciting causes, more specifically, are morally powerful ailments [including] unrequited love, . . . acute disturbances of the soul, . . . a violent fit of jealousy, . . . powerful grief, . . . acute disappointment. . . . The nervous constitution and the unhealthy condition that precede and facilitate the development of attacks are caused by excessive masturbation.[18]

For a reader of Flaubert, the content of this entry is striking, for it describes Emma Bovary's condition quite accurately: her tendency to convulsive affections from an early age is shown by Flaubert in the flashback to her convent days, when "her nature, positive in the midst of its enthusiasms" (28), had led her to devotional excesses; every word used to define the "hysterical character" is also used at some point in the novel to refer to Emma; she falls into fits after she suffers various emotional shocks—for example, her violent chagrin at Rodolphe's letter or her dread of imminent bankruptcy after he turns down her request for money; and her nervous constitution, although not directly attributable to masturbation, is directly alluded to by herself, by Charles, and even by Larivière.

To point out that Emma acts like an hysteric, however, is to do no more than Baudelaire did one hundred years ago. One needs to clarify the extent of this analogy. Is Flaubert borrowing only the overt representations or symptoms of hysteria, or is he also making use in some way of the logical and rhetorical presuppositions peculiar to clinical medicine? To answer this question requires taking a short detour to elucidate these presuppositions, with their complex interplay—evident in the entry just cited—among terms such as *predisposition, character, constitution*, and *exciting causes*.

The particular figure of hysteria, together with the conceptualization of disease in general, changes enormously between roughly 1780 and 1810, the period coinciding with the emergence of the twin disciplines of modern clinical medicine and morbid anatomy under Bichat's leadership. In the earlier eighteenth-century paradigm, medical classification tends to characterize disease according to two distinct systems of causation: one internal and animistic, relying on the notion of *temperament*, the other mechanistic and external, resting on the principle of *constitutional sympathy*. One can illustrate the concurrence of these two etiological factors by examining how hysteria is conceptualized before Bichat's time. Eighteenth-century nosographers, following the great English physician Sydenham's example, regard hysteria as an endogenous, essentially psychosomatic disease growing out of a mutually reinforcing imbalance between bodily fluids (or "vital spirits," in the Cartesian system) and the passions. This etiology, in turn, depends on the ancient medical concept of "temperament," which originally designates the particular mixture of humors in an individual, but that in the eighteenth century begins to refer to the relation between emotions and the body. As the historian Paul Hoffmann has pointed out, this reduction of hysteria to a problem of temperament condemns the female hysteric of the period to be "la prisonnière d'une sort de causalité réciproque, qui joue entre les esprits et l'esprit, entre la passion et le corps."[19]

During the same period, however, a second causal basis for hysteria is articulated by early, mechanistically oriented neurologists, who correlate the disease with a supposed qualitative effect on nervous fibers by climate, diet, and other so-called "non-naturals." Abrupt or capricious changes in the weather, the reasoning goes, communicate sympathetically with the body's fibers, gradually softening or moistening them until they completely dissolve and hysterical fits occur. Rameau's nephew repeatedly invokes this meteorological etiology, blaming the "maudites circonstances" of a "nature bévue" that "grimaced, then grimaced again and again," communicating its distortion to the nephew and leaving him as a "misshapen image" with unstrung fibers.[20] Philological evidence allows us to date this medical appropriation of climatic factors: the word *constitution*, originally used to describe the state of the atmosphere (*constitution atmosphérique*), comes at this time to stand for the observable and statistically tabulated rapport between environment and pathology.

Preclinical medicine thus understands disease as caused by the passions (through temperamental imbalance) as well as the environment (through constitutional sympathies). Not until after the emergence of pathological anatomy and clinical medicine in the early years of the nineteenth century, however, are the two causal networks linked. The key conceptual development for the emergence of clinical discourse is the elaboration of the concept of "sensitivity." Defined as the involuntary but active response by an organism to a positive stimulus, sensitivity becomes for nineteenth-century clinicians the sine qua non for gauging the condition of a living being. Bichat's contemporary, Cabanis, sums up the new centrality of this concept by paraphrasing Descartes: "Vivre, c'est sentir [To live is to feel]."[21]

When sensitivity becomes the primary property of living beings, the central terms of eighteenth-century pathology—*temperament* and *constitution*—are semantically transformed. Temperament, which previously signified a quantitative balance of fluids or spirits, is redefined as the spatial organization of sensitivity, the three-dimensional relationship between "centers" of sensitivity within the body. "The difference of temperaments," according to Cabanis, "depends upon the difference of centers of sensitivity, of relationships of strength, weakness or sympathetic communications among various organs."[22]

In medical discourse, the temperament thus comes to be the expression of "primitive functions" of sensitivity at work inside and between organs, in what Bichat calls the "organic life" of the individual. But sensitivity is not limited to the internal viscera, the organic life, alone; it is also affected by the relations established between a creature and its environment. This second set of relations constitutes what Bichat christens "animal life." Animal life differs from organic life in that its condition is open to some change under the control of the creature. Unlike organic life, which allocates its forces of sensitivity at birth, animal life has at its disposition a "somme déterminée de force," a vital force that can be channeled by the will or by external stimuli into the development of sensitivity in one organ or another.[23]

Finally, in Bichat's new framework, the term *constitution* ceases to refer to a sympathetic or qualitative similarity between the body's fibers and the external environment. Instead, an individual's constitution is to be understood as the total structure of sensitivities—a complex, constantly evolving web of "rapports" between the fixed temperament of the organic life and the variable pressures of the animal life. The web metaphor will be taken up self-consciously and in great detail by George Eliot in *Middlemarch*, as we shall see, but a second metaphor growing out of this new conceptualization of the self-as-constitution is equally popular both in medicine and in nineteenth-century culture. In this other metaphor, the constitution represents the results of what might be thought of as an investment policy pursued by an individual using his or her vital force as a kind of capital. A wise (or lucky) investor, understanding that limited funds set limits to the possible development of organs, will prudently invest vital capital in those organs whose sensitivity needs strengthening if they are to perform the tasks imposed on them by the individual's situation. What this metaphor makes clear is that, from the medical point of view, there can be no such thing as a Renaissance man with a constitution for all seasons; on the contrary, specialization is quite literally a fact of life. Any organ's gain in power can only be achieved at the expense of another organ, a dilemma pointedly illustrated by Bichat's remark that "on châtre les hommes pour changer leur voix."[24]

As this specific example indicates, the investment capital of vital force easily can be, and to some degree is, identified with sexual force. The concrete form of sexual force (at least for men), seminal fluid, comes to stand for vital force just as money stands for capital. Of course, as Shakespeare's sonnet 129 shows, the belief that "Th' expense of spirit in a waste of shame / Is lust in action" had long been a popularly established notion. In nineteenth-century culture, however, a veritable obsession arises over the dangers of excessive sexual "spending," an obsession marked by the growth of a rhetoric of sexual economics that has been well documented by modern critics.[25] The nineteenth-century interest in this topic, I would argue, derives at least in part from the medical identification of the sexual with the vital, and the subsequent warnings to the public about the dangers of "les pertes seminales," the title of a popular book by the French physician Lallemand.[26] A strong constitution means a strong bodily economy, and requires the investment of vital force in organs, not its exhaustion in sexual expenditure.

Masturbation, which weakens the constitution by siphoning off necessary funds of energy, thus begins to be cited in treatises and medical dictionary entries as a predisposing factor for hysteria. To see how the conceptual field underlying hysteria has been altered with the effect of opening up a place for sexuality and masturbation, one need only compare the medical dictionary quoted above, which dates from 1820, with the following quotation from a medical textbook published in 1775: "The exacerbation of desires evidenced in masturbation, adultery, etc., which is one of the signs of hysteria, *is not a cause*, but is the effect of the repercussion of a disordered movement of the spirits upon the organs of generation" [my italics].[27] Only when all the terms used here have been replaced—*spirits* by *sensitivity*, *movement of spirits* by *vital force*, *disordered movement* by what Pinel's successor Georget will call *hyperexcitability*[28]—will sexual activity cease to represent the *result* of a preexistent, direct sympathy between environmental and physical "disorder," and begin to appear as a contributing *cause* of hysteria.

By Freud's time, the sexual drive will have subsumed all other forms of vital force as a causal factor in hysteria, which itself will be reconceived as a phenomenon of the unconscious. Insofar as Freud's work accomplishes the transformation of the term vital force into sexuality, it is the culmination of a century-long tendency within the paradigm of pathological anatomy to equate the sexual with the vital: indeed, as early as 1853, four years before *Madame Bovary* is published, the English physician Robert Brudenell Carter already defines hysteria as a faulty "discharge" of "the sexual passion" in fits rather than in the service of reproduction.[29] Carter's work, however, is at the cutting edge of its time, and far from representative; for most clinicians, sexuality constituted only one among many causes of hysteria.

Pinpointing the status of sexuality in nineteenth-century medical explanations of hysteria, although interesting in itself (and even salutary, insofar as it historicizes what is all too often defined—especially in feminist criticism—as a sexual disease *tout court*), would be out of place here, however, if it did not help clarify how Flaubert imagines Emma Bovary's sexuality and its relationship to her illness. Masturbation cannot be represented in fiction during this period, but Flaubert seems to go further than he needs to in actively resisting any reduction of Emma's desire to sexual desire. Neither marriage nor adultery are seen by him as adequate outlets for what ails Emma—and this is not because she is sexually insatiable, but because it is her vital force, not her sexuality, that is constitutionally flawed. Ten years after Madame Bovary, her guttersnipe cousin, Zola's Thérèse Raquin, will suffer from a passion almost exclusively sexual, so much so that Henry James complains about Zola's tendency "to leave out the life of the soul, practically, and confine himself to the life of the instincts, the more immediate passions, such as can be easily and promptly sought in the fact."[30] For Flaubert, like Bichat and Cabanis, the two lives of the soul and the body—in medical parlance, the "moral" and the "physique," or the organic and animal lives—coexist in a tissue of rapports, irreducible to a sexual drive, which constitute the self.

Two important consequences follow from this tissular view of the embodied person, consequences evident both in nineteenth-century clinical medicine and in Flaubert's conception of character. First, one's constitution can no longer be attributed to the immediate, aleatory effects of external environmental causes (as in *Rameau's Nephew*), nor can it yet be seen as an effect of the internal repression of sexuality. In Flaubert's late short story, "Saint Julien L'hospitalier," both these hypotheses about the cause of Julien's sickly constitution are explicitly advanced so as to be rejected: "Le mal de Julien," his doctors assert, "avait pour cause un vent funeste, ou un désir d'amour. Mais le jeune homme, à toutes les questions, sécouait la tête."[31] In *Madame Bovary*, similarly, the weather is a constant presence, but its moods never directly mirror the state of Emma's soul, as would be the case in a typical romantic novel.[32] For example, throughout the novel, wind blows— from the breath that raises the tissue paper covering an engraving in one of the earliest views of Emma, to the whirlwind that rises in Emma's soul as she feels herself approaching madness, to the gust that blows away a maiden's skirt in the blind tramp's final obscene song— yet Emma's psyche only registers an indirect effect at most. The fog in

Emma's head, unlike the chaotic fibers in Rameau's nephew's brain, is not created by a single atmospheric imprinting.

Instead (and this is the second consequence of the new conception of the self in nineteenth-century medicine), the development or formation of a constitution must take place through a long, drawn-out, incremental process of stimulation from within and without. Stimuli or desires may act upon the embodied self, but they cannot act directly and cataclysmically. A kind of "interior distance" (to borrow a phrase from Georges Poulet) exists within everyone. This *medical* interiority, however, is not a pure, phenomenologically certain locus for the cogito, as Poulet would have it, but a highly organized and evolving system. Every impulse of vital force from the will or stimulus from the environment is disseminated through a network of various centers of sensibility and thus each stimulus can modify the whole only slightly.

In the case of hysteria, the constitution is thought to undergo four distinct steps in its slow process of pathological formation.[33] To grasp these four stages, one might think of them as material analogs to the four tropes of metaphor, metonymy, synecdoche, and irony, whose sequence Hayden White has proposed as providing a framework for the overall narrative movement of Flaubert's *L'Education sentimentale*.[34] In the first stage, a stimulus from passion or the environment is transmitted to the cerebral cortex, in a kind of metaphorical translation. Next, the force of sensation, having arrived in the brain, is relayed to the brain's different centers of sensibility, as significance would be relayed metonymically. Third, the organs of the brain in turn affect the whole range of bodily organs by means of what one important physician terms "interior sensibility," a radiating effect similar to what is said to occur semantically in synecdoche. Gradually, the various parts of the body accumulate sensitivity, until they are saturated, reaching a state of "hyperexcitability" in which any stimulation whatsoever is intolerable. At this point, in the fourth and last stage of the development of an hysteric's constitution, the system of rapports connecting the nervous system has become a collection of "hyperexcitable" components, an ironic (but literal and material) dissociation of sensibility that predisposes the patient to suffer hysterical attacks at the slightest provocation.[35]

Emma's development follows these steps, and more generally, all Flaubert's characters exhibit complex constitutions. Flaubert, of course, does not use the medical terms I have been describing. Rather, he translates these terms into metaphysical and psychological ones more appropriate to the novel, while retaining clinical medicine's conceptual structure and emphasis on embodied sensation. For the physical constitution he substitutes memory; for the centers of sensibility or intellectual functions deployed through the body or brain, he substitutes the representations of which memory consists; and for vital force, he substitutes desire.

The Flaubertian self, in other words, is readable as a complex psychophysiological "constitution," a constantly evolving relation between present sensation and an always already existing set of memories. At moments when the interchange between sensation and memory becomes problematic—for example, during the transition between consciousness and sleep, or during a hallucination—the Flaubertian self can disintegrate into independent sets of memories (equivalent to the different functions into which the hysteric's constitution ironically breaks down during a fit). Dissociation, for Flaubert, is inherent in the human condition, not only a problem for sensitive types or women. It affects all his characters, even those as dull-witted and boringly masculine as Charles Bovary: "Charles from time to time opened his eyes but his mind grew weary, and sleep coming upon him, he soon fell into a doze wherein his recent sensations blending with memories, he became conscious of a double self, at once student and married man, lying in his bed as but now, and crossing the operation theatre as of old" (9).[36]

Whether overtly pathologized or not, then, the Flaubertian self is thus neither given nor unitary. And, as with a medical constitution, this self is capable of slow drifts into decomposition or transformation. As memory erodes or shifts, Flaubert's characters find themselves changing as well, sometimes even in spite of their efforts to avoid such a change. Charles, for example, finds that "while continually thinking of Emma, he was nevertheless forgetting her. He grew desperate as he felt this image fading from his memory in spite of all efforts to retain it" (252). Beyond and sometimes in spite of intention, memory (like the physical constitution) adjusts and reconstitutes itself.

Such are the vicissitudes of every embodied memory. For those who become ill, however, memory does not merely adjust, but develops in the same way that a patient's physical constitution does. In the case of hysteria, Emma does what Freud and Breuer will later say all hysterics do: she "suffers mainly from reminiscences."[37] Flaubert once described his own hysteria as "an illness of memory,"[38] and he anticipates Freud in psychologizing the disease. But Flaubert's presuppositions are Bichatian rather than Freudian, and Emma's illness follows a different course than does that of Dora. Emma's stages of consciousness correspond at a mental level to the four-stage series described above. These four steps occur again and again in a kind of cyclical spiral, each time preparing Emma's mental constitution for its recurrent disintegration in hysterical fits.

Because the first three steps toward constitutional hypersensitivity tend to resolve themselves in most instances without causing any dramatic breakdown of the self, these formative or "predisposing" steps are best observed in local instances such as paragraphs and brief episodes, rather than in the broad arc of narrative. A close reading of such passages—whose free indirect style takes us into Emma's consciousness—shows how the kind of language Flaubert uses to describe Emma's tug-of-war between sensations and memories contains the tropes one would expect for each stage of her developing hysteria. Like every medically defined person, Emma incorporates experience into memory by first metaphorically converting her sensation into feeling, then extending that feeling metonymically in imagination, and finally dissipating it in a plethora of representations stretching synecdochically through her memory as a whole.

Metaphors are sown most thickly in *Madame Bovary* where Emma's sensibility responds to an influx of sensations. The metaphors in this gorgeous paragraph, for example, seem intended to imitate Emma's consciousness during the first moments after sex:

> The shades of night were falling; the horizontal sun passing between the branches dazzled the eyes. Here and there around in the leaves or on the ground, trembled luminous patches, as if humming-birds flying about had scattered their feathers. Silence was everywhere; something sweet seemed to come forth from the trees. She felt her heartbeat return, and the blood coursing through her flesh like a river of milk. Then far away, beyond the wood, on the other hills, she heard a vague prolonged cry, a voice which lingered, and in silence she heard it mingling like music with the last pulsations of her throbbing nerves. (116)[39]

Within the space of three sentences, Flaubert packs three distinct metaphors, each addressing a different sense, as if to emphasize the dominance of sensation within Emma's consciousness at this stage.[40] A similar transfusion of excitement, and one that is more clearly followed by a psychological retrenchment, occurs when Emma incorporates her experience at the Vaubyessard ball. In her first encounter with luxury, she is overwhelmed by the vivid sensations, which cancel (or at least obscure by their intensity) her previous memories: "In the splendor of the present hour her past life, so distinct until then, faded away completely, and she almost doubted having lived it. She was there; beyond the ball was only shadow overspreading all the rest."[41] On her return home, we later learn, "she devoutly put away in her drawers her beautiful dress, down to the satin shoes whose soles were yellowed with the slippery wax of the dancing floor. Her heart resembled them: in its contact with wealth, something had rubbed off on it that could not be removed." This simile signals the onset of an obsession: "The memory of this ball, then, became an occupation for Emma." In clinical terms, one would say that a sensation has made its way into Emma's cerebral centers of sensibility and has begun to work upon them.

Once Emma's sensation has been received, medical discourse teaches, its force need not remain bound to the representation that originally carried it. Like all direct impressions, Emma's images of the ball soon fade, as Charles's image of Emma fades: "Little by little the faces grew confused in her remembrance. She forgot the tune of the quadrilles [like the music that mingles with her nerves during her se-duction by Rodolphe in the passage quoted earlier, this music has been absorbed into her nervous system]; she no longer saw the liveries and the guest-houses so distinctly; some of the details faded but the wistful feeling remained with her" (40). Emma's desire, like the power of sen-sibility or a vital force that can be aroused by a stimulus, then becomes capable of being redirected metonymically onto other memories, that is, other images. In this second phase, Emma seeks imaginary satisfac-tion for her own desires. Like her lover, Léon, who in her absence displaces his passion for her onto other objects, Emma applies this wistful feeling—the echo of her sensation, as it were—to substitute objects like the Vicomte's cigar box, whose odors and needlework re-activate sensation on an imaginary plane. This strategy of metonymic displacement of psychic force from physical to imaginary objects is effective, at least in the short run: "The memory of the Viscount al-ways cropped up in everything she read. She made comparisons be-tween him and the fictional characters in her books. But the circle of which he was the centre gradually widened round him, and the aure-ole that he bore, fading from his form and extending beyond his image, lit up her other dreams" (41).[42] Unfortunately, Emma's psychic energy has been invested in mere representations that in being ex-tended synecdochically, always dissipate that energy: "At the end of some indefinite distance there was always a confused spot, into which her dream died." In the same way, the vital force of a future hysteric remains unfocused and simply fans out into the confusion of the body's or brain's organization, where it raises the general level of hyperexcitability. Prolonged imaginary investment leads, that is, to what Flaubert describes in Emma as "an expansion of selfishness, of nervous irritation," as her stock of energy is exhausted without return in the form of any new sensation: "Each morning, as she awoke, she hoped it would come that day; she listened to every sound, sprang up with a start, wondered that it did not come; then at sun-set, always more saddened, she longed for the next day." As Emma's extreme responsiveness to the slightest sound shows, she has become saturated with hyperexcitability. Given her condition, Flaubert's next two sentences come as no surprise: "Spring came round. With the first warm weather, when the pear-trees began to blossom, she had fainting spells" (45).

What *is* surprising about Flaubert's description of Emma's breakdown is his insistence, at a moment of crisis for his heroine, on noting even the most minute specifications of the environmental conditions—"when the pear-trees began to blossom"—attending this event. The detail here could perhaps point to the pathos in Emma's situation: spring, which should bring love, instead yields only a nervous breakdown. But then why pear-trees, specifically? One answer commonly given is that the obsession with detail *qua* detail defines Flaubert's realism. As Jonathan Culler has argued, Flaubert's details, unlike those of his predecessor Balzac, do not lend themselves to symbolic recuperation, at least not in a fully satisfying way.[43] They supposedly work instead to produce what Barthes calls "l'effet de réel," a sense of sheer, unmotivated *thereness*. But if they are symbolically unrecuperated, Flaubert's descriptions remain, I would suggest, *discursively* recuperated, just as his characterizations are.[44] Flaubert's choice of descriptive techniques, in other words, is a second major consequence of his adopting a medical point of view. To see why this should be so, we need to note that Bichat's clinical notion of the self as a complex constitution implies that it will always be hard to determine which specific stimulus causes a predisposed constitution to go over the edge into actual breakdown. When all the centers of sensibility have become hyperexcitable, the "threshold of sensibility" drops so low that even sound or odor can trigger an attack. In such cases, as one prominent physician of the time cautions, it is often "impossible to find the immediate cause" of the breakdown.[45]

Because of this proliferation of possible exciting causes, the clinician must deepen his observation and analysis of the patient's environment to include the most trivial details if he wishes to fully understand how the disease progresses. This new epistemological imperative in medicine expresses itself in the emergence of the modern case study, which replaces the older, eighteenth-century record that correlated disease with statistical information about environmental conditions. In the case study, as opposed to the earlier mode of analysis, details provide the doctor with a web of possible connections, some spurious, some significant, that he must weave and unweave in order to make sense of the patient's illness.[46]

Merely accumulating details would be a waste of time, of course, if the physician had no epistemological guide to the pathways of illness within the body. Such a guide is provided by the new discipline of pathological anatomy, whose founder, Bichat, catalogues the various ways in which different "concatenations of phenomena" can lead to death, or more generally to the onset of an illness. In his masterpiece, *Recherches sur la vie et la mort* (a book with which Flaubert was familiar), Bichat illustrates the diagnostic implications of pathological anatomy with an example that is strikingly appropriate to *Madame Bovary*: "The simple action of a poisonous substance on the nerves of the lungs can have a very marked effect on the [physical] economy, and is even capable of disturbing its functions in a palpable way: somewhat like an odour, which striking simply upon the pituitary, acts sympathetically upon the heart, and determines the occurrence of a fit; just as the view of a hideous object produces the same effect."[47] A good doctor, Bichat concludes, must collect his details and observations carefully to have any chance of distinguishing between attacks caused physically by odor and those induced psychologically by the view of an object arousing strong emotions.

Madame Bovary teaches Bichat's lesson, using the exact same example. In the episode that culminates in Emma's hysterical fit, she receives a farewell letter from her lover, Rodolphe, hidden in a basket of fruit sent to the Bovarys as a going-away present. The shock of discovery about Rodolphe's infidelity raises Emma's sensitivity to its height, but she controls herself enough to come down to dinner. At the dinner table, however, Charles encourages her to taste the fruit, unaware of her hyperexcitability at the moment:

> "Smell them! Such perfume!" he insisted, moving it back and forth under her nose.
> "I am choking," she exclaimed, leaping up.
> By sheer willpower, she succeeded in forcing back the spasm.
> "It is nothing," she said, "it is nothing! Just nerves. Sit down and eat."
> For she dreaded most of all that he would question her, try to help and not leave her to herself.
> Charles, to obey her, sat down again, and he spat the stones of the apricots into his hands, afterwards putting them on his plate.
> Suddenly a blue tilbury passed across the square at a rapid trot. Emma uttered a cry and fell back rigid on the floor (150).[48]

Like Bichat, Flaubert offers two alternative causes of Emma's fit—either the odor of the fruit or the view of a hideous object (the tilbury is Rodolphe's). Moreover, Flaubert's laconic transcription of the events leading up to Emma's syncope follows the epistemological rules of a good case history: it does not attempt to judge causes but only to describe as faithfully as possible the details, both psychic and physical, that might be taken as causes of Emma's attack. Although Flaubert weights the evidence in favor of a psychic causation by making the physical apricots themselves into psychically "horrifying objects" for Emma, who links them with the letter she has just received, the novelist is careful to record the temporal proximity linking the smell of fruit with Emma's sensation of choking (a symptom that our medical dictionary of the period tells us marks the preliminary stage of an hysterical paroxysm), so that we are forced to consider the odor as data. Just as in the passage quoted earlier—which associated the blossoming of pear-trees with Emma's fainting spells, but only did so by contiguity, so here Flaubert registers the possible exciting causes, leaving to the reader the task of determining which details are significant.

Flaubert, however, does more than simply observe with what Freud would later formalize as *gleichschwebende Aufmerksamkeit*, poised attention. He seems to go out of his way to present Emma with possible exciting sensations, odors to sniff and fantasize upon, from "the mystic languor that exhales from the perfume on the altar," to the Vicomte's cigar box, to the Oriental pastilles she burns after she shuts herself up in her room. By adopting a pathologist's attitude toward his heroine, Flaubert ironically fulfills the wish expressed by Homais, who, upon learning that Emma had been smelling apricots when she was stricken, remarks fatuously: "Some people are so terribly sensitive to certain odours. The subject would well repay study, in its pathological no less than its physiological aspects."[49] As usual, Homais is pseudomedical, as well as behind the times, for such studies were well under way by Flaubert's time, as the quotation from Bichat shows. Doctors increasingly sought not merely to observe symptoms and understand the factors leading to the formation of a pathological constitution, but also to manipulate the environment so as to experimentally induce pathological effects on the bodies of their patients. In this regard, Homais mentions a Pavlovian-like dog that "goes off into a fit if anyone holds out a snuff-box to him," a susceptibility that the dog's owner has "often demonstrated experimentally in the presence of friends." In the notes of one of Charcot's students, an exact human counterpart to this demonstration is recorded: "The subject exhibits hysterical spasms; Charcot suspends an attack by placing first his hand, then the end of a baton, on the woman's ovaries. He withdraws the baton, and there is a fresh attack, *which he accelerates by administering inhalations of amyl nitrate*. The afflicted woman then cries out for the sex-baton in words that are devoid of any metaphor: 'G. is taken away and her delirium continues.'"[50] Homais's overall response to Emma's seizure registers in parody the tactics of nineteenth-century therapists. He recognizes that "it is quite possible that the apricots caused the syncope," that odors act by stupefying the senses, and that women's greater sensitivity makes them more susceptible to "irregularities of the nervous system." At the same time, he imitates Charcot, trying to make Emma "come to" by using aromatic vinegar. Unfortunately, this smelling salt had been declared totally ineffective in reviving patients in a treatise on hysteria written in 1850. Homais's other suggestions for treatment continue the medical charade. He recommends the administration of sedatives, emollients, pacifiers, and a strict diet. None of these therapeutic steps requires any special medical skill, and each has the added advantage of requiring drugs sold at the chemist's own shop. These treatments at least correspond to medically approved efforts to suppress the somatic causes of hyperexcitability. But Homais's final suggestion is beyond the competence of both the chemist and the officier de santé:

> Then, don't you think we might attack the imagination?
> —In what way? How? said Bovary.
> —Ah! That is the question! That is, indeed, the question! *"C'est là la question!"* as someone said in the newspaper the other day.
> But at this point Emma, waking up, shouted, "The letter! The letter!"
> They thought she was delirious; by midnight she *was* delirious; she was declared to have brain fever.[51]

Emma offers the clinically correct answer to Charles's question about how to work on the imagination, but unfortunately neither Charles nor Homais know how to read her delirium (Homais's reading, in fact, is limited to the newspaper, while Charles, as we have seen, never reads the medical dictionary). They see no clear connection between words and the imagination, and can think of no way to prevent brain fever by manipulating the representations available to the patient. Pre-Freudian analysts of hysteria, on the other hand, *did* see a connection between reading and illness. Exposure to the wrong kinds of representations, Georget warns, can increase the danger that dangerously heightened emotions will be brought to bear on the constitutions of those who, like young women, are already naturally weak: "En résumé, une jeune femme de la bonne société, de constitution nerveuse, n'accomplissant pas de travaux manuels et menant une vie oisive entre les concerts et la lecture des romans, est le sujet idéal, prédisposé à l'hystérie."[52]

The moral therapy initiated by Pinel in France and by the Tuke brothers in England, although not firmly grounded theoretically in the conceptual field of official clinical medicine, did offer doctors specific ways of attacking the imagination by controlling access to the letter, and indeed to any stimulus whatsoever. Some of these techniques, in fact, find their way into Charles's medical dictionary, which counsels that

To prevent the onset of hysteria, the following treatments are prescribed: exercise, manual labour, the study of natural science, continual occupation of the mind; in addition, one should avoid all occasions and anything that may be the cause of exalting the imagination, exciting the passions, and filling the head with illusions and chimaeras; one should also prevent dreams and of course the habit of masturbation.

Emma never undergoes such rehabilitation in any thorough way, and when she does go out for exercise—at Charles's suggestion, to improve her health!—she becomes involved in an affair with Rodolphe that exalts her imagination even further. Flaubert seems to imply that Emma's vexed relationship to her representations would not have been adequately dealt with by the moral treatment.[53] Far from undermining the connection between Flaubert's work and medical discourse, however, Flaubert's rejection of this method of treatment only confirms that his concept of hysteria involves a more complex, more *anatomical* notion of imagination and memory than that entertained by the moral managers and psychiatrists. His medical genealogy, that is to say, stems from Bichat and Cabanis rather than from Pinel.

The Author as Clinician: Situating Flaubertian Realism

Flaubert thus integrates medical presuppositions into his writing to an extraordinary degree and in extremely complex ways. He does not, however, "actualize" them in Riffaterre's sense. They do not provide a linear series of consequences forming the plot of *Madame Bovary* (as Riffaterre's presuppositions about adultery do). Rather, these medical presuppositions are taken up by Flaubert as directives about technique: in characterization, for instance, where Flaubert is guided by the medical presupposition that the individual develops as a complexly embodied constitution; or in description, where the novelist accepts the medical presupposition that alternative causes must be considered during diagnosis of hysterical attacks. More generally, *Madame Bovary* marks the emergence of a mode of writing in which the real has become medical, in which the relation between author and text is modeled on medical precepts, with the author viewing characters and situations as a doctor views patients and cases.

But stating things in this way raises further questions about the role and status of the author within the intertextual field of discourses. Why does Flaubert rely on medical discourse, rather than, say, legal, or religious, or military discourse? More specifically, why does he make Emma an hysteric? And why does he write about a situation in which that discourse is posed as unavailable, so that Emma is not treated effectively?

I will conclude by sketching out two broad answers to these questions. Both involve the internal hierarchy and social status of medicine discussed in the first half of the chapter. One answer is biographical, concerning Flaubert's personal encounter with hysteria and with the medical profession; the other is sociological, concerning the historical situation of the profession of literature within a society in which the profession of medicine also was evolving.

One fact about the concept of hysteria not yet mentioned is that in nineteenth-century medicine, hysteria and epilepsy are gender variants of the same basic disorder of the constitution. In fact, Flaubert himself suffered from a nervous condition that was diagnosed as "hystero-epilepsy." Determining what Flaubert's disease really was, an old and hoary issue in Flaubert criticism, is irrelevant here.[54] But it *is* relevant that Flaubert perceived his own illness in the terms provided by nineteenth-century clinical medicine, and in particular by his own father, Dr. Achille-Cléophas Flaubert, who studied under Bichat as well as under the great surgeon Dupuytren and who treated Flaubert.

That Flaubert understands his own form of hysteria in the clinical terms his father must have used is evident from his account of one seizure in a letter to Louise Colet:

> Each attack was like a hemorrhage of the nervous system. Seminal losses from the pictorial faculty of the brain, a hundred thousand images cavorting at once in a kind of fireworks. It was a snatching of the soul from the body, excruciating. (I am convinced I died several times.) But what constitutes the personality, the rational essence, was present throughout; had it not been, the suffering would have been nothing, for I would have been purely passive, whereas I was always conscious even when I could no longer speak.[55]

In another letter, Flaubert repeats the same image used here, describing how "sometimes, within the space of a single second, I have been aware of a thousand thoughts, images and associations of all kinds illuminating my brain like so many brilliant fireworks" (letter to Louise Colet, Tues., 6 July 1852). The grafting of medical or scientific terms ("seminal losses," "pictorial faculty of the brain") with psychic terms ("images," "soul," "rational essence") shows Flaubert's tendency to translate freely between medical and psychological codes. Equally important, however, such passages provide direct evidence that Flaubert understands Emma by projecting his own experience onto her. The metaphor of fireworks, for example, turns up in his description of Emma's hallucination as well as of his own:

She remained lost in stupor, and only conscious of herself through the beating of her arteries, that seemed to burst forth like a deafening music filling all the fields. The earth beneath her feet was more yielding than the sea, and the furrows seemed to her immense brown waves breaking into foam. All the memories and ideas that crowded her head seemed to explode at once like a thousand pieces of fireworks. She saw her father, Lheureux's closet, their room at home, another landscape. Madness was coming upon her. (228)[56]

Emma's dementia, one should note, involves an inverted, ironic return of the kind of metaphorizing that characterized her perception after intercourse with Rodolphe. Here, the music and her veins seem to explode from within, and the hyperconsciousness implied by the earlier metaphors gives way to its opposite, stupor. In the present context, however, what is most striking about this passage is that Emma's symptoms are an almost verbatim transcription of Flaubert's.[57]

Perhaps this symptomatic identification between novelist and character is what Flaubert had in mind when he remarked that "Madame Bovary, c'est moi." Certainly Flaubert was eminently qualified to portray Emma's fate from the point of view of a patient. Yet, at the same time, Flaubert also adopts the point of view of a doctor, with respect to his own illness and that of his characters, thinking in the terms and with the diagnostic presuppositions of a clinician.

Flaubert's peculiar experience of illness both as delirium and as knowledge deeply informs *Madame Bovary*. More generally, this same experience constitutes the phenomenological root of the bifurcated style that Albert Thibaudet, among others, sees as the essence of Flaubertian realism.[58] The novelist himself recognized that in the act of writing he became, in his own words, "literarily speaking, two distinct persons: one who is infatuated with bombast, lyricism, eagle flights, sonorities of phrase and lofty ideas; and another who digs and burrows into the truth as deeply as he can, who likes to treat a humble fact as respectfully as a big one, who would like to make you feel almost physically the things he reproduces." Traditionally, this passage has been adduced as evidence of Flaubert's vacillation between two styles, one romantic and the other analytic. Given what we now know about Flaubert, however, it may be more appropriate to speak not of romantic and analytic, but of hysterical and medical perspectives in tension. The hysterical aspect of Flaubert's prose appears in what he calls the "throbbing of sentences and the seething of metaphors," stylistic events that, like the river of milk Emma feels in her veins, "flow from one another like a series of cascades, carrying the reader along." The medical side of Flaubert's style is evident from the anatomical and surgical implications of the second half of the quotation above, and can be supplemented by Flaubert's aspiration in another letter for "a style that would be precise as the language of the sciences . . . a style that would pierce your idea like a dagger."

Prescient in this as in so many other things, Sainte-Beuve was the first to recognize the predominance of the anatomical element in Flaubert's style, in the now-famous remark that "M. Flaubert wields the pen as others do the scalpel." The critic also recognized that to write in that way was "a sign of enormous power." We can now specify the nature of that medical power and the way in which it is exercised. It is the power to act upon, to control, and ultimately to constitute its intellectual object—the embodied self—without coming into direct contact with it or even being visible to it. Flaubert's ideal of stylistic power is exactly this kind of medical panopticism: "an author in his book must be like God in the universe, present everywhere and visible nowhere. Art being a second nature, the creator of that nature must behave similarly" (letter to Louise Colet, 9 Dec. 1852).

Certainly, as the plight of Charles Bovary's unread medical dictionary shows, the medical perspective of the author is visible nowhere in the world represented in *Madame Bovary*—or almost nowhere, for there is one competent medical figure who does appear at the end of the novel (although too late to redeem the world and save the doomed Emma with his healing power). That figure is Dr. Larivière, and as one might expect, there are many affinities between him and Flaubert. Larivière's relation to those outside the profession mirrors Flaubert's relation to the characters he portrays: both doctor and writer assume the status of deities. As Flaubert remarks about Larivière's arrival in town on the eve of Emma's death, "the apparition of a god would not have caused more commotion."

Larivière and Flaubert mirror each other in their personalities as well. The doctor is one of those

> who, cherishing their art with a fanatical love, exercised it with enthusiasm and wisdom. . . . Disdainful of honors, of titles, and of academies, hospitable, generous, fatherly to the poor, and practicing virtue without believing in it, he would almost have passed for a saint if the keenness of his intellect had not caused him to be feared as a demon. His glance, more penetrating than his scalpels, looked straight into your soul, and would detect [the French word is *désarticulait*, disarticulated in the anatomical sense] any lie, regardless how well hidden. (233–34)

Flaubert, similarly, is fanatical in his devotion to his art; he, too, disdains academies and honors, as is evident from his sarcastic award of the Cross of the Legion of Honor to Homais, as well as from comments in his correspondence (for example, "How honors swarm where there is no honor!" [letter to Louise Colet, 15 Jan. 1853]); he, too, feels that he acts charitably to the poor; he, too, is interested in burrowing and penetrating into the truth. And, like Larivière, who "belonged to that great school of surgeons created by Bichat," Flaubert claims to "feel at home only in analysis—in anatomy, if I may call it such" (letter to Louise Colet, 26 July 1852).

Both Emma and Dr. Larivière, hysteric and physician, thus are projections of Flaubert's own personality. In this sense, *Madame Bovary* might be described as a "disarticulated" autobiography. As Jean Starobinski argues, following Emile Benveniste, autobiography characteristically contains an inherent tension between historical and discursive subjects, between the self who lives and the self who makes sense in writing of that life. This structural tension between lived experience and (self-) knowledge, according to Starobinski, is usually mediated in narrative by some radical change in the life of the autobiographer, such change most often taking the form of a conversion into a new life.[59]

In *Madame Bovary*, however, the relevant tension arises between hysterical and discursive subjects, between lived-experience-as-illness and medical knowledge. Instead of finding resolution in a new life, the *bios* in a medically defined autobiography must by definition ultimately die. As Bichat's dictum puts it, life is that which resists death. Flaubert echoes this sentiment: "How annihilation stalks us! No sooner are we born than putrefaction sets in, and life is nothing but a long battle it wages against us, ever more triumphantly until the end—death—when its reign becomes absolute" (letter to Louise Colet, 31 March 1853; Steegmuller's translation). And the corollary of this premise, as Bichat points out, is that although the truth of life only becomes evident in death, when the anatomist disarticulates the body, illness is already a form of dissection. In this sense, Emma is dead even before the novel begins, and the novel itself is a patient anatomization.

This seems somewhat sadistic, and one may well wonder why, after all, Emma is denied medical treatment. Why, in other words, does Larivière come too late? For Jean-Paul Sartre, the reason is clear: Larivière's knowledge—and medical knowledge more generally—is foreign to Emma's existential pain, as it is to Flaubert's art. The doctor, according to Sartre, "*knows* the horror scientifically but does not *feel* it," because his medical knowledge is grounded in utilitarianism.[60] But this, I would suggest, is a philosopher's misreading (albeit a strong one), based on a distortion of actual medical knowledge into philosophical categories. Larivière represents not utilitarian but medical philosophy: Bichat is his mentor, not Bentham. Moreover, Larivière's professional *impassabilité*, imposed on him by the requirements of his clinical epistemology, does not destroy all feeling in him, as Sartre claims. The great physician's objective veneer cracks just enough at the sight of the horror to hint at a human interior: "this man, accustomed as he was to the sight of pain, could not keep back a tear that fell on his shirt front" (234).

This tear resembles those that Flaubert claimed to have himself shed over Emma while writing *Madame Bovary*, and marks another link between novelist and ideal doctor. But it also points toward a more complicated biographical connection between the two. For Larivière's tearfulness when faced with Emma may remind one that Flaubert's father wept over Gustave during the early days after his son's first "epileptic" attack. Several other characteristics link Achille-Cléophas with Larivière—both physicians served under Bichat, both wear cloaks that identify them as somewhat eccentric, both attempt to maintain a stern late-Enlightenment moral stance. These similarities have prompted several critics to argue that Larivière is a fictional depiction of Flaubert's father.[61] If Larivière represents Flaubert's *knowledge* confronting in Emma the novelist's *being*, Larivière as father figure must also be the focus of a second autobiographical problematic: the Oedipal tension between father and son.

Sartre's mammoth biography of Flaubert has dissected in great detail the intimate strains between Gustave and his father, stemming in large part from Achille-Cléophas's refusal to allow his younger son to follow in his footsteps and become a doctor. Flaubert's eventual breakdown, Sartre contends, was due to his medical disinheritance, and provided him with the freedom to write. Flaubert then used this freedom to gain his revenge against his father by portraying him—in what Sartre considers a less than flattering way—as Larivière in *Madame Bovary*. Seeing the filial tie as one of *ressentiment* depends upon accepting Sartre's claim that Larivière's portrait is laden with sarcasm. This claim, however, is based on an oversubtle reading of the textual evidence.[62] My less elegant but clearer reading interprets Larivière as positively representing Flaubert's father and the heritage of medical knowledge—but also recognizes that Larivière to some extent represents Flaubert himself. The son thus accedes to his father's place, in that he performs—as a writer—all the functions of a doctor.

In addition to its simplicity, this interpretation of the father : son relationship has another advantage over Sartre's: it accounts for not only two but three generations of medical genealogy in Flaubert's life as well as in his text. If the first medical generation is that of Bichat (recall Flaubert's description of Larivière as one of a "great line of surgeons that sprang from Bichat"), the second generation is that of Flaubert's father and Larivière, both of whom studied under Bichat. The third generation, then, belongs to Flaubert and . . . surprisingly enough, to Charles Bovary. No wonder Flaubert says that Larivière's kind of surgeon is now extinct. Neither Charles nor Flaubert is a successful physician. In this sense, Charles represents Flaubert's failed ambition to become a doctor—and indeed one can trace many of the signifiers of failure borne by Charles (stuttering, falling into stupors, and so on) back to Flaubert, the idiot of the family. At the same time, however, Charles's medical ineptitude makes it possible for Flaubert the writer to act as a doctor in monitoring the progress of Emma's illness. In the gap left by Charles's incompetence, the novelist can note Emma's symptoms, elicit her delirium, supervise her fantasies, and probe the constitution of her memory. Flaubert makes himself the true heir to Bichat's anatomical insights. By extending the anatomicoclinical concepts of constitution and diagnosis into the psychological domain, he secures his own position within the Bichatian genealogy.

Flaubert's choice of a novelistic situation in which medical knowledge is not available thus makes biographical sense as a response both to his personal experience of illness and to his family ties to medicine. The sociological issue, however, remains: given the literary strength of Flaubert's medical realism, what accounts for its authority? Why should the medical point of view become such an appropriate one, at this moment in history, for the task of representing reality?

The answer to this question has to do, I think, with the development of the professions—including the profession of letters and the profession of medicine—during the first half of the nineteenth century. This is an extraordinarily complicated event, to be examined in more detail in the following chapter, but the general results of the professionalization process can be summed up here. By the 1850s, literary and medical workers have reached the end of a period during which they sought professional status from the public. While the doctors by and large succeeded in gaining control over their market, the writers failed to control the vast new market for literature that opened up during the 1820s and 1830s. By the time Flaubert begins to write, it has become clear that instead of a unified reading public under the domination of men of letters, a stratified market has formed, with some writers knocking off what Sainte-Beuve disdainfully refers to as "industrial literature" intended for consumption by the newpaper-reading public, and a small elite group of novelists writing for Stendhal's "happy few."[63] The change can be indexed by the fact that Balzac is one of the first to write in the new large-circulation journals, and eagerly sets forth to conquer that market (although eventually he, too, turns against journalism with a vengeance, most scathingly in his *Monograph on the Paris Press*, published in 1842), while Flaubert disdains and despises journalism.

In turning away from the mass reading public, Flaubert in effect accepts literature's marginal status as a profession. Unlike Balzac, he makes no ideological appeals to his readers—he does not loudly proclaim, as Balzac does, that he is a "doctor of social medicine" ready to heal the wounds of postrevolutionary French society.[64] Instead, Flaubert focuses on technique. But with this new emphasis in realism on a medicalized style (rather than on the persona of the doctor), and more generally on the importance of technique, is not Flaubert now appealing to successful doctors, and indeed to the professional class as a whole, for whom technical skill rather than ideological purity or personal authority is fast becoming the relevant measure of value? Given that the professional class—which would include literary and medical men, as well as lawyers, engineers, and architects—is the rising class during this period, Flaubert's realism would seem to be very much of its time, marginal only in the sense that a professional elite is marginal.[65]

Reading Flaubert in this way, as affiliated with a rising professional class, becomes possible only if one extends Riffaterre's concept of intertextuality beyond what semiotics contemplates. The discursive intertextuality I have traced not only links literature and society together in a much finer historical weave than does Riffaterre's ideological intertextuality, but also permits one to begin to address the much-vexed question of the influence Flaubert's social context has on his textual production. Semioticians have tended to leave this question—framed for them as one about the ideological determinants of literary form—to the Marxists, who in Flaubert's case (as Sartre's endless project reminds us) have had enormous trouble tying the writer's forms to his class situation or conjuncture. The classic working-through of the "Flaubert problem" in Marxist criticism, of course, occurs in Georg Lukács's work. For Lukács, literary texts qualify as "realistic" only insofar as they accurately represent, through types, the inner dynamic of historical development: the coming-to-power of an emerging dominant class (or at least, of that emergent class's ideology). The only possible progressive class in the modern age, however, is the proletariat, a class hardly visible in Flaubert, much less blessed by him. If the proletariat fails to materialize historically in the failed revolutions of 1848, this merely excuses Flaubert from responsibility for what Lukács must nevertheless ultimately regard as artistic failure. Flaubert, in this view, is denied the very possibility for success by his social and historical belatedness.[66]

Archaeological analysis suggests that although Lukács's conclusions are false (and his own agonizing over Flaubert indicates that even Lukács was troubled by the evaluation he found himself forced to make), his aesthetic principle remains sound. In order to claim that Flaubert is a realist in Lukács's sense, one need only substitute discourse for ideology and loosen the definition of class a bit. Flaubert may not be representing the ideology of the proletariat, but he *is* projecting the discourse, and with it a certain ideology of an emerging dominant class, that of professionals.[67] The drama and the dynamic thus map themselves textually not so much in the clash of typical characters, but in the impersonal, authoritative exercise, the powerful demonstration, of Flaubert's narrative technique, his point of view, and his control of knowledge. It is this power, the power not so much of capital or of labor as of information, that one should recognize in Flaubert's medicalized realism.

THREE

PARADIGMS AND PROFESSIONALISM

BALZACIAN REALISM

IN DISCURSIVE CONTEXT

FLAUBERT WAS IN THE MIDST of composing *Madame Bovary* when he wrote to Louise Colet, on December 27, 1852, "in the grip of a ghastly terror." This sensation had been provoked, Flaubert went on to explain, by his discovery of an uncanny resemblance between Balzac's *Louis Lambert* and his own experience: "Lambert is, in all but a few particulars, my poor Alfred. I have found some of *our* sentences (from years ago) almost word for word: the conversations between the two school friends are our conversations, or analogous. There is a story about the manuscript stolen by the two of them, and remarks made by the schoolmaster—*all of which happened to me*, etc. etc."[1] To find one's life anticipated in this way was frightening enough in itself, but what made matters even worse was that Balzac seemed to have anticipated Flaubert's *text* as well: "My mother showed me a scene in Balzac's *Un Médecin de campagne* [*sic*] (she discovered it yesterday) *exactly the same* as one in my *Bovary*: a visit to a wet nurse. (I had never read that book, any more than I had *Louis Lambert*.) There are *the same details*, the same effects, the same meaning." Recognizing that he had been unconsciously transcribing *idées reçue*, Flaubert found himself on the brink of panic. Only his confidence that his style eclipsed Balzac's gave him the strength of mind to quell the anxiety he felt at discovering his realist predecessor's version of a novel including a country doctor: "One would think I had copied it, if it weren't that my page is infinitely better written, no boasting intended."

That *Le Médecin de campagne*, of all Balzac's novels, should give rise to such a strong anxiety of influence in Flaubert is surprising, in view of that novel's relatively marginal status in the Balzacian canon.[2] Despite Balzac's own claim that it formed the keystone to the entire *Comédie*, *Le Médecin* has been relegated by most literary critics to secondary status. Tagged as one of Balzac's utopian fictions, it is not considered an important realistic novel of the caliber of *Le Père Goriot*, *Illusions perdues*, or *Eugénie Grandet*. Literary histories of realism usually broach the comparison between Balzac and Flaubert by citing one of these latter novels. Yet for Flaubert himself, *Le Médecin* was the novel that most urgently forced him to assert a stylistic identity distinct from his literary forefather's. Flaubert's aesthetic anxiety raises a number of questions for anyone interested in discriminating not only among various realisms, but between realism and utopianism as literary modes. What relationship can be established between this supposedly utopian novel and Balzacian realism in general? If *Le Médecin* and *Madame Bovary* share certain sentences in common (as well as certain aspects of setting and character conveyed through these sentences), can we move beyond Flaubert's defensive value judgment about how his prose is "infinitely better written," to clarify the differences in generic presuppositions that make the same sentence function as a different statement in the two novels?[3] Can we then rely on these differences to develop some nonaxiological precepts about the nature of Balzacian realism? If, as I suggest in the previous chapter, Flaubert's realism can be described as "medical," and if Balzac's utopianism stands in some close relation to that medical perspective, Balzac's realism may also turn out to be medical in its own distinctive way—a way that makes it possible for Balzac to imagine a utopia where the physician rules as hero, rather than (as with Flaubert) only a realistic world premised on the absence of that heroic physician.

I shall return to these questions later in this chapter. Here I simply would like to stress how such questions fit into the larger debate about the history of the realistic novel. That Balzac and Flaubert belong within a single literary tradition called realism has been relatively firmly established by critics of widely varying persuasions. But in agreeing on a coherent line of descent, modern critics have hardly escaped the anxiety Flaubert himself registers about his relation to Balzac. Critics cope with their anxiety, most commonly, just as Flaubert does—by making a value judgment in favor of one or the other novelist, so that each stands as the negation or antithesis of the other. Thus Balzac is "classical," Flaubert "modern"; Balzac is "readerly," Flaubert "writerly"; Balzac lacks Flaubert's style, Flaubert lacks Balzac's energy; Balzac's realism is "critical," Flaubert's is "merely descriptive."[4]

Such "simple abstractions" (to borrow a phrase from Marx) may soothe one's angst, but they do not go very far in providing satisfactory answers to the general questions that anyone interested in realism is likely to ask: If Balzac inaugurates nineteenth-century realism, how does that realism differ from earlier and later fictional modes, from Sir Walter Scott's historical fiction or Victor Hugo's romanticism, from Conrad's or Joyce's modernism? And is there any reason why Balzac's particular kind of realism appeared when and where it did?

To begin to answer these questions, one needs a working definition of the formal characteristics of Balzacian realism—a definition sufficiently narrow to exclude previous types of fictional practice and yet broad enough to apply to Balzac's work in general. Balzac's own assertions about his literary method, unfortunately, cannot be taken as gospel; he says little on the subject, and, as I will show, what he does say is at times incoherent and at other times self-contradictory on such important issues as characterization and representation. But even if Balzac did provide a working definition of realism, one would still need to measure that definition against the realism demonstrated in the novels themselves.

Literary critics, on the other hand, have identified a number of disparate formal characteristics distinguishing Balzac's realism from that of his predecessors and successors. Two major lines of thought concerning Balzac's approach to mimesis have emerged. The first, exemplified in the work of structuralist-oriented critics like Barthes, Culler, and Heath, has taken Balzac's claim that his language corresponds to reality as an accurate one that is indispensable for understanding his realism. The second, championed by historicizing critics such as Lukács and Auerbach, has focused instead on the correspondence between subjective and objective experience within the novels themselves.[5] Together, these two approaches have highlighted three major identifying features of Balzacian realism. First, it aims at what the novelist himself calls "the rigorous transcription of reality,"[6] presuming that language can be transparent to the reality it represents (a naïve presumption, for the structuralists, insofar as it implies wrongly that language is not itself part of reality—as Barthes puts it, Balzacian realism can be defined as asserting its truth "not by the origin of the model, but by its exteriority to the word that accomplishes it"). Second, Balzac's mimesis is impelled by a drive to penetrate into the "hidden meaning," the *sens caché*, of reality, not simply to reproduce its surface but to grasp its inner mechanism, to know it not only contemplatively but practically, not only as a chaotic set of characters in flux but as a unified, value-laden, and dynamic whole—what Lukács refers to as a "totality." Finally, realism in Balzac works to generate what the novelist calls "types," characters whose subjective lives are inextricably linked to their objective, social existence and who thus participate in the social dynamic.[7]

In these three fundamental aspects of Balzacian mimesis—representation as transparency, meaning as totality, character as type—one has at least the rudimentary elements of a working definition of Balzac's realism. To fuse these elements into a single satisfactory definition, however, will be far from easy. For although each points to something essentially true about Balzac's realism, the truth in each case stems from a distinct epistemological framework. The impasse here is starkly reflected in the different Balzacs found in structuralist versus historicist interpretation. For the structuralists, understanding the truth claims of Balzacian realism means defining his theory of meaning as a reflection theory of language. For the historicists, in contrast, the issue of truth—the question of just what the "real" in Balzacian realism *is*—concerns not whether words comply with their referents, but whether man interacts with his historical conditions.

To have any hope of grasping the interrelatedness of Balzac's concepts of representation, totality, and the type within a single realistic practice, one must begin by setting aside the epistemological presuppositions of structuralism and historicism—by viewing Balzacian realism apart from whatever "realistic" theory of language or "realistic" theory of man in society Balzac's writing may more or less embody. The point is not to substitute some third philosophical system that would explain the truth Balzac must have had in mind. Rather, it is to pose the question of truth more humbly in historical terms. For a given notion of the type (or of totality, or of transparency), what are the systems of knowledge, the "scientific" contexts, that during Balzac's own time might have endowed this notion with the value of truth? Having identified these contexts, one may reopen the larger question of the unity of Balzac's realism by correlating these systems of knowledge, these partial epistemological contexts, within an epistemological field or paradigm.

As I shall show, such a paradigm—which one can proleptically designate as that of early French psychiatry—did exist, although its coherence was both tenuous and brief; now almost forgotten, it constituted an evanescent historical context within which the disparate truth claims for Balzac's realism become intelligible. The very fragility of that paradigm, however, raises the question of why Balzac should have opted to rely on it. What sort of authority and persona does this paradigm bestow on the novelist, if the potency of its truth is so dubious? The answer to *that* question, in turn, will help explain how *Le Médecin de campagne*, despite—or rather because of—its peculiar utopianism, deserves to be seen as the keystone to Balzac's realism.

Physiognomy, Phrenology, and the Balzacian Type

Discussions of typification in Balzac usually begin by citing the novelist's own comments on the subject in the "Avant-Propos" of the *Comédie*. There Balzac sets out to distinguish his own concept of character from that of his immediate Romantic predecessors, in particular Scott. While the romantic novelists created their representative characters or types intuitively, Balzac claims, he derives his representative characters scientifically, reuniting traits common to many individuals. Balzac's types, consequently, are not *mythical* but *social* constructions: not allegorical figures but quasi-statistical amalgams. As Peter Demetz has shown, however, Balzac's distinction ought not to be taken at face value, not only because it seems overly schematic, but also because earlier in his career he had claimed that his novels included statistical *and* allegorical types.[8]

Demetz points out this inconsistency in part to chastise Georg Lukács, who draws far-reaching conclusions from the assumption—based in large part on Balzac's comments in the "Avant-Propos"—that Balzac's types are never scientific or statistical.[9] For Lukács it is precisely the *non*statistical basis of Balzac's types that distinguishes him from "naturalists" like Flaubert and Zola, making him at once a more humane and (more relevant for our purposes) a more *realistic* novelist. But if Demetz is right to argue that Balzac mixes his types after all, creating some that are traditional and others that are scientific, then how can both kinds of typification be integrated within a single overall practice of Balzacian realism?

To understand how Balzac's realism reconciles scientific and mythical types, one must first describe the conflict between these notions of type a bit more precisely. The mythical type favored by the Romantics stands, in Charles Nodier's words, as "le signe représentatif d'une création, d'une idée."[10] Its essence lies in an ahistorical passion, energy, or moral value—a force so strong that it transcends circumstance, shining forth from the character incarnating it no matter what the context. The mythical type, thanks to this transparency, can be (and often is) recognized by a single trait, a kind of physicalized epithet signaling the essential quality of the character who bears it. The scientific type, in contrast, embodies a passion inextricable from milieu: the environment expresses the man. Rooted ontologically in his surroundings, the scientific type can only be represented through the correlation of statistically accumulated traits.

These distinctions, as spelled out by Demetz (relying on Balzac's explicit pronouncements in the "Avant-Propos"), seem absolute. Yet there must exist some underlying poetic principle that permits Balzac to shift as he does from one mode of characterization to another, from conceiving the type as the allegorization of innate forces to conceiving it as a product of social pressures. Underlying these two conceptions is a prior assumption: of *direct and harmonious expressivity*. A singular interior expresses itself in the character's exterior, even if exterior and interior are somewhat differently defined in the two cases. Thus, the scientific type may summarize a large number of traits, but Balzac does not statistically weigh these details or worry over how to evaluate their relative significance, nor does he depend on metonymy or narrative action to make them meaningful, as does Flaubert. Instead, for Balzac, every trait in a type is immediately allusive, whether to a class of mythical passion or to a kind of scientific animality.

Scientific and traditional types both presuppose, in other words, what Auerbach brilliantly labels the "harmony-thesis," an accord among traits that secures a congruence between milieu and the *"coeur humain."*[11] Auerbach traces the roots of this Balzacian thesis to two general sources: the biological theories of St.-Hilaire and the historicist attitudes associated with Michelet and Scott. But he does not follow through in any great detail on his *aperçu* about Balzac's stylistic debt to science. For the philologist, it is sufficient to describe Balzac's biologism as "mystical, speculative, and vitalistic," and to conclude that the "unity of the milieu" that types require "is not established rationally" (471). Indeed, the very *ir*rationality of Balzac's supposedly scientific method of typification is what enables him to blend his scientific types smoothly together with allegorical ones in what Auerbach calls "romantic-magical" or "demonic" realism. In this view, Balzac's grasp of typicality depends not upon scientific method but upon what Sainte-Beuve called the novelist's "physiological intuition."[12]

Balzac's scientific ideas may indeed be irrational and thus as much magical as scientific, at least from the perspective of modern, rationalized scientific method. Yet to dismiss them for being irrational is a strangely antihistoricist move on Auerbach's part, for during Balzac's time the biologistic ideas he adapted to literary ends were considered scientific within at least a certain segment of the scientific and medical community. To understand the constraints of truth under which Balzac's types take shape, one must define more precisely than does Auerbach the epistemic situation of the quasi-scientific ideas Balzac uses to generate types. Among these ideas, Balzac was most enthusiastic about two particular kinds: physiognomical and phrenological.

In their nineteenth-century versions, physiognomy and phrenology had intellectual life spans almost identical to Balzac's. Both disciplines were constituted as "sciences" at the turn of the century, and both were largely discredited in the scientific community by the 1850s. During Balzac's lifetime, they enjoyed both popular and quasi-scientific legitimacy, being accepted by some (although by no means all) doctors and many laypersons as scientific ways of understanding character. Despite all these similarities, however, phrenology and physiognomy were conceptually distinct forms of knowledge, differing—in ways that matter greatly for Balzac—from each other as well as from the dominant symptomatology of clinical medicine.[13]

Physiognomy, the art of judging character by examining the face and body, had been practiced informally for many centuries, but was revitalized in the 1790s under the extraordinary influence of Lavater's *Physiognömische Fragmente*. Lavater, a Swiss pastor, based his physiognomy on two principles, both of which were as much religious as scientific. First, he assumed that human beings' outward appearance manifested their inner selves, selves that Lavater defined neither by their rationality nor by their drives but as moral essences—virtue, vice, sensitivity, nobility, and so on. Second, he assumed that "each part of the body contains the character and essence of the whole," so that "all features and contours, all passive and active motions of the human body—in short, everything whereby one reveals one's person is a matter of physiognomical interest."[14] Every detail is significant, but significant in the same way. The human body, and more generally, the milieu surrounding an individual, Lavater conceived as a homogeneity, a whole bound together and bound to the soul of the individual by what Lavater called "harmony." Only by assuming that the milieu could be apprehended as a harmonious whole, in fact, could Lavater maintain that every sign points to the soul's essence. Auerbach's postulate of a harmony-thesis in Balzac thus has its counterpart, and even its uncanny foreshadowing, in the Lavaterian system. Moreover, insofar as this notion of harmony implied that every type constituted an aesthetic whole, Lavaterian physiognomy tended to conflate human characteristics with artistic (and especially religious) images, at one extreme, and with animal species, at the other—a double tendency also evident in Balzac's typifications.

Like physiognomy, phrenology is an art devoted to deducing inner being from the external signs of character. But the similarity ends there, for phrenology involves a conceptual basis radically different from that of physiognomy, a difference intimately related to the fact that while Lavater began as a pastor, the founders of phrenology—Gall and Spurzheim—began as physicians. Like Lavater, they based their science on an analogy, but where Lavater's analogy equated external signs and the soul, Gall's and Spurzheim's analogies equated the outer organization of the body with the inner structure of the brain. Borrowing their assumptions from the then newly dominant paradigm in medicine—Bichat's pathological anatomy—Gall and Spurzheim postulated that the brain, like the body, was organized as a set of physiological functions. Each area of the brain, in this view, served as the organ, the physical substrate, for a specific mental faculty: "instincts, sentiments, penchants, talents, and, in general, the moral and intellectual forces."[15] If this principle of cerebral localization was correct, the phrenologists concluded, one should be able to characterize an individual by measuring and comparing the sizes of different parts of the brain. An enlarged sector of the brain would imply an excessive influence of one faculty over the others, a disproportion or relative excess that could denote some sort of abnormality—perhaps genius, perhaps mental illness, perhaps both.

Phrenology, then, derived from a respectable scientific discourse, physiognomy from a religious one. In principle, phrenologists would rely only on cranial traits in determining the psychic status of an individual, and would regard the inner man not as a spiritual essence but as an effect of physical organization, and thus could see their discipline as a kind of diagnostic tool. In fact, the phrenologists—whose ranks included some physicians whose scientific legitimacy had been jeopardized by their espousal of this dubious practice, as well as many less well-connected "general practitioners" who saw phrenology as a ticket to such legitimacy in the first place—took great pains to distinguish themselves from the physiognomists on these grounds. To the public, however, the two disciplines remained confused and conflated with each other, as they do to this day.[16] There is little wonder in this, for although conceptually and discursively different, in practice both physiognomists and phrenologists drew immediate connections between the appearance and internal condition of individuals. And although phrenologists did not believe that *every* feature of the body revealed the soul, they shared with physiognomists the assumption that a single trait—a bump on one's forehead, or the shape of one's nose—could provide a telltale sign of one's type.

After this long detour, one might well ask: how do these nuances help to clarify what Balzac is doing with his types? To begin with, the differences between physiognomy and phrenology could provide evidence to support Demetz's view that Balzac creates traditional and scientific types. Because physiognomy defines the inner man in moral terms, for example, one might expect Balzac to use it to shape his mythical or allegorical types. Indeed, Félix Davin, in the 1835 introduction to the *Etudes de moeurs*, suggests that Balzac "has put into action the maxims of La Rochefoucauld, that he has given life to the observations of Lavater in applying them."[17] But things are a little more complicated than Davin makes them out to be: although Balzac uses physiognomical indicators liberally when representing mythical types, such types cannot be reduced to Aesopian instanciations of ahistorical maxims about character. In fact, Balzac conceives of Lavater's physiognomy in a quasi-materialist way, suggesting in *The Curé of Tours* that "everyday life makes the soul, and the soul makes the physiognomy."[18] Physiognomy reveals a moral essence, but an essence that Balzac then treats as itself a product of social forces; there is a harmony between soul and physiognomy, but also a potential for dissociation.

Phrenology, on the other hand, might be expected to structure Balzac's supposedly scientific characterizations, as one method in the construction of "statistical" types. But phrenology is not a statistical discipline, and Balzac, like the phrenologists themselves, tends to use phrenology not in order to evaluate character statistically by sifting out and weighing the different traits against one another, but rather as a kind of diagnostic shorthand allowing him to penetrate directly into the essence of character, as he does for example by describing Père Goriot's bump of paternity. The hermeneutic complexities of symptomatology or typification based on pathological anatomy—the sense of the difficulty involved in moving from symptoms to internal structure—may constitute a fundamental aspect of Flaubert's work, but Balzac's phrenological characterizations do not offer these particular kinds of interpretative challenges.

Like moral and scientific methods of typification, the physiognomy and phrenology that inform them thus shade into each other, in Balzac's work as in the public mind. They mark relative points on a single spectrum of characterization, rather than two incommensurable descriptive techniques. Balzac himself speaks of physiognomy and phrenology as "twins, of which one is to the other as cause to effect."[19] As this statement implies, these two disciplines serve Balzac not because they provide a grounding scientific framework (their frameworks are incompatible with each other, in fact), but because they permit him to conflate their frameworks. Like mesmerism, to which they are assimilated by the novelist in *Ursule Mirouet*, phrenology and physiognomy imply a world at once material and spiritual, a matter of fact and of fate: "the science of Lavater and Gall," Balzac claims in *Une Ténébreuse affaire*, "proves beyond question that . . . there are signs in a man's face that reveal not only his character but his destiny."[20] An indissoluble unity of inner and outer lives, Balzac's type stems from this religious cum scientific perspective.

Invoking the prestige of religion and science in the same move has obvious ideological advantages. But the very shrillness in Balzac's claim that the scientific question has been settled indicates that perhaps it has not really been settled after all. In fact, phrenology and physiognomy were considered only marginally scientific even during Balzac's lifetime. Given the positivist and empiricist bent of clinical medicine, with its stress on the visibility of its corporeal object, and given the scientific authority this medicine enjoyed at the time, phrenology, physiognomy, and mesmerism were bound to remain suspect as spiritualist, pseudo-scientific disciplines.[21] Only in one field, the nascent medical specialization of psychiatry, did such disciplines find a sympathetic hearing. This peculiar fact needs to be considered further, but for the moment it is worth pointing out that the predominant antagonism that official clinical medicine showed to phrenology, physiognomy, and mesmerism did not go unnoticed by Balzac himself, who dramatized it (and betrayed his own scientific preferences) through the dilemma faced by Dr. Minoret in *Ursule Mirouet.*

Minoret, who had served as Robespierre's physician, is both a very successful doctor and a confirmed atheist who scoffs at what Balzac calls "the science of imponderable agents"—a science that capaciously includes phrenology, physiognomy, and mesmerism. In his ignorant dismissiveness, however, Minoret is not alone, for Balzac admits that "the Academies of Medicine and of Sciences roared with laughter" at such dubious disciplines. Minoret later converts to mesmerism (after a demonstration—even the science of imponderable agents claimed to and needed to be empirically verifiable!). To believe in mesmerism, phrenology, and physiognomy, however, means to accept that "the Finite and the Infinite . . . existed one in the other," and for Minoret this spells the ruin of "all his scientific theory." The struggle between official and marginal sciences ends in the triumph of the marginal, at least in Balzac's imagination—hardly a surprising result, since as we have seen, Balzac uses the tools of these marginal sciences to create his own types.

But this struggle, with its projected victory of a marginal scientific perspective over an entrenched one, is not only a scientific dispute for Balzac; it is an ideological one as well, in which each scientific perspective is saturated with values, as can be seen from the effects on Dr. Minoret of his acceptance of mesmerism, phrenology, and physiognomy. He not only admits these disciplines as true, but undergoes a more fundamental change of heart, rejecting "Voltairean old age" in favor of "Catholic youth." Like several other physicians in the *Comédie* (Benassis in *Le Médecin*, Desplein in *La Messe de l'athée*), Minoret becomes a late convert to Catholicism—a fate that indicates how strong are the crosscurrents between the scientific and the ideological in Balzac's work. In fact, Balzac's tendency to choose between competing scientific ideas on ideological rather than scientific grounds must strike anyone who reads the opening pages of the "Avant-Propos," where the novelist defends St.-Hilaire's biological theory against that of Cuvier. St.-Hilaire's system, which assumes that all living things stem from a single original being, must be correct, argues Balzac. Why? Because "the Creator works on a single model for every organized being." (St.-Hilaire, by the way, eventually loses his battle against Cuvier, just as the mesmerists, phrenologists, and physiognomists lose their battles for scientific status.[22] Balzac backs not only marginal but doomed avant-garde sciences.)

Whatever Balzac's ideological motive for preferring phrenology and physiognomy to the official diagnostic techniques of clinical medicine, there is no doubt that he relies on the tools these marginal disciplines provide. In this he differs radically from Flaubert, whose methods are clinical through and through. The two passages below, in which Balzac and Flaubert describe the effect of love on their heroines, Eugènie and Emma, nicely illustrate the difference in methods:

> From that day on, the beauty of Mlle. Grandet took on a different character. The grave thoughts of love by which her soul had been gently invaded, the dignity of the woman who is loved, gave to her features that sort of brightness which painters represent by a halo. Before the arrival of her cousin Eugènie might have been compared to the Virgin before the Conception; when he left, she resembled the Virgin Mother: she had conceived love.[23]

> Never had Madame Bovary been as beautiful as at this period; she had that undefinable beauty which results from joy, enthusiasm, success, and which is nothing more than the harmony of temperament with circumstances.[24]

In his helpful study, *Physiognomy in the European Novel*, Graëme Tytler treats these passages as two of a kind, considering both as illustrating the same thing: the literary use of physiognomy to achieve lyric effects. This seems to me to miss the discursive point: unlike Balzac, Flaubert interprets the effect of emotions on physical appearance in radically *non*physiognomic terms.[25] For Balzac, it is a matter of a "soul" (defined by emotional and ethical qualities) giving rise to a definite, typical image; inner and outer lives resolve themselves into a unity of soul and form. For Flaubert, on the contrary, it is a matter of a specific circumstance combining with a certain temperament to give rise to something so complicated and unstable that, far from constituting an icon, it is undefinable. The Flaubertian dialectic between temperament and circumstance derives in turn from his clinicoanatomical orientation, as I argue in the previous chapter.

One way to distinguish Balzacian from Flaubertian realism, then, is by exposing the phrenological/physiognomical underpinnings of Balzac's method of characterization. By asserting that inner psychic states correspond to outer physical appearances, they give scientific support to Balzac's oft-repeated dictum that the self is to its appearance as an oyster is to its shell. The self, however, differs from an oyster in one fundamental way: rather than remaining static and closed off from its environment, the self moves, changes, and develops in the world. In neither phrenology nor physiognomy, nor the types

Balzac creates using these disciplines, can one find a systematic vision of this world. Phrenology does not try to explain how the causes of disease could be mapped; Balzac's types in themselves do not imply any conception of social totality as a dynamic causal system in which they emerge. How Eugènie comes to be endowed with the soul she possesses; how Goriot's bump of paternity evolves; how saintliness or fatherliness grow out of historical conditions, or how they will fare: these questions remain unanswered within the terms of Balzac's characterizations.

Despite having identified subsystems of knowledge that contribute something to Balzac's realism, we seem to be back where we started at the beginning of this chapter—unable to correlate the type and totality (not to mention that third Balzacian characteristic, transparency) within one overall conceptual system. Phrenology and physiognomy, however, did not exist as isolated systems of knowledge during Balzac's lifetime. The psychiatrists who used them supplemented them with theories of the causes, development, and treatment of mental illness. These etiological and therapeutic frameworks, taken together with the symptomatology provided by phrenology and physiognomy, comprise what one medical historian has called the "synthèse aliéniste," the alienist synthesis.[26] Could this synthesis provide any clue to how Balzac might have integrated his techniques of typification into a dynamic vision of totality?

Alienist Synthesis, Balzacian Totality

The paradigm synthesized by French psychiatrists in the 1820s and 1830s brought together in a single discursive contrivance at least four distinct concepts—two etiological, two therapeutic. Each of these four concepts, in turn, may be thought of as helping shape that enormous, dynamic totality that is the *Comédie Humaine*.

"Incessant Capriciousness": The Etiology of Milieu

If phrenology and physiognomy postulated that the inner man harmonized with his physical appearance or immediate environment, this diagnostic assumption neatly dovetailed in early psychiatric thought with an etiological one: the idea that environmental conditions could directly impinge on that inner man, causing illness. For the alienists, such a causal relationship between pathological milieu and mental illness was shaped by the psychological models they had inherited from late eighteenth-century Hartleyian associationism and sensationalism.[27] The sensationalists had argued that human beings' ideas arise from their sensations, and that the association of ideas therefore depends on the type and frequency of external stimuli or "impressions." Psychiatrists simply drew out the etiological consequences of this psychological proposition, arguing that because what Pinel's successor Esquirol called "the power of association of ideas with external objects" was strong, disturbances or abnormalities in the milieu must necessarily cause dissociations or abnormalities in one's thoughts.[28] The wrong environment, defined in terms of the sensations it provided, could be pathogenic.

The notion that environment could cause mental illness, of course, was nothing new: it can be found as far back as Hippocrates, and as I mentioned in the previous chapter, earlier eighteenth-century medicine already made much of this connection, seeing it as determining for physical as well as mental illness. Unlike the psychologists upon whom the alienists relied, these earlier physicians argued that the link consisted in the translation of qualities from nature into the internal "humours." Hot, moist weather, for example, would soften the body and mind, while cold, dry weather might cause an accrual of phlegm. In contrast, the sensationalist model implied that a milieu posed dangers not because of its *quality*, nor even because of its specific, positive content, but simply because of its *disorder*, an anarchy communicable through the nerves into the mind of the individual.

In the psychiatric theory developed during the early decades of the nineteenth century, then, the natural environment, especially weather and climate, continued to be seen (as it had been in the earlier medical paradigms) as a cause of illness—but only insofar as its capriciousness might translate into inner disturbance or disruption. The older medical idea that environment caused illness by transmitting its qualities to the self—an idea abandoned both by physicians and by psychiatrists—survived into Balzac's time (and still has some currency today) in scientifically degraded form as a popular belief. Balzac, so often a precise registrar of the historical shifts and stratifications of these sorts of beliefs, marks this one as well, in *Le Médecin de campagne*, for example, where a young woman named La Fosseuse is afflicted by the weather. Doctor Benassis tells us how she thinks about this meteorological etiology: "La Fosseuse is sensitive and highly strung. If it is close and hot, and there is thunder in the air, La Fosseuse feels a vague trouble that nothing can soothe. She lies on her bed, complains of numberless ills, and does not know what ails her. In answer to my questions, she tells me that her bones are melting, that she is dissolving into water"(116). The doctor, of course, knows better: although there *is* a direct link between La Fosseuse's mental aberrations and the weather, her body is not really melting, but is responding to meteorological variability. As he patiently explains, La Fosseuse is "a victim to highly-strung nerves, to an organization either too delicate or too full of power. . . . I have made a study of her temperament, recognized the reality of her prolonged nervous attacks, and of the swift mysterious recurrence of her moods. I found they were immediately dependent on atmospheric changes and on the variations of the moon, a fact I have carefully verified" (116). By Flaubert's and Eliot's time Benassis's lunatic etiology of nervous disorders will be recognized as quackery, but for Balzac and his psychiatric contemporaries such an analysis is on the cutting edge of science, and Balzac thus presents it without a hint of irony or sarcasm, through the persona of an authoritative physician. For him, it is not bêtise, but perfectly acceptable knowledge, part of the real(istic) truth.

The sensationalist model of environmental causality did more than simply provide an alternative to humouralism, however. It permitted one to regard social disturbances as causes of illness, thus enormously extending the purview of psychiatric intervention. Every social encounter must involve a certain shock of sensation, and for the fragile person, such shocks may be extremely disordering.[29] La Fosseuse exemplifies this type of patient, susceptible as she is both to natural and to social excitement: "She belongs to the small minority of women whom the slightest contact with others causes to vibrate perilously," Benassis warns a visitor. The good doctor goes on to indict La Fosseuse's social environment for causing her illness by its inconsistent, unsettled character. Taken up as a young girl by an aristocratic family, La Fosseuse "was, during this time, the victim of all the caprices of the rich, who, for the most part, are neither constant nor consistent in their generosity: beneficent by fits and starts, sometimes patrons, sometimes friends, sometimes masters. . . . Treating her by turns as a companion and as a chambermaid, they made of her an incomplete being."[30] As this discussion of the dangers of being déclassé shows, the psychiatric concept of pathogenic milieu carried with it some strongly inflected ideological implications, generally of a reformist, Saint-Simonian bent. The focus on social disorder as pathological cause meant that revolutions and the uncontrolled conditions of capitalism had to be condemned—not because they threatened the interests or rights of either the dominant or the oppressed classes, but because both these social processes led to anarchy and hence, psychiatrists argued, to outbreaks of mental illness.[31]

Like the alienists in this as in so many other regards, Balzac too asserts that social disorder poses a danger to the self. Such disorder for him appears most evident and hazardous to one's health in Paris, a milieu he describes as "ceaselessly dissolving, ceaselessly recomposed, . . . without bonds, without principles, without homogeneity."[32] The city's maelstrom-like environment can only give rise to a "pathology of social life" (the title of one of Balzac's projected but unaccomplished works), a life following the lines of the Balzacian plot, with its inherent unpredictability and coincidence.[33]

Balzac's vision of the social, in sum, takes its pathological bearings from the same psychiatric paradigm that informs his types. To say this, however, is to force a rethinking of the issue that has vexed Balzac's readers since Marx: the relation between Balzac's politics and his realism. The usual practice of leftist critics has been to rejoice in the revolutionary kernel in his realism—his representation of the real and *necessary* disorders accompanying the rise of capitalism—while at the same time condemning his manifestly reactionary political opinions, in particular his Catholic monarchism. If Balzac's perspective on social disorder is quasi-psychiatric rather than directly political, however, the contradiction between the manifest and the latent content of Balzac's representation of society vanishes. The stress on disorder-as-evil both in Balzac and in the alienists, it is true, coincided with the fear of disorder in conservative political thought—but the psychiatric/realist perspective entailed an overall response to social problems that differed enormously from that of the political conservatives. In essence, where conservatives tended to see social disorder as something to be condemned and repressed, Balzac and the alienists saw disorder as an object of study—something first to be understood, tamed into a *cognitive* or *discursive* order, and then treated.

Put more precisely, the alienists believed that the social milieu, however disordered or chaotic, necessarily gave rise to its own counterorder of pathological species, a perverse double of the healthy natural order that required a psychiatric Linnaeus to classify and clarify it. Describing a pathological milieu thus entailed two apparently contradictory epistemological steps: first, distinguishing the pathological from the normal, the disordered from the ordered environment; then, defining and controlling this disorder through classification. Balzac shares with the alienists this double gesture toward society. Life in metropolitan, capitalist society is indeed chaotic, but Balzac insists that this very corruption and disruption in the social milieu generates its own "laws of social consciousness, [a consciousness] which bears no resemblance to consciousness in the state of nature."[34] The "doctor of social medicine"—a title Balzac claims for himself in the introduction to *La Cousine Bette*—finds that social disorder produces an order of consciousness with its own laws and its own set of types, an order and a set he must describe, analyze, and treat in his narrative.[35]

"An Excess of Desire": *The Etiology of Passions*

For the alienists, the idea that a pathological milieu could cause illness was justified by sensationalist psychological principles. But environment alone could never be the sufficient cause of illness, or everyone placed in the same milieu would automatically fall sick in the same way and to the same degree. In order to account for such empirical variability while retaining the sensationalist model of environmental impingement, psychiatrists had to postulate a second, internal source of disturbance. A similar need to elaborate an inner cause of illness was felt by clinicians, as seen in the previous chapter. Both clinicians and psychiatrists, as it turned out, defined this inner cause in quasi-metaphysical language, Bichat and his followers speaking of "vital force" or internal sensibility, Esquirol's school speaks of "volonté." But the two branches of medicine understood the causal *process* in fundamentally different ways. In clinical medicine, vital force was thought to act upon an individual—for good or for ill—through a complex network of tissues, a network made visible by the pathological anatomists who opened up bodies and traced the hidden pathways of disease. For the clinicians, it was not the vital force itself that was responsible for illness, but the particular and varying way that force was deployed through the body, strengthening some organs at the expense of others and leaving some internal pathways open to the invasion of disease under certain environmental conditions. For the psychiatrists, on the other hand, volonté was more like what we would call a passion or idée fixe, a desire not deployed contingently or freely (Esquirol and his followers would speak in materialist terms of "a lesion of the will"), but always already tied to a specific object.

Critics have long recognized the importance of such fixated passions in Balzac's work, although no one (to my knowledge) has tied Balzac's conceptualization of passion to the psychiatric theory of his age.[36] Appetency in itself, however, is a psychological given but not necessarily a pathological one. What really ties Balzac to the alienists is the way both assimilate this supposed psychological condition into their systems of pathology. For Balzac and the alienists, all humans are "egotists," driven to gratify their particular desires ("all passions are essentially jesuitical," as Balzac puts it), so that appetency, per se cannot be considered pathological; indeed, "the great law of Self for Self," Balzac tells us, is simply the universal condition not only of man but of any animal. But in a badly organized social milieu, appetency, far from being curbed from excesses, might even be encouraged. There, egotism becomes pathological: "The condition of society makes of our needs, our necessities, our tastes, so many wounds, so many sicknesses, through the excess to which we are carried, pushed by the development thought impresses upon them; there is nothing in us through which they are not betrayed. Hence this title [*Pathology of Social Life*] borrowed from medical science. Where there is no physical sickness, there is moral sickness."[37] The pathological symbiosis between passion and milieu could not be more clearly stated than in this passage. Given chaotic social conditions, intellectual disorder inevitably results, and this inner disorder of thought will in turn communicate its violent energies to the passions—or rather to whatever passion dominates the individual in question.

The psychiatric name for psychic excess, of course, is mania, and it is hardly surprising that the 1820s witnessed a new and intense psychiatric interest in that disorder. The near-maniacal interest in mania culminated in the creation of an entirely new category of mental illness—the monomanias—corresponding to the belief that even an otherwise normal individual might suffer from a single excessive passion.[38] In monomania, the alienists argued, one suffered from a ruling passion that expressed itself only when the patient was dealing with the object of that passion, or more accurately with a particular train of thought directed toward that object. Thus, a patient could appear perfectly normal when his or her milieu exercised faculties that remained undiseased, but would display symptoms of mental illness if the milieu allowed the obsession to be focused on.

Balzac once again follows the alienists' line very closely. "What is madness," he asks in *La Peau de chagrin*, "if not the excess of a desire or of a power?" And Balzac is the first great novelist to place great weight on the idea of monomania, most overtly in his depiction of Balthazar Cläes (hero of *La Recherche de l'absolu*) and Louis Lambert.[39] But unlike the alienists, Balzac at least registers the ambiguities inherent in the psychiatric categories he invokes. Lambert and Cläes, for instance, are classic monomaniacs, but monomaniacs whose passions are directed toward an ideal (in Lambert's case intellectual, in Cläes's case aesthetic), so that the two men may also be labeled geniuses. In an ideal world, these monomaniacal geniuses would thrive, but in the degraded environment of French society they can only sicken and die. For Balzac, then, the category of monomania enjoys only a relative validity—not only because in a society of excessive passions everyone could potentially be defined as monomaniacal, but also because the term does not distinguish between ideal and egoistic passions.[40] Balzac even admits that it may be abused, turned by the unscrupulous and greedy against those who remain faithful to an ideal. In "L'Interdiction" Balzac presents a case of just such abuse by the Marquise d'Espard, who attempts to have her husband put away because he insists upon paying off a debt of honor the Marquise prefers not to acknowledge. The dénouement of the story, however, reveals the limits of Balzac's critique of monomania: the concept itself is ratified as correct, even though it may require professional authority (in the form of the legal-medical team of Judge Popinot and Dr. Bianchon dispatched to examine the Marquis) to certify that it is being used properly.

From physiognomy and phrenology, then, come the conceptual equipment Balzac needs to make types; from psychiatric nosology comes a coherent view of social order within which these types exist; and from psychiatric etiology come assumptions about pathogenic milieu and volonté that lend the social order its *sens caché*, or inner sense. One can extend this remarkably tight correlation between the elements of Balzacian realism and those of psychiatric discourse still further by turning to the therapeutic regimen contemplated in the *synthèse aliéniste*. As might be expected, therapy consisted in a two-stage attack on the environmental and passional causes of illness. In the first stage, that of *isolement*, isolation, the mental patient was to be prophylactically removed and protected from his pathogenic milieu. In the second stage, the patient—now sheltered from the capriciousness of the social milieu—was to be subjected to what came to be called the *traitement morale*. What are the assumptions guiding these two therapeutic practices, and how, if at all, do they structure Balzac's fictional practice?

"Isolement" and the Outlines of Balzac's Utopia

Championed by Esquirol beginning in the early 1820s, the doctrine of isolation derived conceptually from the same sensationalist principles as the theory of pathogenic milieu. If the social environment could cause mental illness, it followed logically that the first step in treating an insane person should be to isolate him or her from possibly harmful environmental influences. Psychiatrists defined these influences in the broadest possible terms: Esquirol, for example, emphasized the need "of removing the lunatic from all his habitual pastimes, distancing him from his place of residence, separating him from his family, his friends, his servants, surrounding him with strangers, changing his whole way of life."[41]

To achieve such a radical displacement, alienists invented a new social space, an artificially created therapeutic milieu purified of all the temptations of the social maelstrom: the modern asylum. The rise of the asylum as an institution is a fascinatingly complex story whose details are not important here.[42] What should be stressed, however, is the utopian quality of the asylum as alienists conceived it before they were granted professional status (and legal authority over the insane) by the French government in a series of laws beginning in 1838. The alienists' contention that they could create a space free of social pressures was naïve at best, and the asylum in practice never did materialize in quite as pure a form as they had imagined it. But if psychiatry was to have any chance of treating and curing patients, and hence of socially justifying itself as a science, such a space had to be imagined nonetheless. The asylum, like many another utopia, provided a conceptual raison d'être, an authoritative fantasy of efficacy as well as an efficacious fantasy of authority, for the group positing it—in this case the emerging psychiatric profession.

This double fantasy, I would argue, finds its exact utopian counterpart in Balzac's *Le Médecin de campagne*. That novel, in short, offers the literary expression of the alienists' therapeutic utopia, complete with isolation and moral treatment.

From the very start, Balzac stresses the isolation of the utopian community in *Le Médecin* from French society as well as from the pernicious influences of "capricious nature." The story begins as Captain Genestas, an old soldier who has come seeking Benassis's help for his sickly child, rides into the valley to which the doctor has chosen to devote himself and discovers "a village which had nothing beyond it, which seemed to border on nothing and to have no connection with anything; its inhabitants seemed to belong to a single family outside the social dynamic, and to be linked to the world only by the tax collector or by the most slender of threads."[43] The few social relations that *do* exist here, Balzac emphasizes, are deeply ingrained and essentially static, uncontaminated by the disturbances and turmoil of modern society that contribute so strongly to that society's pathology: "Political events and revolutions had never reached this inaccessible country—it lay completely beyond the limits of social stir and change." Thus, like the psychiatrist in his asylum, Dr. Benassis finds (or at least imagines he finds) in this country village "a *tabula rasa*. . . . My ideas did not clash with people's prejudices" (58). In its isolation, the village is a natural asylum, the perfect place to demonstrate a social therapeutics. The only possible source of "mental and physical contagion" to the community comes from a colony of cretins, whose inbred isolation provides a negative lesson illustrating both the power of isolation to effect change and the need for therapeutic oversight to direct it. The good doctor acts preemptively to isolate them more completely from the village community whose health is his primary concern. In what to us may seem a chilling move but to Balzac is clearly for the good of all, Benassis has the cretins transported by night, leaving the village a clean, pure environment in which treatment may proceed unencumbered.

"The Father of Us All": Moral Treatment as Medical Paternalism

If isolation placed the patient in a milieu free from disorderly social influences, the regimen known as moral treatment developed by Pinel, Tuke, and others in the early years of the nineteenth century aimed at re-creating in that artificial, blank space the simulacrum of an ordered, "normal" social environment, thus providing what one historian has called "a rational structure to annul disorder."[44] Given such a structure, it was believed, the asylum could over a period of time implant new and healthy habits of thought into the patient's mind and rehabilitate his or her psyche.

But what does rehabilitation aim at, if competitive egoism is both socially normal and pathogenic? As Robert Castel has shown, alienists resolved this dilemma by identifying mental health in juridical terms, as an ability to participate in free and rational exchanges as a member not of a competitive but a "contractual society." To be judged incapable of acting as a legal, contracting subject—contract being understood as both economic and social—was to become, instead, a subject of moral treatment. If sane, one came under legal jurisdiction; if insane, one would be placed under the jurisdiction of French psychiatrists within the walls of their asylums, a legal power granted alienists in 1838.

Children, of course, are the most common class of subjects considered disqualified from engaging in legal or contracting processes, and hence it is hardly surprising that alienists should model the doctor-patient relation in moral treatment upon the nineteenth-century form of the familial relation between parent and child: what alienists called a *relation de tutelle*. The ideal psychiatrist, as the historian Jan Goldstein remarks, was in effect "modelled on the nineteenth-century paterfamilias, a fact which Scipion Pinel tacitly acknowledged when he observed that only the asylum-doctor who felt himself to be 'a father' and his patients to be 'a family' would be gratified by a psychiatric career, would 'find charm in this existence, so barren in appearance.'"[45]

This paternal role, it turns out, is precisely what Balzac projects for his ideal doctor. Benassis hopes through his work in a small village "to develop all the resources of this country, just as a tutor develops the capacities of a child." As this sentence implies, Benassis's paternalism extends to all aspects of his social medicine. But the primary resources he aims at developing are human, and it is in relation to the villagers that his (and Balzac's) paternalism displays itself most clearly. He tells us, for instance, that his favorite patient, La Fosseuse, is "as simple as a child, and, like a child, she is carried away by her tastes and her impressions." The medical paternalism here obviously works along gender lines and reinforces patriarchy.[46] But La Fosseuse's individual condition of ignorant innocence emblematizes the condition not only of women but of the entire village, and indeed of society as a whole, in Benassis's view. Because social life is pathological, medical prudence dictates that "the masses should be kept in tutelage for the good of society" (151). And in Balzac's utopia, at least, the villagers accept this medical paternalism: the novel ends with the erection by the village of a monument marking Benassis's grave, on which the doctor is eulogized as—what else?—"the father of us all."

Tutelage is clearly enough a form of power. But it is an odd one, not overtly political or even repressive. The tutor does not brutally dominate or exploit a weaker party in the interests of his own class. Rather, as Foucault has suggested, the power involved in the tutelary relation is productive.[47] In the case of the mental patient confined in an asylum, moral treatment is intended to produce normality—defined as the ability to perform functions and fulfill obligations in a contractual society. This means that instead of squelching or destroying the egotism that makes one sick, moral treatment aims at turning individual attention, based on self-interest, toward "positive" personal and social objects.

A similar rechanneling of the forces of "diseased ambition" is evident in Balzac's utopia in the way he attempts to develop the village's economic life. He does this not by preaching altruism, but by appealing to the self-interest of the peasants, "to make them see where their real interests lie," in the doctor's words. A chiasmatic symmetry thus links the "healthy type" of character found in the village and the pathological type such a character might become if Balzac were to release him or her into Parisian society. For example, the usurer Taboureau would be a millionaire in Paris, Benassis tells us, but here in utopia his greed is both restrained and guided by the doctor's tutelage. Taboureau is able to imagine acting as a character would in a realistic novel. He tells Benassis a story, for instance, in which he himself is the main character, and in which he reneges on a contract in order to make a profit; we could be in any one of a dozen Balzacian novels. But it turns out that Taboureau in fact is the injured party in the story he tells. He has simply reversed the roles in order to make sure that Benassis (and the law) will agree that he is acting properly. Balzac's utopian narrative, like the asylum world on which it is modeled, is the realistic turned inside out.[48]

For Balzac, however, reentry into contractual society as constituted, with its egotistical gratifications and its built-in potential for tragedy, is at best a stopgap solution, The tutelary relation ultimately implies, and aims at, a more radical social solution, in which the structures of exchange and contract would be superintended and if possible superseded by the structure of the family emblemized by the doctor-patient relationship. Benassis's patients, if he has his way, will never escape from the tutelary relation, which itself becomes the standard of a healthy society. "The family," Benassis proclaims, echoing Balzac's own words in the "Avant-Propos," "will always be the basis of human society. Law and authority are first felt there; there, at any rate, the habit of obedience should be learned" (76). The good habits of the family discipline the dangerous freedom of contractual society, channeling the innate propensities of desire into healthy activities. Thus the ultimate cure for La Fosseuse is to assume her role as mother, for "motherhood, which develops the whole of a woman's nature, would give full scope to her overflowing sentiments" (115). Similarly, in the society as a whole, Balzac implies that the family structure should be translated into larger institutional and organizational units, and specifically into those of the professions, where authority derives not from mere strength but from a paternal wisdom. General Genestas, Dr. Benassis's visitor from the "real" world, functions within Balzac's utopia in part as an emblem for this generalizing of the tutelary relation beyond the medical, occupying the same position with respect to his troops that Benassis does with respect to his patients: he makes "a family of his regiment" (36) and calls his soldiers children.

It would be imprecise to reduce such paternalism either to an archaic patriarchy or to bourgeois ideology, to "a means by which society attempts to bring into harmonious alignment patterns of passion and patterns of property."[49] Balzac's paternalism devolves not upon the bourgeoisie or men as such (as it might well have), but upon professionals.[50] Benassis never considers going into business, but he does debate "whether to become a curé, a country doctor, or justice of the peace" (60), and claims to have "the courage of the schoolmaster" (55)—all service occupations that can be conceived as tutelary, with the professional as benevolent father figure. Le Médecin's insistent paternalism needs to be seen as a contribution to an emerging ideology of professionalism—an ideology, one might add, whose paternalistic, Dr. Welbyesque imagery has only recently begun to show its age.[51]

Tutelage must be relatively autonomous from intellectual structures, since so many distinct professions invoke it. But in the particular case of early psychiatry, that autonomy seems extremely slight. Psychiatry's paternalism develops in remarkably close coordination—even symbiosis—with the profession's paradigm. Phrenology and physiognomy, pathology of milieu and of passions, isolation and moral treatment—these elements specify for the doctor a tutelary position and mode of power over his patients, while the ideology of paternalist professionalism projects that position and that power as legitimate. This intimate link between ideas and ideology in French psychiatry has prompted the suggestion that, in Goldstein's words, the concepts of psychiatry were in effect "tailored to the extrascientific needs of the new profession."[52] One striking bit of evidence lends credence to this claim: following the passage of the 1838 asylum laws giving legal sanction to psychiatry, the paradigm I have laid out disintegrated with astonishing rapidity. By the 1850s, phrenology and physiognomy had been scientifically discredited and abandoned by most psychiatrists in favor of pathological anatomy, while hysteria (understood in pathological-anatomical terms) had replaced monomania as the quintessential disease of desire.

This paradigm shift, as I have argued in the previous chapter, occurs within realism as well, with Flaubert's adaptation of the principles of pathological anatomy to his own literary practice.[53] Although sharing with Balzac a general perspective as a realist oriented toward the pathology of social life, Flaubert thus exhibits a much stricter stylistic control that stems from his reliance on a more rigorous medical paradigm, as does his decision to write about an hysteric, Emma, rather than about a monomaniac like Monsieur Grandet. But if the earlier psychiatric paradigm was indeed as conceptually weak as it appears to have been, and if it was sustained at least in part because it served extrascientific needs, what were those needs? And can one describe similar professional needs on Balzac's part that might help to explain why he makes use of the psychiatric paradigm in his practice as a novelist?

Real Charisma: Professionalism as Ideology and Ethos

This is hardly the place, nor do I claim the expertise, to launch into a full-scale comparative sociological analysis of either the profession of psychiatry or the profession of letters during the first half of the nineteenth century. In any case, I am interested less in the conditions of professional labor under which Balzac and the psychiatrists worked than in how these conditions gave rise to a particular rhetoric: a rhetoric of what might be called militant professionalism. This rhetoric, I shall show, promotes the notion that psychiatrists and novelists deserve to be treated as authorities on the basis not of their technical skill or scientific standing—as one might expect—but of their charisma. But the oddity of such an overblown claim for authority can be accounted for by the historical moments to which it answers: the births of psychiatry and fiction writing as professions. At these moments, the rhetoric of militant professionalism provides the crucial shield for the would-be professional against dangerous questions about his or her competence or credentials. It also provides an equally crucial sense of personal identity and mission—an ethos—for the would-be professional self.

Because my primary interest lies in this rhetoric—and specifically in how it inflects Balzac's project as a realist—I shall touch upon the economic and institutional aspects of professionalism in only the most superficial way, relying heavily (but not uncritically) upon a number of works by sociologists of literature and of the professions for my information. My only purpose here is to make clear the structural homology between the professions of letters and of psychiatry at a particularly pivotal historical moment for both, and to sketch out the ideological imperatives and rhetorical strategies—what Larson calls the "professional project"—that responded to these structural conditions.[54]

Charismatic Exactitude: Professionalizing Ideology in Balzacian "Representation"

For any would-be profession, the ideal social condition is autonomy—independence from the demands and constraints of outsiders upon the "free activity" of the professional.[55] In any culturally well-established profession, like medicine or "high" literature, one takes such autonomy for granted: doctors are expected to make their decisions about how to treat a patient without considering anything except the innate complications and aspects of the patient's case; likewise, great writers are assumed (and most writers continue to demand the right) to pursue their calling without pandering to the reading public's appetite or the censor's requirements. But this kind of autonomy of thought and practice is not something that has always been a matter of course, or even conceivable. In fact, the serenity of the professional only becomes possible after a period of struggle during which his or her profession carves out an economic, social, and intellectual territory of its own. As many writers have learned to their dismay, however, intellectual and social autonomy—twin conditions of the independent writer's creative freedom—in themselves are insufficient.

From a sociological point of view, the isolation and poverty of so many modern literati signifies the failure of the profession of letters to establish the economic autonomy characterizing real professions. Like it or not, the struggle for economic autonomy is as much a feature of the profession of letters as is the struggle for freedom of thought.

Many of the most crucial campaigns for economic autonomy were fought by literary and psychiatric professionals in the first half of the nineteenth century. This economic history is a complex and sometimes arcane one, conducted largely between impersonal entities—professional associations, state agencies, licensing boards, universities, cultural organizations, and the like. Individuals, of course, also participate in this history—Balzac, for example, served as one of the first presidents of the "Société des gens de lettres" and was an early proponent of the concept of copyright (or what he called more precisely "propriété littéraire"), while Pinel, Georget, and Esquirol were extremely active in agitating for professional power through political and social channels.[56] The history of professionalization has predominantly been understood, however, not as the work of heroic individuals, but rather in terms provided by the sociology of institutions. At least this is the case for medicine and psychiatry.[57] The history of literature's professionalization, on the other hand, remains largely unwritten, but what has been produced does not begin to try to integrate what we know of the professionalizing efforts of such prominent literary figures as Balzac, Dickens, and Eliot with their individual projects as writers.[58] When historians of literature notice such efforts at all, they tend to write them off as external to the concerns of literary criticism (or even to the social history of literary ideas).

But construing the struggle in this way, sociologizing it as an external or institutional or "purely economic" battle, runs the danger of underestimating the tactical importance, in that battle, of ideology. The battle for economic autonomy on the part of the profession involved gaining control over their markets, to be sure; but success depended on persuading the public that doctors, psychiatrists, or writers deserved this authority. The struggle for professional status had to entail an appeal for legitimation—an appeal that depended upon the rhetorical abilities of these professionals, and which should not be divorced from the other supposedly "creative" or "scientific" or "intellectual" activities they engaged in.

The outcomes in these struggles, as everyone knows, were far from identical. Psychiatrists, and more generally the medical profession as a whole, succeeded in creating a public image as the only legitimate authority on health, to such an extent that even today medical legitimacy is hardly disputable; novelists, on the other hand, ultimately failed to convince the public that realism could meet the needs of all readers, for reasons I shall examine later. But despite their different fates, psychiatrists and realist novelists shared in their professional beginnings a similar socioeconomic profile, and evolved analogous rhetorical strategies to justify their claims to authority.

Psychiatrists and novelists were responding to mutations in the structure and extent of their markets during the first half of the nineteenth century, changes that for the first time made a professional career imaginable. In the previous century, psychiatrists (and doctors as well) had faced a divided marketplace—psychiatrists sharing authority over the mentally ill with religious institutions,[59] while the medical marketplace was vertically stratified, with physicians' guilds serving the social elite and the surgeons treating the lower classes.[60] In the literary marketplace, a similar stratification of the marketplace existed: the upper-class reading public was served by a small elite of polite, humanist writers dependent to a large extent on patronage or local reputation, while less sophisticated readers constituted a separate market for an impoverished group of scribblers and chapbook writers who eked out their living on Grub Street or its Parisian equivalent. This division was enforced by economic mechanisms and class distinctions,[61] rather than by explicit guild regulation as with medicine, and within London and Paris a few writers (most notably Sterne, Johnson, Diderot, and Rousseau) were attempting to overcome it. But blurrings at the limits should not blind one to the underlying market similarities between the nascent professions of letters and clinical medicine.

During the fifty-year period between 1790 and 1840, as part of what Karl Polanyi has called "the great transformation," fundamental changes occurred in the institutional and technological conditions of the marketplaces for these two occupations, resulting in a shift—both for medical men and for novelists—from a relatively small and divided market to a unified mass market for their services. In medicine, as seen in the previous chapter, the French Revolution destroyed the guild system, creating for the first time the possibility for what would take shape in England more hesitantly as a "general practice."[62] Psychiatrists in particular benefited as well from the decline of clerical authority during the revolutionary period. In the literary marketplace, as Williams writes, "the real break to a very rapid expansion did not come until the 1830's," spurred by the rapid growth of a middle-class reading public, as well as by the lifting of what Kathleen Tillotson calls "the general embargo on novel-reading" by moral authorities.[63] Perhaps of even greater importance were the technological innovations introduced during this period, including the rotary steam press, new methods of binding, and the development of railroads. Such material advancements reduced the prices both for books and for magazines, making them accessible to a mass public for the first time, and thus opening up the vista of a truly national market for writers. Publishers like John Dicks almost immediately began to exploit this new market by issuing enormous quantities of sensational fiction and cheap editions of the classics.[64] And the word *enormous* is no exaggeration: Dickens (who came closest to saturating the market) could reach up to one hundred thousand readers in serialization (not including those who read the many plagiarized editions of his novels), a figure far beyond that available to writers in the previous century. "All classes, in fact, read Boz," as G. H. Lewes noted at the time.[65] Like Dickens, Balzac was present at the creation, being the first author serialized in Emile de Girardin's fabulously successful journals. Moreover, Balzac himself recognized the possibilities for profit inherent in the new literary marketplace, and even tried to exploit it by sinking a large amount of his own capital, like Scott before him (and Twain after him), in a printing venture; as with Scott and Twain, Balzac's firm soon failed, leaving him with enormous debts he was to spend the remainder of his life attempting to recoup through the labor of writing.[66]

For aspiring professionals, as well as for speculators in publishing, these new market conditions presented both enormous opportunity and enormous danger. A unified mass market held out the potential for a new order of professionalism, in which the psychiatrists, doctors, or writers, having established their authority and tamed the marketplace, could practice their vocations and pursue their careers in relative security. More ominously, in the absence of monopoly (or at least hegemony) the free market could only degenerate into a fierce competitive battlefield. The nightmare image of this sort of field for literature is, of course, familiar from Balzac's *Les Illusions perdues*. What needs emphasizing here is that Lucien's is a specifically *professional* nightmare rather than a nightmare of life under capitalism, as is often suggested. Lucien's fate was shared not only by other writers, but also by many of Balzac's contemporaries who had sought a career not in literature but in medicine—especially in those fields of medicine (like psychiatry) that had not been granted full scientific status. In America, where medical professionalism was stymied until late in the century, the correlation between medicine and writing as laissez-faire professions was crystal-clear: "like literary labour," the *Medical and Surgical Reporter* noted in 1861, "medical attendance is worth in the market what it will bring." Needless to say, the rewards of a medical or literary career under these circumstances were both uncertain and likely to be meager.

Novelists and doctors thus felt a crying need to transform the new marketplace from a competitive to a professional one. To do this it was necessary, first and foremost, to persuade the public that the alienist or the realistic novelist constituted the single legitimate authority for what should be considered as proper treatment or good literature. But on what basis could such claims could be made to stick? Max Weber distinguishes three possible grounds for authority, three basic modes of social justification or legitimation: tradition, rationalization, and charisma.[67] Hardly surprisingly, the different aspiring professions asserted their claim to authority in all three of these ways, ascribing to themselves the weight of tradition, the clarity of rationalization, or the intensity of charisma whenever they felt it might help them win the confidence of the public. For emerging professions like letters and psychiatry, however, the legitimation provided by tradition—the sense that an alienist or novelist ought to be granted authority because it has been ever thus—was not really available; on the contrary, such habitualized public support tended to militate against would-be professionals, since it was already invested in the non- or preprofessional kinds of writing or health care that the alienist and the novelist were trying to replace.

The new professions, then, found themselves justifying their authority primarily on legal-rational and charismatic grounds. Today, we take for granted that the authority of a professional is based primarily on rational criteria—that he or she is objectively better at what he or she does than a nonprofessional, a mere amateur, could be. That is obviously true of the medical profession, whose cognitive basis is supposed to be scientific; but it also holds to some extent for literature, especially realistic fiction, which is so often postulated as an instrument of demystification, a repository of truth. Whether or not medicine and realism actually *are* cognitively superior, more rational, or true, in any objective sense is irrelevant to the argument I am pursuing here, of course, which is about ideology rather than philosophy. What matters is only that psychiatrists or novelists *claim* that they are more true to life or more accurate, and that in doing so they seek to establish their professional authority. It is quite possible that medical ideas or literary techniques may be more rational than alternatives and yet not gain acceptance; conversely, as the alienist synthesis shows, the ideas themselves may be rather wacky, and yet the profession may convince the public that they make rational sense, even in the absence of cures.[68]

One way to help assure the public of a profession's rationality is by pointing to certain standards of skill—what Weber calls "functional 'competence'"—guaranteed to the public in each practitioner and transmitted through a process of credentialing.[69] For the medical profession, the epistemic validation comes today very explicitly in the form of university and medical school educational requirements. In nineteenth-century medicine, however, "institutionalized, standardized programs of education and licensing [which] conferred authority upon all who passed through them" emerged only slowly and unevenly in Europe over the course of the century (and in America, not until 1910). Clinical medicine, it is true, came into its own to some extent in revolutionary-era France, when publicly financed teaching hospitals and a national system of public health controlled by clinicians were established; as seen in the previous chapter, Charles Bovary is one product of this rationalized system for the production of professional rationality. In the subdiscipline of psychiatry, however, the institutional enfranchisement was much slower in developing: as already noted, the first laws mandating a national asylum system under psychiatric control did not pass until 1838, and France was far more advanced than were either England or the United States in this regard.

For would-be literary professionals, on the other hand, the idea of regulating entry into the field of publication was a pipe dream of the 1830s and 1840s, a dream to which Sainte-Beuve (himself a student at the Paris Faculty of Medicine before he became a spokesman for literary professionalization) gave eloquent voice in appealing for the creation of new literary associations. "In order for literature to have a whole and consistent life," he argued,

> there must be a certain stability which is not stagnant; there must be, for the competition, a circle of competent and elite judges, something or someone who organizes, regularizes, moderates and sets limits, who the writer keeps in mind and whom he wishes to satisfy; without which he is completely unrestrained, dissipates his efforts, and loses his essence. . . . The great literary ages have thus always had a judge, a tribunal dispensing judgment which the writer feels some dependence on, some balcony . . . from which palm-branches and awards are handed down.[70]

In the absence of this sort of rationally judged credentialing of the producers, Sainte-Beuve predicted, pure competition would lead to the proliferation of "la littérature industrielle"—with novelists as proletariat.

Under conditions in which alienists and writers could see the potential and the need for limiting competition within their markets by stressing the rationality of their competencies, hyperbolic claims to truth naturally abounded. Balzac's notoriously apodictic rhetoric of truthfulness, his insistence on the literalness of his "reproduction littérale de notre état social" ["literal reproduction of our social state"], needs to be understood at least in part not as a misguided theory of representation, but as a strategic effort to stake out professional territory on the literary battlefield. A vexed effort, one should immediately add, since such claims—whether by Balzac or by the phrenologists—were unsupported by institutionalized credentialing. Without adequate backing for their claims to rationality, and unable to appeal to traditional bases for authority, the emerging professions of letters and psychiatry thus were forced to invoke Weber's third brand of justificatory rhetoric—that of charisma—even as they continued stridently to maintain that they were rational and scientific in their procedures.

Every successful professional image must to some extent include charismatic qualities, if only because, as Sennett and Cobb put it, "all professionals are priests; they interpret mysteries which affect the lives of those who do not understand."[71] The professional's competence must be taken on faith. In bedside medicine, however, where one places that faith not in the ability to argue well or to construct a bridge that will not fall down but in the treatment of one's own body, in the efficacy of an intimate laying-on of hands, an extrarational mystique seems particularly necessary. And this is all the more so when no one has quite established the scientific basis of this treatment. Hence, as Paul Starr writes of American medicine, "before the profession's authority was institutionalized in the late nineteenth and early twentieth centuries, physicians might win personal authority by dint of their character and intimate knowledge of their patients."[72] In France and Britain, where the institutionalization of medical authority occurred earlier than in America, doctors still relied on their tactfulness and charismatic personal qualities at least through the first half of the century. Indeed, another historian of medical professionalism points out, "right through to the middle of the nineteenth century . . . the high status [of physicians] within the wider society . . . was rarely, if ever, justified" by claims to specialized knowledge.[73]

Writers, on the other hand, have always found it useful to claim some sort of charismatic, bardic authority based on their intimate knowledge of character or the human heart. Balzac is no exception. But in Balzac this charismatic posturing is often juxtaposed bizarrely in his writings to what we would think of as its antithesis—a claim to be writing scientifically. At one moment, he invokes the rhetoric of scientific precision, of the "exactitude," of his representation of reality; at the next, he stresses the nonrigorous, qualitative nature of his realism: "This word 'exactitude' requires an explanation. The author did not thereby mean to incur the obligation of giving the facts one by one, dryly, and in such a way as to show how far one could make a story resemble a skeleton whose bones have been painstakingly numbered."[74] In impugning the legitimacy of rationalized (and here, even anatomical) ways of working, Balzac would seem to be contradicting his own self-identification as a physiologist. The appeal to sensibility, however, although it may be opposed to the hardness of some sciences, need not be taken as absolutely antiscientific. In fact, Balzac wants his reader to see this waffling on "exactitude" as a sign both of his charismatic understanding and of the particularly difficult science he is practicing in writing about human beings. The vacillations involved in this double move can be wonderful, as in this passage (from a preface written by Balzac under a pseudonym—a neat way to promote one's charisma without seeming to be tooting one's own horn!): "The most important determinations occur in an instant; [Balzac] wanted to represent rapidly conceived passions, which submit all existence to some thought of the day; but why should he try to explain logically what must be understood by feeling? . . . Although social life may, like physical life, possess apparently immutable laws, you will nowhere find either the body or the heart as regular as the trigonometry of Legendre."[75] The argument veers: first championing rationality, determinations, submissions, and temporal localization; then abandoning this rationality for sensibility, suspending the very need for explanation by asking a rhetorical question; then once again reasserting the rational, law-governed basis of social processes (a statement that Balzac makes without qualifications in many other places); finally, appealing on the basis of the unformalizable irregularity of his object.

The consistency binding together such wildly varying claims is not intellectual but ideological. They all serve to legitimate Balzac's authority as a professional. And as Balzac's reference to "le corps" and "le coeur" implies, this way of legitimating one's professional authority is common to medicine as well as to realism. In either discipline, the innate uncertainty or irregularity of the object the professional works with means that his labor must be both law-governed and unformalizable, both rationalized and irreducible to a set of reified intellectual steps.

Here, then, is finally an explanation for the third major characteristic of Balzacian realism—its claim to represent reality transparently and exactly. The claim about representation makes sense only if one sees it as deriving from ideological claims to rational and charismatic authority that stem from Balzac's quest for professional legitimation. That quest is an analogue of the quest of physicians for the same sort of authority, as Balzac seems to acknowledge by posing the problem of representation in medical terms.

The need to assert charismatic authority, however, makes itself felt not only in the way professionals define the nature of their work or knowledge, but in the way they define themselves as working or knowing subjects—in what might be called the icons of early professionalism. As one might expect, such icons rehearse the contradictory logic of rational/charismatic appeal, with a stronger stress on the charismatic. Indeed, it is difficult to think of these ideal figures as "professionals," imbued as they are with transcendental attributes that seem to call into question the very need for rational justification. Balzac's Benassis—whom most critics have recognized as a mouthpiece for Balzac's own political and social ideas—exemplifies this almost antiprofessional figuring of professional authority. Having been educated at the scientifically advanced Ecole de Médecine in Paris, Benassis possesses the necessary credentials. But despite this training, Benassis makes diagnoses that, as we have seen, would have been scoffed at by any clinician of the time. For Balzac, it is more important that Benassis be marked as having rational knowledge than that he actually exercise it, for it is the legitimating authority of the Ecole de Médecine that Balzac wishes to appropriate above all.[76] In fact, the training and qualification that constitute the rationalization of medicine ultimately are dispensable for Benassis/Balzac: what makes a good doctor (and a good writer as well, one might add) cannot be taught, Benassis insists, only gained from experience. (It is worth noting that Benassis's counterpart in the military profession, Genestas, feels the same way about his own work, confirming that we are dealing with a professional ideology not restricted to medicine alone, although most centrally articulated for Balzac there.) The various cases Benassis treats reveal how much weight Balzac places on the power of irrational, charismatic empathy rather than on rational competence. In treating a mentally disturbed patient, for instance, he admits that "those musings of her are so profound that you fall under the spell of them." By Flaubert's time, such an admission on the part of a doctor would appear unthinkably unprofessional (when Larivière in *Madame Bovary* looks into your soul, Flaubert tells us, he disarticulates it without blinking an eye). In the early period of novelistic and medical professionalization, however, the seemingly antiprofessional, charismatic attitude serves paradoxically to reinforce the authority of the professional, and, by extension, of his profession.[77]

Stressing the importance of charisma in Balzac's image of the professional helps to make clear the structure of the ideology of professionalism. But it also helps make clear how Balzac's *Le Médecin de campagne* promotes that ideology by presenting a utopian fantasy of professional authority achieved. As we have seen, Benassis embodies that authority, but Balzac's profound yearning for such power leaks into the text in other ways as well, especially in the almost obsessive references to that most charismatically charged figure of the postrevolutionary French imagination, Napoleon. No other novel in Balzac's corpus is so fixated on the *esprit napoléonien* as this one:[78] Genestas has served under the Emperor; Gondrin, a veteran and hero of the Russian campaign, lives by the memory of being embraced by Napoleon and the hope that someday his leader will return; Napoleon's name alone, Balzac tells us, has penetrated from French society into the minds of the inhabitants of the utopian valley. The central chapter of the book, in fact, consists of a series of mythical stories about this "Napoleon of the people." For Balzac's biographer, André Maurois, this excursus on Napoleon is simply a digression that "has no bearing on the subject of the book."[79] But Dr. Benassis's utopian assumption of charismatic authority is greatly enhanced by the favorable comparisons drawn again and again between the doctor and Napoleon.

Utopian Realism: *Le Médecin de campagne* as a Novel of Professional Vocation

In presenting Benassis as a figure of charismatic power who creates a healthy society under the dominant but benign rule of a professional elite, Balzac was offering a potent fantasy in which the wishes for authority of aspiring professionals (including Balzac himself, of course) could find fulfillment. A closer look, however, reveals that this fantasy, like most wish fulfillments, is innately ambiguous. Here the ambiguity centers on the identity and origin of the professional himself. As a charismatic leader, the professional is marked as a man apart, as both different from and superior to the average person. But who is this professional man? How does he define himself? If his desires and motives distinguish him from others, what are they, and how are they articulated in the experiences that form him? How has he become the omnipotent figure he is? What is his past, where are his origins? In short, how can the professional be understood—and how can he understand himself—as at once a fantasized icon of authority and a human being like other human beings?

Questions of this kind tend to be elided in the professional fantasy itself. For insofar as an ideal figure is charged with charisma, his individuality and personality must veil themselves within what Barthes has aptly termed the *numen*. Somewhat like Benjamin's "aura," the numen typically appears in a gesture of a specific kind—a gesture that, Barthes explains, even though it shows, points, or acts, "has nothing human about it; it is not the gesture of a worker, *homo faber*, whose totally habitualized movement runs through him in search of its own effect; it is a gesture immobilized in the least stable moment of its course; it is the idea of power, not its density, which is thus eternalized. The hand which rises slightly, or comes to rest gently, the very suspension of movement, produces the fantasmagoria of a power alien to man. The gesture creates, it doesn't merely carry out an order."[80] Barthes has in mind here the kind of gesture made by Napoleon in many hagiographic paintings executed during the First Empire. But pictorial images of doctors during the same period (and in many cases within the same hagiographic paintings!) closely mimic the Napoleonic pose,[81] and as I pointed out earlier, Benassis himself is closely associated with Napoleon. Indeed, Benassis's actions reveal the same qualities of transcendent power that Barthes recognizes as the essence of Napoleon's numen. Benassis acts, but not like a workman; he embodies the idea of power, but not the mastery of complex, rationalized medical techniques; he (re)creates the village he adopts, but not through any massive or overt intervention.

What structure and intention of the self could Balzac possibly rely upon to motivate this kind of activity? Certainly not those of egotism and appetency, the categories of selfhood that define Balzacian types. For the numenous self, any project must be oriented not to self-gratification but to an ideal end. A term bequeathed by religious discourse captures this notion of selfhood: one speaks of such a person as having a "calling" or a "vocation."

As Weber has shown, the religious concept of "vocation," as redefined by Luther, played a crucial role in the forging of the Protestant work ethic that helped make possible the rise of capitalism.[82] Once the new economic formation had been consolidated, however, the Protestant underpinnings of the vocational self—the emphasis on what Weber calls "worldly asceticism," the salvational necessity for work— quickly gave way to a less stringent ethic of "worldliness." This may explain why the vocational model of the self elucidated by Luther was not taken up by most novelists during the eighteenth and early nineteenth centuries.

With the rise of professionalism during the first half of the nineteenth century, the need for an imagined self that could be in the cruel world of competitive capitalism but not of it became pressing, and under that ideological pressure the older idea of vocation as an ethos, a model for the self, reemerged. Once the professions had established themselves—by roughly 1860—the vocational self could not only be imagined, but imagined with a full (although retrospective) sense of the difficulties, temptations, and obstacles it had faced in a world that was incompletely professionalized and at times hostile. What Alan Mintz has called "the novel of vocation" then emerged to represent this now realistically imaginable self.[83]

Balzac's *Le Médecin de campagne*, of course, is about a doctor who has a calling, as is the book that Mintz considers the first true novel of vocation—Eliot's *Middlemarch*. Benassis thus might be thought of as a preliminary sketch or rough draft of the vocational hero, a prototype for Lydgate (and after Lydgate for Deronda, Jude, Stephen Dedalus, and so on). But Balzac, writing during a period before the professional class had carved out its niche, did not have available to him the conditions necessary to imagine in a realistic way the career of a vocational self; such career lines had not yet been regularized in the culture, and thus could hardly constitute a set of probabilities to be determined within the gradual unfolding of a realist plot.[84] Of the many committed professionals represented in the *Comédie*—for example, the physician Bianchon, the writer D'Arthez, or the surgeon Desplein—none is permitted more than an ancillary narrative role. Their careers do not constitute realistic stories for Balzac. With Benassis, on the other hand, Balzac—who at this point was just setting out on his own perilous career as a serious writer—seemed determined to tell the story of a committed professional, and to make that professional's career the story, despite the formal difficulties this might entail. *Le Médecin* ultimately succumbs to these difficulties; when all is said and done, it represents a fantasy, a utopia, rather than a realistic fiction. But that utopia takes a peculiar form, a form that bears the traces of Balzac's intense desire to imagine the professional existence as a realized one, his straining toward a reality that is not yet realistically narratable within the novel. The formal solution Balzac found for the problem of representing professional vocation was to reinvoke a different, more archaic narrative structure, the first, as it happens, in which the vocational self found literary expression of any sort: the conversion narrative.

The most striking feature of conversion narrative is the rigid structure of the self it implies. Unlike the novel, which can be thought of as a series of beginnings that gradually transform and individualize the self, conversion narrative involves a single radical discontinuity of the self, at the moment of conversion when God calls the hero to his vocation. Prior to this moment, the old self resembles the novelistic self, governed as it is by appetency and self-interest rather than by some compelling mission; this may explain why the preconversion section of the paradigmatic conversion narrative—Augustine's *Confessions*—is so often read as a protonovel.[85] Upon converting, however, the old egoistic self renounces its desires while accepting a vocation. This moment constitutes the unique, kerygmatic origin of the vocational self, a singular crisis in being. Once the vocational self has been created, he or she lives an attenuated, shadowy existence: postconversion experiences cannot threaten or transform anything essential in one's self, and it is not uncommon for postconversion narration to leave behind the self altogether for exegesis, as occurs in the last six books of Augustine's *Confessions*.

If the major difference between confessional narrative and the novel of vocation is that the former pivots around a "before" and "after" of a religious conversion, while the latter *begins* with the assumption of a professional vocation, Balzac's *Le Médecin de campagne* stands as a sort of missing link between the two. Balzac's narrative begins neither with conversion nor with the need for a conversion to come, but rather with all the signs that promise a typically realistic Balzacian novel: a panoramic sweep in the opening pages, the insistence on mysteries or secrets hidden within the souls of the central characters, a glimpse of the hero on his rounds. In making these descriptive, hermeneutic, and characterological opening moves in his narrative, Balzac seems anxious to convince readers that Benassis is a realistic character in a world somewhat better than, but not essentially different from, the realistic world that French readers of Balzac's other fiction would recognize as their own. If we are in a different sort of landscape, Balzac wants us to recognize that nevertheless "it was a beautiful country, it was France!"[86] But as soon becomes evident, this "belle France" differs from the Paris of the opening pages of *Le Père Goriot*, as it does from all those other annunciatory landscapes in Balzacian realism. Jameson tells us that Balzac's realistic landscapes usually invoke utopian values needed "to secure the reader's consent, and to validate or accredit the object as desirable, before the narrative process can function properly."[87] In *Le Médecin*'s world, however, no real narrative process ever gets under way. The novel instead offers a series of vignettes, exemplary representations of the therapeutic virtues of the physician. And the physician himself, who in a realistic narrative would take his cue from the desire built into the utopian dimension, seems to lack even the minimum libidinal investment necessary to make him a novelistic hero. Sexually celibate, indifferent to food, beyond personal ambition, Benassis is completely absorbed by the work he performs.

What redeems Benassis as a character from this numenous flatness—and thereby constitutes the novel as a fiction rather than a daydream—is Balzac's modulation of literary form in the last third of the book, in a long chapter, "Confession of the Country Doctor." *Le Médecin*, which reads like a utopian novel masquerading as a realistic one for the first two hundred pages, reveals itself at last to have been all along what might be called an inverted confessional narrative. The self-abnegating professional turns out to have a history after all, a history that links his utopian self to the Balzacian real as a convert might be linked to his own sinful past.

The typical Balzacian hero is rapidly propelled by egotistical ambition or appetency through a series of experiences—a career in the more archaic sense—toward death or success, toward the fate of a Lucien de Rubempré, Raphaël de Valentin, or Rastignac. Like these characters, Benassis turns out to have followed this typical trajectory: a young, ambitious man from the provinces set loose amid the temptations of Paris, he is gradually "drawn into the dissipated life of the capital" and falls victim to his own worst impulses, eventually abandoning the loving woman who bears his child. But Benassis's life ultimately takes a different turn from that of other Balzacian heroes. Although he begins with egotistical impulses joined with the "vast intellectual capital" typical of Balzac's young men, a series of chastisements—including the deaths of his wife and son and the breaking-off of a second engagement when his fiancée discovers Benassis's mistreatment of his first wife—leads him to renounce his egotism and to convert his personal ambition into an ambition for the good. It is this second form of ambition, this vocational desire, that sets Benassis apart from Balzac's other characters as a new type of hero—a professional with a calling.

The "Confession" thus provides Balzac with the formal framework within which a vocational self can at least be imagined as related to the real by negation. But as the tendency of publishers to reprint the "Confession" as an independent story indicates, the fusion between the confessional and the utopian is incomplete. One is left with the impression that Benassis lives realistically only in his past life—after he confesses it, in fact, he dies. In the last analysis, then, *Le Médecin* fails as a novel of vocation. But that very failure is an instructive and fascinating one, for it shows how Balzac's literary possibilities are historically determined by the immature social and ideological conditions of the professions of his day. The very tenuousness of the connection between Benassis's past life and his existence as a professional corresponds precisely to the tenuousness of the professional self-image during a period when psychiatrists—and writers—were struggling to realize professional autonomy and the sense of identity that such autonomy entails. *Le Médecin* remains one of the purest expressions of the dreams and ideology that fueled this struggle, a struggle in which Balzac was on the front lines.

It at last becomes clear why Balzac considered *Le Médecin* to be of such importance within the *Comédie* as a whole, despite its queer utopianism amid the realism that comes to surround it. The key lies in the historical collusion between the ideology of professionalism so profoundly registered in Balzac's utopia and the psychiatric paradigm so fundamental to his realism. To recognize that collusion required analyzing Balzacian realism as a systematic set of procedures for the production of knowledge, analogous to a scientific paradigm. Balzac's literary procedures in fact were discovered to mimic those of early

French psychiatry. But paradigms and ideologies, discourses and strategies, knowledge and power work synergistically. Defining Balzacian realism as a paradigm necessarily led to the question of which dreams of power invested it, and which historical exigencies might have fueled these dreams. The conjuncture I have described for Balzacian realism, that of incipient professionalism, differs from that emphasized by Marxists such as Lukács or Jameson. But I think it allows a more accurate assessment both of the technical variety and of the visionary, dynamic thrust of this realism.

FOUR

"A NEW ORGAN OF KNOWLEDGE"

MEDICAL ORGANICISM AND THE LIMITS OF

REALISM IN *MIDDLEMARCH*

B ETWEEN BALZAC AND FLAUBERT there is at once a hiatus
and a continuity: a pertinent difference that permits one to
recognize a passage as quintessentially Flaubertian or Balzacian, even as one acknowledges both Balzac and Flaubert as realists.
One of literary history's tasks is to cope with such paradoxes of identity and difference by specifying the conditions and nature of literary
change. In practice, to be sure, literary critics tend simply to declare
that Woolf's or Stein's modernism marks a distinct shift from the modernism of her near-contemporaries, or to describe Austen as a novelist
of manners, or to say that *The Portrait of a Lady* rewrites *Middlemarch*,
without worrying over the status of these claims. When they do address the issue of how to theorize change in literary history, they prof-
fer models of change that are predominantly linear, stagist, and sub-
ject-oriented: tradition versus the individual talent, or a strong poet
struggling against the influence of his predecessor, or new forms of
subjectivity and objectivity emerging in a procession of genres or literary modes (romanticism gives way to realism, realism to modernism,
and modernism to postmodernism, just as Enlightenment rationality
gives way to historicism, historicism gives way to reification, and so on).

A different approach to literary history is possible, however—one
that focuses not on the subjectivity of the writer or the general intellectual or ideological tenor of his or her time, but on specific intellectual practices. Changes in a literary genre or mode can be charted by
tracing the itinerary, and determining the relative status, of these
practices as they are taken up by a succession of writers. The literary
history that then emerges will be more concerned with divergences,
subordinations, and reorientations than with originality, secondar-
iness or greatness. In the previous two chapters, I try to show how
such an approach might help explain how nineteenth-century realism
can accommodate writers as temperamentally opposed as Balzac and
Flaubert. Realism is a literary practice informed by medical principles
and attitudes: both Balzac and Flaubert compare themselves to "medi-

cal" observers, asserting that their writing constitutes a medical view of life, and an analysis of their methods reveals these comparisons to be valid ones. But the two novelists incorporate this viewpoint into their works in strikingly different ways. Balzac pursues the analogy between medicine and literary creation by way of a quasi-medical paradigm, that of French psychiatry; this scientifically weak paradigm provides a kind of discursive template for Balzac's style. But if Balzac invests so deeply in the medical analogy, he does so not only because the medical point of view offers certain technical possibilities, but also because that point of view additionally entails an ethos of professional authority that he desperately needs. Flaubert, on the other hand, pursues the medical analogy through a much more firmly established paradigm, that of pathological anatomy and clinical medicine. His writing, in consequence, does not develop the ideological theme of professional authority so fundamental to Balzac's medical perspective as a realist. Instead, Flaubert's realism aims at demonstrating the epistemological and heuristic authority of the medical paradigm itself, the controlled technical power of the clinical gaze.

Without question, Flaubert's demonstration succeeds: the medical point of view (which is also that of the realist) reveals its immanent power to penetrate and know the embodied self it treats. For both the physician and the novelist, however, this power can be exercised only at a cost. When the clinical point of view is adopted, a new, absolute gap, an ironic distance, must open up between the knowing subject (doctor or writer) and the object of knowledge (patient or character). To know the truth about a patient no longer means to understand how he or she feels, but to locate where it hurts; the doctor treats the person who is ill, but seeks to isolate the embodied disease from the person, and this requires a certain withdrawal, a reticence, a repression of the impulse toward identification with the patient, a silencing of one's sympathy so as to permit the disease to speak for itself. (This withdrawal reflects itself, incidentally, in the distinction developing during this period in diagnostics between *symptoms* subjectively reported by the patient and *signs* registered directly in the body.) Similarly, to know the truth about a character no longer means to live through that character, but to record strictly its vicissitudes, and this requires an alert yet hidden omniscience that approaches absolute impersonality.

In short, as the epistemological assumptions common to medicine and realism are transformed, the knowing subject (whether the physician in the text or the author implied by it) becomes more and more difficult to represent as a *human* subject, a multidimensional self with feelings, aspirations, and desires other than the pure will to knowledge. Within the purview of knowledge, the tangle of political, ideological, moral, and ethical motives basic to character is mooted; for the strict clinician or the impassive realist, the only interests at stake in the doctor : patient or novelist : character relationships are what Kant, in a different context, called "the interests of reason."[1] To see that this emergent kind of knowing subject resists representation as a human subject, one need only compare Balzac's physician to Flaubert's. In Balzac's world, the physician, although a utopian figure, can still be represented—and even emphatically so—as hero of the keystone novel of the entire *Comédie Humaine*, *Le Médecin de campagne*, because he is a paragon of feeling and ideological fervor, rather than of technical knowledge. In *Madame Bovary*, on the other hand, where the physician Larivière knows the medical truth about Emma, he does not— and, I have argued, *cannot*—appear as a character participating in a meaningful way in the plot. As a figure of knowledge, he resists representation. And what is true of the physician is true of the author. Although both Balzac and Flaubert pose as doctors, they present radically opposed figures to the imagination. Balzac appears (in Rodin's sculpture most clearly) as the embodiment of gargantuan energies of assimilation, prowling the streets of Paris at all hours and throwing himself into immense political, social, and literary projects. Flaubert's name, on the other hand, barely conjures up an image at all, unless that of the cloistered and self-isolated writer, disdainful of the outer world and intent only on his craft.

In spite of these major differences in their conceptions of the medical-authorial subject, however, Balzac and Flaubert share one overriding characteristic: neither is able to represent in his fiction a completely realized and historicized figure who combines (without conflating) knowing and feeling as ethical factors.[2] Neither Benassis in *Le Médecin de campagne* nor Charles Bovary in *Madame Bovary* is portrayed as a medical man who confronts in any depth the specific ethical issues raised by his devotion to his scientific knowledge and the more common ethical problems of the self dealt with in novels—love, money, marriage, social status, or politics. In *Le Médecin*, as we have seen, Balzac avoids the question of how such a character could be portrayed by splitting his doctor's life into two parts, allocating Benassis's love problems to one and his moral activities as a physician to the other. In *Madame Bovary*, on the other hand, Flaubert denies Charles the capacity for truth and knowledge required of a good physician, instead introjecting these qualities himself and making them the essence of his literary style. It is almost as if a medical vocation provided its own rewards (for Balzac moral, for Flaubert epistemological), making it unnecessary, and perhaps impossible, to conceive of a novel of vocation centrally concerned with the ethical, psychological, and existential problems inherent in any effort to sustain the pursuit of a secular calling like medicine.[3]

Tertius Lydgate, the unfortunate doctor whose choice of wife proves fatal to his scientific aspirations in George Eliot's *Middlemarch,* is the first modern physician to be represented with this sort of depth in fiction. That is not to say, of course, that physicians never appear in Victorian novels published before 1871. As Q. D. Leavis has pointed out, the doctor, as "a modern figure concerned not for private practice among the well-to-do but for public health and the scientific advancement of medicine, a figure as disinterested as the cleric and visibly more important in the new social conditions," serves as a potent symbol for English novelists during the 1850s,[4] as it had for Balzac in the new, professionalizing social conditions of France in the 1830s. But what characters such as Woodcourt in *Bleak House,* Tom Thurnall in Kingsley's *Two Years Ago,* and Physician in *Little Dorrit* symbolize is less a medical-scientific consciousness than a reforming impulse.[5] None of the doctors mentioned by Leavis actually represents medical science at work, despite the fact that they stand for scientific advancement; rather, like Balzac's Dr. Benassis, the progressive doctor in Victorian novels before *Middlemarch* is most often depicted as a quasi-religious model of feeling. Dickens can claim of Physician that "where he was, some thing real was," but that real is manifested not so much by the ironic disinterestedness of scientific discernment as by charismatic understanding, "an equality of compassion no more disturbed than the Divine Master's of all healing was."[6]

In contrast, Lydgate's distinguishing characteristic as a physician is not his compassion (both Dorothea and Farebrother outdo him in this regard) but the degree to which Eliot specifies and valorizes his intellectual activity—the sense he conveys that, to put it bluntly, he knows what he is doing.[7] Borrowing a phrase from Eliot's "Prelude," one might say that Lydgate represents a "function of knowledge" in the world of the novel. More precisely, Lydgate represents the form of knowledge familiar from our analysis of Flaubert: pathological anatomy, a scientific discipline instituted, as Eliot takes pains to inform us, around 1800 through the work of Bichat. Like Larivière, Flaubert's medical proxy in *Madame Bovary,* Lydgate follows in Bichat's footsteps, exploring "the dark territories of Pathology," "a fine America"[8] discovered by the pioneering anatomist. Lydgate's aim, we are told, is to go beyond Bichat by resolving the tissues of the body—for Bichat, the ultimate objects of anatomical analysis—into a single fundamental element, a "primitive tissue." This is a laudable project, a natural extension of Bichat's work, and one for which Lydgate is extremely well qualified, having studied in the avant-garde medical schools of Paris and Edinburgh. He is even willing to use a microscope to see beyond Bichat, who always refused to let observation go beyond that available to the scalpel and the naked eye.

This brief sketch of Lydgate might lead one to conclude that Eliot considers clinical vision worthy of scientific status, of the epistemological privilege Lydgate claims for his Bichatian exploration of the continent of the body. One indication of Eliot's approval is that in contest against the therapeutic methods and diagnostic techniques used by the other Middlemarch doctors, Lydgate's clinical knowledge shows itself unequivocally superior: he corrects Dr. Wrench's diagnosis of Fred and recognizes that what another physician had called tumor was merely cramp. More generally, Lydgate's exchanges with those outside his profession ironically highlight the stupidity and ignorance of received opinion on medical matters. Again, like Flaubert's Larivière, Lydgate knows more than those he treats, and, conscious of his intellectual predominance, remains reserved in the company of the unenlightened. The most obvious evidence for Eliot's approval of the medical gaze, however, comes from her own treatment of character and society, her own representational practice, in which she self-consciously appropriates the very system of description—based on the metaphor of the body personal or politic as an organized network compounded of sensitive and irritable tissues—that she ascribes to Bichat and Lydgate. Like Flaubert, and even more overtly, Eliot would appear to be a realist whose "real" is allied to the medically defined "reality" of Bichat's body.

As any reader immediately senses, however, Eliot's realism differs markedly from Flaubert's. To begin to understand how it differs, one needs to clarify the status of clinical discourse in her work. That Eliot acknowledges the epistemological superiority of the clinicoanatomical gaze is clear enough—she even theorizes her own practice as a matter of analyzing webs of organic relations—but she never makes the medical view of the embodied self an absolute principle of authorial representation in the way Flaubert does. On the contrary, Eliot's major innovation is to contextualize and historicize, for the first time in the realist novel, the clinical epistemology to which she—as a realist—must remain committed. As I shall try to show, Eliot delimits this scientific "point of view," not only by ascribing it to a character—Lydgate—whose fate can then be thought of as an allegory of the fate of clinical medicine as a human science, but also by supplementing her own formal use of the clinical notion of the body with others that are valid without being medical. Although the clinical perspective remains central, the novel makes room for entire sets of characters and plots imagined according to rules that do not match those of the clinic but that nevertheless have the ring of truth.

What is involved in *Middlemarch*, I am suggesting, is an elaborate worrying over medicine's—and by extension realism's—claim to scientific truth and the authority that stems from such truth. The challenge takes two forms. First, medicine's epistemological value comes into question as it is surrounded by other sciences (embryology, evolutionism, cell theory) whose truths seem incompatible with those of medicine. Second, the Bichatian perspective loses the autonomy from the social that it enjoyed in Flaubert's work, appearing now to be bound to nondiscursive social and psychological conditions that support or threaten it. In the process, medicine's security is undermined, for it no longer appears capable of supplying either a necessarily triumphant or ultimately truthful vision of human beings, as it did respectively in the realisms of Balzac and Flaubert. Eliot, however, remains a realist bound to the same kind of study of the embodied person that medicine continues to pursue, and hence this epistemological humbling of the medical perspective does not lead her to abandon that perspective altogether. Instead, the ethical side of medical (and novelistic) practice, submerged in Flaubert's more confident medical realism, reemerges in *Middlemarch* as an important, if vexed, characteristic of a realism in which the medical perspective (and the narrative it authorizes) is supplemented by other equally valid perspectives with other narrative possibilities.

"Disentangling Reflection": The Predicament of Medical Discourse in Middlemarch

At first glance, nothing would seem less epistemologically insecure than Eliot's prose. Take for example the famous parable of the pier-glass that begins chapter twenty-seven of *Middlemarch*:

> An eminent philosopher among my friends, who can dignify even your ugly furniture by lifting it into the serene light of science, has shown me this pregnant little fact. Your pier-glass or extensive surface of polished steel made to be rubbed by a housemaid, will be minutely and multitudinously scratched in all directions; but place now against it a lighted candle as a centre of illumination, and lo! the scratches will seem to arrange themselves in a fine series of concentric circles round that little sun. It is demonstrable that the scratches are going everywhere impartially, and it is only your candle which produces the flattering illusion of a concentric arrangement, its light falling with an exclusive optical selection. These things are a parable. The scratches are events, and the candle is the egoism of any person now absent. (194–95)

Eliot's interpretation of her own parable seems on first reading to be perfectly appropriate, a simple, straightforward explanation, and

many critics have accepted it as such. The sentences that immediately
follow this passage apply the parable to Rosamond: the candle, it is
said, represents her egoism, the self-centeredness that leads her to
imagine that providence has created a real romance involving her and
the prepossessing young Dr. Lydgate. In fact, the narrator tells us, she
is projecting her own wishes onto contingent events—Lydgate is not
really courting her. Rosamond's egoism, however, is only one instance
of "the egoism of any person now absent"; even those characters who
lay claim to knowledge rather than romance—Casaubon, for instance,
or Lydgate himself—are merely egoists on a different scale, just as lost
in the labyrinth of knowledge as Rosamond is in the labyrinth of her
romantic plots.

This conception of character as intellectually and emotionally limited is familiar from Flaubert, whose word for such a condition is *bêtise*.
In *Madame Bovary*, only the narrator and Dr. Larivière transcend
bêtise, and both do so by occluding themselves, as much as possible,
from the world of characters. In contrast, in Eliot's parable (and in
Middlemarch as a whole), both the narrator and her scientific friend
(identified by N. N. Feltes as Herbert Spencer)[9] appear gregariously
within the fiction itself, posing as figures who claim to be able to critique objectively the process by which less knowing characters project
their own interpretation of things onto an empirically meaningless reality. The scientist, like the narrator, views things in a "serene light"
that, unlike the candlelight of egoism, illuminates a "demonstrable"
fact—a fact, moreover, that is "pregnant" with truth. Scientist, narrator, and reader can share in this truth beyond egoism and subjectivity,
seeing things as parables, moving unproblematically from representation to reality.

In a sense, then, the parable narrated by Eliot colludes with a
smugly positivist science, taking the scientific viewpoint as the proper,
omniscient alternative to a cognitively and morally suspect egoism, as
the guarantor of a naïve realism. Like most parables, however, this one
can give birth to more than one interpretation, and it is possible to
read the parable—and Eliot's realism as well—deconstructively, so as
to find it (after a good deal of reflection) not arrogantly confirming
science's transcendence of egoism, but subverting the very distinction
between scientific objectivity and egoistic subjectivity. For one could
easily show that the scientist and the narrator are just as compromised
by the position they occupy in viewing the scene as the egoistic candleholder is compromised by her position in viewing the mirror. The
"serene light" of scientific reflection (Eliot here may be referring
obliquely to the moonlight that Spencer uses instead of a candle as his
light source in his earlier version of the parable) is still light, and
hence, one might speculate, is liable to the same distorting condition as

is the candlelight of egoism. Despite his claims to the contrary, the scientist does not (indeed, cannot) illuminate everything in his serene light. Even as it makes his particular insight possible, it must blind him to certain features of reality. Like the egoist, he must see reality through an "exclusive optical selection," because what J. Hillis Miller calls "the same projective, subjective, even egoistic act" is involved whether one is a scientist, a novelist, or an adolescent girl.[10] Here, for instance, the scientist sees the scratches on the pier-glass, but takes no account at all of the demonstrable fact that because a pier-glass is not simply a piece of steel but a convex mirror, there will appear behind the scratches an image (albeit a distorted one) of the person holding the candle to it. One might then interpret *these* things as a parable not of the egoistic subject but of the phenomenological subject. The parable's meaning would be that reality not only presents us with contingent events but also supplies us with an image of our real phenomenal selves. The scientist, and perhaps the narrator as well, misses this subjective truth within reality because his point of view reifies reality, seeing (as through a glass darkly) only scratches, only random events, not the subjective meaning within those events.

But Eliot's view of science is even more complicated and entangled than this, as becomes evident when one defines more precisely the narrator's position within the parable's scenario—her relation to the scientist, the reader, the mirror, the candleholder, and even the maid. Far from intending to subvert the scientific viewpoint, she presents herself as a mediator between her philosopher friend and a reader who is assumed to have both furniture and a housemaid; more generally, Eliot's fiction could be said to aim at transmitting scientific truth to bourgeois culture. As mediator, she attempts to educate the reader by representing the same fact that the scientist has shown her. Yet even after the lucid scientific explanation and the assertive firmness of the equations in the last two sentences of the parable, Eliot remains troubled enough to define "these things" as a *parable* rather than a scientific instance or example or illustration of some truth or theory. And the rhetoric of the passage sustains this qualifying of the science that it at the same time promulgates. In reminding us that "the candle is the egoism of any person now absent," for example, Eliot explicitly excludes herself and the reader, while just as clearly intending to remind us, in a gently ironic way, that we are really no less egoistic than is Rosamond. But Eliot's remark includes a further irony, and one that with all her wisdom she may not have intended. The eminent philosopher among Eliot's friends, who is the original source of and guarantor of Eliot's knowing commentary, must be included among those who are now absent, although it seems clear that Eliot wishes he were here.

This kind of epistemological shakiness, the uncertainty in the narrator's own voice about the distinction between knowledge and egoism, firm truth and what Nietzsche would call "perspective knowing," shows more clearly and acutely in Eliot's treatment of Lydgate, since he is the primary representative of what passes for knowledge in the world of *Middlemarch*. Just as Eliot tacitly distances herself from her own interpretation and relativizes the certainty of her own knowledge in her handling of the parable, so she problematizes Lydgate's Bichatian view of the body even as she hails Bichat's achievements. After honoring Bichat for having discovered the "dark territories" of the body, for example, Eliot points out that "there was still scientific work to be done which might have seemed to be a direct sequence of Bichat's" (110). The "might have seemed" here is telling, for as W. J. Harvey has pointed out, Eliot writes from an historical vantage point permitting her (and her readers) to know that although Bichat is a seminal figure whose anatomical paradigm dominates medical thought in the first half of the nineteenth century, following Bichat does not lead to the discovery of "the primitive tissue" sought by Lydgate.[11] The problem, as Eliot goes on to define it, is that even though Bichat does make possible the science of pathological anatomy, giving rise to a number of different avenues of research, those who follow Bichat and attempt to discover a primitive tissue cannot put the question "quite in the way required by the awaiting answer," which is that the primitive tissue is the cell.

The direct sense of Eliot's comment is that Lydgate will not discover something just waiting to be discovered. At the same time, however, her way of putting Lydgate's predicament, her rhetoric of dialogue, of question-and-answer, points to two organizing assumptions about the nature and limits of knowledge, assumptions that seem to complicate the very notion of scientific discovery as involving an "out there" where things might be waiting. The first of these assumptions is that thought and perception, although distinct from language, are organized through (or at least according to the same rules as) the language or sign system one uses—that, in G. H. Lewes's words, "thoughts differ from sensations as signs from things signified; but the process by which they are combined is of the same nature."[12] For Lydgate, medical thought and even medical sensation depends on the Bichatian sublanguage of webs, tissues, and organization. Pathological anatomy, in other words, provides him a specific way of putting questions (and hearing answers) as well as a way of seeing the embodied self. But the grounding of knowledge in particular discourses implies that coming to know a science (or conversely, failing to grasp a science one seeks to know) is a metalinguistic or rhetorical event, a (re)orienting or interpellation of the self in language.

Scientific enlightenment, in particular, must consist in a moment of accession not only to new or more finely grained perceptions, but more fundamentally to a newly acknowledged discourse. In *Middlemarch*, at least, this is precisely the case: Lydgate's initiation into pathological anatomy takes the form of a conversion experience, a transfiguration within the self that Eliot presents as at once linguistic, intellectual, and perceptual. As a child trapped inside the house on a rainy day, Lydgate notices "a dusty row of volumes with grey-paper backs and dingy labels—the volumes of an old Cyclopaedia which he had never disturbed,"[13] and which he must stand on a chair to reach:

> But he opened the volume which he first took from the shelf: somehow, one is apt to read in a makeshift attitude, just where it might seem inconvenient to do so. The page he opened on was under the head of Anatomy, and the first passage that drew his eyes was on the valves of the heart. He was not much acquainted with valves of any sort, but he knew that *valvae* were folding doors, and through this crevice came a sudden light startling him with his first vivid notion of finely-adjusted mechanism in the human frame. A liberal education had of course left him free to read the indecent passages in the school classics, but beyond a general sense of secrecy and obscenity in connection with his internal structure, had left his imagination quite unbiassed, so that for anything he knew his brains lay in small bags at his temples, and he had no more thought of representing to himself how his blood circulated than how paper served instead of gold. But the moment of vocation had come, and before he got down from his chair, the world was made new to him by a presentiment of endless processes filling the vast spaces planked out of his sight by that wordy ignorance which he had supposed to be knowledge. (107)

Part of the resonance of this passage stems from its relationship to an underlying theme in *Middlemarch*: the recasting of what Mintz calls the ethos of Protestant vocation in secular form, with science taking the place of Christianity as the transcendental discourse. The important point for our purposes, however, is not that Eliot secularizes the moment of vocation in the passage above, but that she treats this moment as a rhetorical event. In doing so, as it turns out, she remains extraordinarily faithful to a pre-Protestant Christian model of conversion, a model that, as I have earlier pointed out, finds its classical expression in the eighth book of Augustine's *Confessions*. Like Augustine, whose conversion occurs through his reading of "the first passage upon which my eyes fell,"[14] Lydgate finds his moment of vocation in a random reading of the first passage that draws his eyes to it. Moreover, like Augustine, for whom, "in an instant . . . it was as though the light of confidence had flooded into my heart and all the darkness of doubt was dispelled," Lydgate is suddenly enlightened by his reading. Most important of all, like Augustine, whose renovated vision results from his reading himself into his text and consequently reading the world itself as a text,[15] Lydgate is converted to a world made new to him through a kind of metaphorical transubstantiation, with the word *valves* conjuring up an architectural correlative for the mechanism in the human frame. By emphasizing Lydgate's reliance on a Latin root, *valvae*, at the moment of vocation, Eliot reinforces our sense of the mediating function of language in this process; in fact, within the passage I have quoted, Eliot herself plays with the symbolic and metaphorical possibilities of "folding doors," as if to suggest that her own writing is a process of discovery governed to some extent by liminal possibilities inherent in the language she employs.[16] If language can be described as obstruction, as wordy ignorance that planks out of sight what lies beyond it, language can also, at certain sensitive points, be a folding door that unfolds and opens a crack, or a crevice, when one opens a book or muses upon a word.

The enabling power of a metaphor, or more generally, of a vocabulary or even a discourse, however, is not absolute, although Augustine may predicate such theological authority for biblical discourse. In Eliot's secularized world, the alternative to wordy ignorance is not pure transcendent knowledge of God but the "disentangling reflection" (554) of science, a knowledge different in content but not in kind from other modes of consciousness and thus bound by certain rules and limits that pertain to any particular language. As Eliot elsewhere reminds us, "We all of us, grave or light, get our thoughts entangled in metaphors, and act fatally on the strength of them" (63), and even if the entanglement in metaphor then makes it possible for one to engage in disentangling reflection, as Lydgate's valve metaphor does for him, one remains tangled in it in a fateful, even fatal, way.[17] Even Eliot's own comment, although thoughtful, is entangled in metaphor—the metaphor of entanglement.

Lydgate's particular entanglement is in pathological anatomy, and Eliot goes on to analyze brilliantly and subtly the necessary closure of this kind of medical thought, the reasons why it prevents Lydgate from putting questions in quite the right way to find waiting answers about the fundamental elements of the body—cells—even though pathology is intimately concerned with bodies. At stake in Lydgate's failure to recognize the cell is a notion usually thought of as postmodern—that a Kuhnian-like incommensurability of paradigms or a Foucauldian epistemological break separates clinicoanatomical medicine from cell biology. It might seem anachronistic to describe Lydgate's predicament in this way, as if Eliot acceded to our modern relativizing of scientific truth. After all, one might argue, Eliot is an eminent representative of a militantly positivist and empiricist age, not a Nietzschean skeptic. But in labeling the Victorians as positivists, we fail to do justice to the sophistication of their epistemology. Eliot's relativization of Lydgate's knowledge, it turns out, can be situated within an intellectual controversy, raging in her own time and close at hand, over the status and nature of truth. Even during that period of Gradgrindian factism, the assumptions of John Stuart Mill's dominant empiricist epistemology were being challenged by Lewes, as well as by the historian of science William Whewell.[18] Against Mill, both Lewes and Whewell argued that knowledge emerges through our interpretation of sensation rather than in raw perception. Lewes, indeed, went further than did Whewell in stressing "our subjective cooperation in the perception of objects," asserting that this cooperation is not only a matter of Kantian "necessities of thought" but of necessities of organic adaptation—of interests that are material and changeable. "We only see what interests us, or has once interested us," Lewes proclaims decades before William James, and these interests, not any a priori truth-value, will determine if something is true for us. "So far from its being marvellous that men of vast intellects should fail to see what to other men are self-evident truths," Lewes concludes, "it is only a case of the general incapacity of the mind for seeing what does not interest it, and of combining ideas that are antagonistic."[19]

For Lewes (and one may presume, also for his spouse and collaborator, Eliot) different sciences express different and even sometimes antagonistic interests, leading those who work within these sciences to ask different questions of nature and to see different things in nature. A science may be "une langue bien faite," as Condillac proposed (Lewes quotes him), but different scientific languages may be well made for different purposes. Nor can one hope that making better *physical* instruments will overcome the different intentions that govern one's scientific language and hence one's perception. Even with more powerful tools like the microscope, which may multiply the range of scientific vision, a scientist will still see what he or she looks for. As Lewes puts it, "No little of what passes for microscopic observation is the substitution of a mental image for the optical image;"[20] mental images are already interpretations, bound to the interests of the scientist's paradigm.

Nowhere is the relative unimportance of technological advances to scientific perception more patent than in the very case that Eliot presents through Lydgate in *Middlemarch*—that of pathological anatomy and the development of cell theory. For although Lydgate, unlike Bichat (as Eliot tells us), eagerly uses a microscope, he still fails to see the cells that are certainly present as optical images. The lesson, once again, is that Bichat and his followers are perceptually limited, not in the sense that they refuse (as Bichat himself did) to even look to see what is there under the microscope, nor in the sense that they cannot see sharply enough, but in the sense that their very insightfulness as pathological anatomists entails a necessary blindness to what the cell represents. Every empirical science is devoted to the ideal of dragging the invisible into the range of the visible, but each science articulates the relationship between the visible and the invisible in its own special way that defines it as a distinct science. For pathological anatomy, this relationship between the visible and the invisible, the perceptible and the questionable, must be framed within the domain constituted by tissues and their organization into organs. If a person shows symptoms of an illness, those symptoms become significant in being traced back to the interiority of the body. One presupposes that the source of disease lies hidden in the minutiae of tissues; in the autopsy, the unfolding of these tissues in the opened corpse, the pathologist expects the disease to become ultimately visible in its pathway from a seemingly innocuous local lesion to the full-blown clinical symptomatology of the disease. And conversely, disease itself makes visible the complex interweaving of tissues, answering questions raised by the anatomist.

Lydgate's own research into the invisible, the "dark territories" of the body, is thus grounded in and limited by his tendency as a doctor to see the body in terms of health or disease. As Eliot puts it, Lydgate's science aims to "pierce the obscurity of those minute processes which prepare human misery and joy, those invisible thoroughfares which are the first lurking-places of anguish, mania, and crime, that delicate poise and transition which determine the growth of happy or unhappy consciousness" (122). Slipping from a physiological vocabulary of minute processes to a psychological (and even Hegelian) vocabulary of states of consciousness, this passage reveals the presumed unity of the scientific and the human, the collusion between the invisible and the symptomatic, inherent in the pathologist's perspective. The faith that sustains Lydgate as a physician-scientist is precisely that the obscure and the minute can be made manifest, and that this operation will yield therapeutically valuable insights, confirming the "direct alliance between intellectual conquest and social good" (108).

But the intellectual conquest Lydgate hopes for cannot be gained by piercing obscurity, by finding, as he puts it, a stronger light "as of oxyhydrogen, showing the very grain of things." The allusion here is, as usual in Eliot, historically precise: oxyhydrogen, introduced as a light source for microscopes in the late 1820s, certainly improved microscopic resolution of details. By this time, however, the cell's general morphology had long been recognized (the first microscopist, Leeuwenhoek, even described the nuclei of blood cells as early as the seventeenth century). To make the discovery of the cell possible, biological researchers needed not a brighter light or more data, but a different way of construing the same data, a rhetoric different from that of morbid anatomy.

Schleiden and Schwann, who by Eliot's era had been recognized as the formulators of the modern theory of the cell, were able to do what no anatomically or medically oriented researcher could have done—conceive of the cell as a fundamental structure to be analyzed in isolation from the body and its conditions of health and illness. They could do so at least in part because the German intellectual milieu in which they worked stressed the importance of forces and elements that exceeded or bypassed human embodiment. In particular, the *naturphilosophen*, who saw all processes in the universe as deriving from the inviolable unity of matter subject to first principles, pointed beyond organization to what Oken called "the primitive matter of which all is organized."[21] Although later scientists, including Schleiden and Schwann, would repudiate the metaphysical underpinnings of the nature philosophers' argument, the doctrine that life must be compounded of minute and repeated vital elements contributed to the marked emphasis in German microscopy on the ideal of resolving organic form into units that would have their own integrity, independent of their anatomical embodiment. It is easy to see how Lydgate, initated into science as an anatomist and a physician, would be unlikely to set aside the anatomoclinical view of life for one in which, as François Jacob puts it, the properties of life "can no longer be attributed to the whole, but to each part—each cell—which in some way possesses an 'independent life.'"[22]

Integrating cell theory into medical science was a long, arduous task, finally accomplished during the latter half of the century through the efforts of physiologists such as Virchow, Claude Bernard, and Pasteur. During the interim, medicine had to continue, even though a fissure began to open between cellular and human life, between the innumerable activities of individual cells and the fluent progression of a disease through the tissues of the body, between the microscopic and the macroscopic constituents of the self. During Eliot's lifetime, cell theory struggled to elaborate corollary sciences to itself, sciences capable of bridging the gap between cell and organism by providing explanations of how a cell developed, evolved, or mutated into something as complicated as a new organ or even a new individual. A new organicism, founded on embryological, cytological, and

Darwinian principles, clearly was needed to supersede Bichat's tissular organicism and give medicine a more fundamental grounding in biology. But such a science was still only a hope in the 1860s, as pathologists lagged behind biologists in defining and accepting the implications of Schleiden and Schwann's theory of the cell. Virchow's *Cellular Pathology* (translated into English in 1860) was still distrusted in England in 1869, when Eliot began work on *Middlemarch*.[23] Hence, when writers like Lewes and Huxley sought to describe the new unity of the cellular organism, they found themselves reduced to the mealy-mouthed conclusion that, as Lewes put it, "every cell in the organism is independent. . . . There is a certain aggregate unity, but it is made up of distinct units."[24]

Aggregate unity is a clinically impoverished way of describing a human body, offering little if any practical help for a doctor faced with a patient's sufferings. Neither cell theory nor evolutionary organicism, in its rudimentary form of the 1860s, could account for, or effectively treat, the medical processes of disease and death that Bichat's pathological organicism explained: one could not put a patient under the microscope (at least not yet), nor could one expect any therapeutic insights from the study of individual cells. Only after the bacteriological revolution would scientific medicine even begin to reap the therapeutic fruits of the discoveries of cell theory. In view of this state of affairs, it is hardly surprising that clinical medicine and cell theory went their separate ways, with the Bichatian perspective of tissue and individual pathology supplemented but not quite superseded by the perspective of the cellular histologist, the embryologist, and the evolutionist.[25]

What I have been describing in perhaps too lavish detail as an epistemological divergence in the specialized domain of sciences of the body may strike some as an irrelevant, local historical epiphenomenon, hardly worthy of notice when set against the broader, supposedly more basic cultural forces—the Industrial Revolution, commodity fetishism, reification, the crisis in religious values, the political enfranchisement of the working classes, or the status of women question—which so clearly impinge upon Eliot's fiction. For Eliot and her circle, however, the issue of organicism, as posed within the biological sciences, constitutes the intellectual horizon or *habitus* (in Pierre Bourdieu's sense) within which cultural and social phenomena come to be understood by Eliot. If the ultimate question about *Middlemarch* (and about realistic novels more generally) remains "What is a body politic or a society?" one can best work one's way out to that question by first asking "What is a body or organization?" In the last instance, Eliot may well be the ideologist of organicism that Eagleton and other Marxists have labeled her; but the complexity of that ideological role demands an analysis that respects the immanent problematics of the first instance—that of the conflict of the sciences.

For Eliot, in fact, the divergence of pathology from other emerging organismic sciences creates profound problems of life and mind to which Lydgate's predicament, and more generally, *Middlemarch* as a whole, stands as a kind of response, or more accurately, an accommodation. Perhaps the most pressing of these difficulties is that of retaining some faith in an ultimate unity, or at least some hierarchical relationship, among the sciences. If, as seems to be the case, medicine and cell theory really are incommensurable sciences, different species of discourse yielding unreconciled versions of the truth about the same object—the body—then the Comteian ideal of a social order crowned and informed by a scientific order (an ideal cherished by Eliot and many of her contemporaries) may be compromised. The schism within science itself, the loss of a sense of a single scientific truthfulness or rationality of which various sciences are the expression, calls into question the very possibility, broached in Eliot's "Prelude," of a unified scientific culture in which scientists could indeed "perform the function of knowledge" in the interest of "coherent social faith and order."

Lydgate's particular predicament, as it would be recognized by the educated reader of the early 1870s, thus makes manifest a strain that is simultaneously epistemological and social, involving the structure not only of intellect but of the intellectual community as well. For just as the community of knowledge symbolized by Lydgate's simultaneous pursuit of medicine and the cell must appear in retrospect as naïve, so the knowledge of community, the ideal of a "scientific culture" (93) that Lydgate believes he will someday be able to enjoy, must by Eliot's time also appear as a fading hope. The 1860s provide much evidence of the disintegration of scientific culture, among which three particular trends may be mentioned: a precipitous decline in the number and popularity of general-knowledge reviews, while journals devoted to distinct philosophical and scientific topics were being founded at a rapid rate; the increasing specialization, institutionalization, and professionalization of scientific work; and the virtual extinction of the amateur scientist. Huxley, who unlike many of his contemporaries rejects the idea of society as an organic totality,[26] is able to hail the passing of amateurism,[27] but Eliot's response, registered in *Middlemarch* through Lydgate's relationship with the amateur naturalist Farebrother, is less sanguine. Between the two men, only the most tenuous (and on Lydgate's part uninterested) scientific exchange occurs, a state of affairs that seems to forecast pessimistically what Huxley gladly accepts: the emergence of distinct social spheres separating the clerisy from the scientists, and both from cultural hegemony.

For Eliot and Lewes these developments are ominous ones. Both writers have large stakes in maintaining and promoting a culture dominated and unified by science. In such a culture, clinicians and cell biologists would answer each other's questions, while Eliot and Lewes, as amateurs, lovers of science, would act as cultural mediators, talking to doctors[28] and scientists on the one hand, to the general public on the other. In his own books, Lewes says, he thinks of himself as assuming "the position of a lecturer addressing a miscellaneous audience. . . . Beside the Medical Student there sits an intelligent Artisan—beside the Man of Letters sits the Mother of a family."[29] We have already seen, with the pier-glass parable, how the narrator of *Middlemarch* presents herself in an analogous position, repeating what she has heard from one friend, a man of science, to another, a bourgeois seeking cultural guidance. A glance at Eliot's diary, or at Gordon Haight's fine biography, reveals that the narrator's concerns match the author's: Eliot's life, particularly during the period of the late 1860s, exemplifies her devotion to the ideal of a culture in which science would play as important a civilizing role as art, philosophy, and music. Consider the following diary entry, a not untypical one from the period during which *Middlemarch* is being written:

> G. and I went to the Museum, and had an interesting morning with Dr. Rolleston, who dissected a brain for me. After lunch we went again to the Museum, and spent the afternoon with Sir Benjamin Brodie, seeing various objects in his laboratories, amongst others the method by which weighing has been superseded in delicate matters by measuring in a graduated glass tube. After Mrs. Pattison took me a drive in her little pony carriage round by their country refuge—the Firs, Haddington, and by Littlemore, where I saw J. H. Newman's little conventual dwellings. Returning we had a fine view of the Oxford towers. To supper came Sir Benjamin and Lady Brodie.[30]

Given this deep an investment of personal energies in matters both scientific and cultural, it is only natural that Eliot's novels, with their projection of a self-confident and wise voice, appear as an act of cultural cementing, an effort to sustain in her art what she also was trying to sustain in her life. But underlying this confident cultural activity, both in her own life and in her texts, lurks a kind of dread, a sense of despair about the possibility of sustaining a culture that could be at once moral and scientific. Her work certainly evokes such dread for her contemporary audience. One reader, for example, writes to Eliot asking if it is possible to reconcile what the reader feels to be a painful gap between science and morality. Eliot's reply is a masterpiece of qualifications:

> The consideration of molecular physics is not the direct ground of human love and moral action, any more than it is the direct means of composing a noble picture or of enjoying great music. One might as well hope to dissect one's own body and be merry in doing it, as take molecular physics (in which you must banish from your field of view what is specifically human) to be your dominant guide, your determiner of motives, in what is solely human. That every study has its bearing on every other is true; but pain and relief, love and sorrow, have their peculiar history which makes an experience and knowledge over and above the swing of atoms.[31]

Bernard Paris has offered this passage as the final word confirming Eliot's adherence to a humanism independent of science.[32] It would seem more appropriate, however, to treat Eliot's comments as symptoms rather than simple statements, for their hesitancy, evident in the choice of such modifiers as "not the direct," "dominant," "solely," "peculiar," and "over and above," points to a masked ambivalence and anxiety within Eliot herself about the possibility of providing any dominant guide whatsoever in a world split between the microscopic and the human.

The brave front of the "Wise Woman" persona she presents as narrator may seem to belie this anxiety, but that anxiety simply surfaces elsewhere, infecting both Eliot's attitude toward her writing and her ability to live a full life.[33] In her letters, for instance, one finds a veritable litany of complaints about her own infirmities and the immense difficulty involved in the act of writing. The peculiarity of Eliot's psychic self-division between putative narrative authority and personal malaise may be clarified somewhat by comparing it with Flaubert's analogous condition as a suffering writer (discussed at greater length earlier in chapter two). Flaubert's pain seems at once more extreme and more controlled than Eliot's, brought under the penetrating scrutiny of artistic-cum-medical consciousness and transformed into an object of literary analysis. The stringent labor of writing provides Flaubert with a way to dominate his pain; for Eliot, on the other hand, writing itself seems to generate a depression, a "paralyzing despondency—in which many days of my writing life have been passed."[34] If writing is the best medicine for Flaubert, allowing him to transcend his own pain in the process of anatomically disarticulating his characters, for Eliot (as for her heroine, Dorothea) the only treatment she can accept is to "clutch [her] own pain, and compel it to silence, and think" of the pain of her characters. And the style in which the two novelists assert their authority thus also differs accordingly, despite their sharing of the same Bichatian principles. Flaubert, secure in his medicalized vision, feels no need for commentary; finding the *mot juste* is all that needs to be done to anatomize. Eliot, in contrast, finds refuge in commentary, using it to fend off her despairing sense that her epistemological and social universes are disintegrating.

Coherence, Pathology, and Evolution: Three Organicisms and Their Narratives

Even with its use of the communal *we* and its maxims, however, Eliot's commentary only partially succeeds in unifying the reality it purports to comprehend. That reality remains fissured along the lines of different scientific perspectives, each of which must be granted a certain insight into the heart of things, a certain truth-to-life. We have already seen one important effect of Eliot's grudging scientific relativism in *Middlemarch*: Lydgate's predicament, his innately limited medical perspective, is an ineluctable consequence of a world where no form of rationality enjoys hegemony. The divergence of scientific discourses manifests itself not only at the level of character, however, but also and more profoundly, I would argue, in the extraordinary multiplicity of *Middlemarch*'s plots. It would be a mistake to confuse such formal multiplicity with the formlessness of James's loose baggy monster; on the other hand, it would be equally misleading to argue, as so many critics have done, that Eliot succeeds in controlling the potential monstrosity of her text and imposing an organic form on her novel. Given the vexed scientific context I have been attempting to establish, the very terms of aesthetic judgment employed here, monstrosity and organicism, become problematic as analytic instruments. The critic's task is neither to celebrate Eliot's achievement of organic form, nor to criticize the ideology of organicism to which Eliot's social vision and narrative form contribute, nor even to celebrate the lack of organic unity in *Middlemarch*, its abysmal monstrosity and incipient textuality. It is to explain how *Middlemarch*'s narrative organization reflects the formal consequences for Eliot's realism of the diverging scientific world in which she finds herself.[35] As a realist, Eliot is deeply committed to a medical perspective and to the kinds of character and plots that such a perspective entails; at the same time, however, her recognition that other scientific perspectives exist leads her to create other kinds of characters subject to different narrative possibilities than those of a purely medicalized realism. Indeed, it is probably most accurate to speak of *Middlemarch* as a polyvalent narrative, in which at least three distinct character-types and plot possibilities may be identified, each drawing on a different scientific discourse of organic form.[36]

The first of these narrative formations depends on what might be called "physiognomic organicism," an approach toward character and environment that we have already seen structuring Balzac's realism and that also figures quite strongly in Eliot's own early work. Traditional organicism assumes an immediacy and transparency of reality, and in particular the reality of character, to the mind of the narrator, which can reflect it in turn directly to us as readers. In *Middlemarch* this mode of realism gives rise to the story of Fred Vincy and the Garths, which we must now look at in more detail.

Fred Vincy, Mary, Caleb, and the rest of the Garth family are all what Balzac called "types." All present relatively straightforward profiles as characters, being essentially open and uncomplicated. As Eliot says of Mary: "Rembrandt would have painted her with pleasure, and would have made her broad features look out of the canvas with intelligent honesty. For honesty, truth-telling fairness, was Mary's reigning virtue: she neither tried to create illusions, nor indulged in them for her own behoof" (84). As the allusion to Rembrandt implies, Mary, and the other characters mentioned above, are realistic in the sense given by a younger Eliot (and her contemporaries) when discussing seventeenth-century Dutch painting. The intelligent, truth-telling qualities of the sitters for Dutch realist paintings, Eliot tells us, parallel the ethos of the artist himself, whose work is dominated by the ideal that art be true to life, mirroring it honestly and openly, eschewing illusionism. Eliot subscribes to such an ideal not only in her early art criticism but also in early novels such as *Adam Bede*, where she promulgates the famous (or for antirealist critics, infamous) definition of her artistic aim: "My strongest effort is to avoid any such arbitrary picture, and to give a faithful account of men and things as they have mirrored themselves in my mind. The mirror is doubtless defective; the outlines will sometimes be disturbed, the reflection faint or confused; but I feel as much bound to tell you as precisely as I can what that reflection is, as if I were in the witness-box, narrating my experience on oath."[37] There may be defects in the mirror, as there may be defects in character, but the narrator in *Adam Bede* remains confident that her faithfulness, like Mary Garth's faithfulness to herself, will yield an adequate account of experience.

By the time she begins *Middlemarch*, however, Eliot has come to recognize that mirrors are not merely defective in themselves but scratched by experience, at least in spots. Neither character nor reality can be witnessed adequately unless one attends to illusions and internal complexities that are foreign to Mary and characters like her (as well as to the confident narrator of *Adam Bede*). In the passage quoted above, for example, Mary's plainness and openness are explicitly contrasted to Rosamond's enigmatic attractiveness, especially that of her eyes of blue "deep enough to hold the most exquisite meanings an ingenious beholder could put into them, and deep enough to hide the meanings of the owner if these should happen to be less exquisite" (83). Such issues of interpretation need not be raised for Mary, nor for Fred nor any of the Garth family; their characters are organized so as to be as close to immediately meaningful as possible.

Caleb, for example, has settled into a relationship with his wife in which any need for interpretation (which looms so large in the Lydgate-Rosamond and Dorothea-Casaubon marriages) has been obviated. Caleb is completely understood by his wife, as he is by us; she knows what he will do from the most minimal signs, and there is no chance of her either being mistaken or of changing his mind once he has made it up. Caleb's very inarticulateness signifies his transcendence of the problems of mediation and construal that vex other characters' efforts to understand each other. For him, as for the Garth family as a whole, "things hang together" (297).

Indeed, Caleb's statement of faith about the coherence of things seems true not only of him and his family but of the social reality he inhabits. In this reality, people and relationships hang together, forming an essentially stable totality, a coherent social order rooted in the presumed steadiness of individual work. Not even crude economic facts, which would seem to show that in actuality things do not hang together in business, can threaten this totality: Garth (and Eliot as well) redefines business itself so as to circumvent its association with capital (185). Instead, it appears as a pure attribute, a synonym for productive work, "busyness": "by 'business' Caleb never meant money transactions, but the skilful application of labour" (402). No contradiction, either social or psychological, mars Caleb's whistle-as-you work world, and even those laborers who feel threatened by forces of business such as the railroad, and who thus might constitute a threat themselves to Caleb's busyness, are dealt with (by Garth and Eliot) as "poor fools" rather than as legitimate antagonists.

The plot predicated by such a conception of character and totality must involve entanglements, mysteries, and vicissitudes that are circumstantial rather than existential, so that time stabilizes rather than destroys or mutates the self. In Fred Vincy's case, for instance, Eliot deploys the familiar early realist plot of great expectations disappointed. One might wish to find in this pattern, as Mark Schorer does, an analogy to what happens to Lydgate's and Rosamond's expectations. Fred's disappointment, however, differs crucially from that of Lydgate and his wife, in that it is only a necessary stage of an essentially redemptive process. A temporally circumscribed and specified episode, it constitutes a chastisement, not a tragedy. The essence of Fred's character and fate is never in danger nor even really in question, for the reader senses from the beginning that the love between him and Mary, a love rooted in early childhood affection, is too natural to be thwarted by time. By the end of the novel, Fred and Mary have taken their places within the immanent social totality they themselves embody, reproducing the family structure of the Garths (Mary as teacher and Fred as farmer) and restoring Fred's inheritance, Stone Court, through "unswervingly steady" work. Our last view of Fred and Mary emphasizes the bucolic fullness of time implied by their romance and the Vincy-Garth plot in general:

> Fred and Mary still inhabit Stone Court— . . . the creeping plants still cast the foam of their blossoms over the fine stone-walls into the field where the walnut-trees stand in stately row—and . . . on sunny days the two lovers who were first engaged with the umbrella-ring may be seen in white-haired placidity at the open window from which Mary Garth, in the days of old Peter Featherstone, had often been ordered to look out for Mr Lydgate. (609)

Time, in this setting, has settled to a stillness in which our first glimpses of Fred and Mary can be recalled in our last, and in which the discontents recorded in the narrative stand revealed as only unnatural, inessential interruptions.

One litmus test for the kind of organic temporality I have been attempting to distinguish in the Vincy-Garth plot is the way it permits illness to enter narrative. Susan Sontag suggests that illness can either impinge from outside the self as penalty or emanate from within the self as expression.[38] In "formal" realism, as I argue in chapter one, both these options are exercised. But the fever that attacks Fred Vincy in the aftermath of the shock he receives at the loss of his expectations operates neither as retribution for his character nor as revelation of it, but only at most as a sort of disciplinary rite of passage. Like Pip in *Great Expectations*, Fred recovers in time to live a healthier, happier, organically stabilized life.

Chronic, developing pathology, on the other hand—Rosamond's

(or Emma Bovary's or Gwendolen Harleth's) hysteria, for instance—pertains to a second kind of narrative, one in which the temporality of plot is in some sense articulated upon the temporality of the body, its organic growth and decay, its duration of illness, its descent toward death, its complicated finitude: the narrative, in short, of a pathological organicism.[39]

To understand how Eliot generates character and narrative possibilities based on the paradigm of pathological organicism, or to be more precise, morbid anatomy, one needs to recall here its two guiding assumptions (discussed in some detail earlier in this book) about the nature of the self: first, the notion that the self carries on two distinct lives—one internal, uncontrolled, and relatively stable (Bichat's "organic" life), the other external, affected by pressures from the environment ("animal" life); and second, the idea of the individual as an economy, powered by a "vital force" that is invested in centers of sensibility, with profitable or disastrous results for the individual. Like Flaubert before her, Eliot translates these assumptions about the body into the domain of the mind: memory substitutes for the body's organic life, consciousness for its animal life, and the imagination for the particular bodily economy, powered by passion.[40] In view of this shared vision of the self, it is hardly surprising that Eliot generates a narrative (the Rosamond-Lydgate-Bulstrode story) remarkably similar to the plot of *Madame Bovary*. Moreover, both Eliot and Flaubert emphasize with remarkably similar characters and scenes the diagnostic/hermeneutic problems created by the Bichatian model of the self. At the same time, however, there remains a striking *difference* between the two plots, between Emma's fate and Rosamond's, Charles Bovary's fate and Lydgate's. This difference, I shall show, stems from Eliot's more extreme (and as we have seen, historically determinate) sense of medicine's innate uncertainty. In stark contrast to Flaubert, Eliot finds that medicine's "pathological doubt" casts into question the value of medicine as a scientific instrumentality. The resulting plot exposes this epistemological insufficiency and stresses the ethical imperative for medicine and medical realism that follows from it.

For those characters—Lydgate, Rosamond, Bulstrode—whom Eliot treats as pathologically organic, the self is what Lewes calls a "resultant,"[41] a double entity rather than a simple unity. Each of these characters possesses a "rational" and conscious self, able to give formal reasons for his or her actions. At the same time, however, each character is also subject to a different self, impassioned and uncontrolled by consciousness, spinning fantasies from within and getting thought entangled in metaphors. This second, inner self often is read by modern critics as a Freud-like unconscious. But it is more accurate, as well as less anachronistic, to equate Eliot's psychology to Bichat's "organic life" of autonomic systems in the body. Both consist of repetition compulsions, habits, desires, reflexes, latent memories, that are both displaced from and beyond the total control of consciousness. As Eliot puts it: "formal reasons . . . are a very artificial, inexact way of representing the tingling returns of old habit, and the caprices of young blood." Not only does the inner life exceed consciousness, but it actually enjoys some priority over consciousness: "there is no human being," Eliot insists, "who having both passions and thoughts does not think in consequence of his passions."

In itself, the priority of passion over thought might not be hazardous. The inner life, however, does not exist in isolation in Bichat's paradigm, but rather is enmeshed with the outer life of an individual—his or her active engagement with the environment. And just as the inner, imaginative life is a process of "spinning that web from [one's] inward self" (238) out of an "excited throng" (568) of emotions, so the outer life is also a web finely spun of a multitude of small, sometimes unnoticeable relationships. To exist as an individual is to mediate between these two different webs, which may be spun unevenly, and which may even be tugging in opposing directions—the inner web tensed by desire, and the outer web by what Eliot calls "the small solicitations of circumstance" (574).

The vicissitudes of Lydgate, Rosamond, and Bulstrode result from their efforts to sustain a coherent image of a unified self, either by suppressing one of these two elements of their being, or by searching for an environment in which a psychic economy—the physiological term, coined by Spencer, is "consensus"—can be sustained. To achieve consensus is to achieve a kind of organic integrity, a state that is ideal not only in life but in art. Eliot, in her "Notes on Form in Art," asserts her own admiration for those who can achieve in their art the kind of biological "consensus or constant interchange of effects among its [the body's] parts" that an accomplished athlete manifests.[42] Consensus, as Eliot sketches it, is thus not a static quality, but a constancy and smoothness sustained in action, whether such action is individual or artistic. Just as an athlete throwing a stone gives form to motion, Eliot argues, so the strong artist arranging events gives form to an emotion.[43] But Eliot's athletic analogy in "Notes," although emphasizing the active and pragmatic quality of consensus, does not sufficiently— as *Middlemarch* does—take account of the struggle consensus demands, or the profound stakes of that struggle. We are not all athletes, yet we all, like Lydgate at the start of his career, face a difficult journey in which, "with all the possible thwartings and furtherings of circumstance, all the niceties of inward balance, . . . a man swims and makes his point or else is carried headlong" (111). Even for the strongest, another point always looms, and eventually everyone must be carried headlong. Life, to recall Bichat's dictum, is resistance to death, and a resistance that is ultimately always overcome; no consensus, no matter how firm, can hold indefinitely, if only because the resources of one's ardour are limited.

The unity of our consciousness, the consensus of our psychic system, is then merely a mode of temporary delay, a "delicate poise and transition" (122) deferring inevitable strains and disintegration within the individual. Eliot's pathological characters achieve short-lived consensus by acting as if the two selves could be quarantined from each other and only one of the two admitted as the true self. Bulstrode, for example, has in his youth performed misdeeds that "were like the subtle muscular movements which are not taken account of in the consciousness, though they bring about the end that we fix our mind on and desire" (503); he finds himself "carrying on two distinct lives," but manages to hide from himself the disjunction within him, spinning justifications "into intricate thickness, like masses of spiderweb, padding the moral sensibility" (451). Lydgate, too, has "two selves within him" (113), the emotional and the scientific, but proceeds as if each of these two selves can exist in isolation both from each other and from the circumstantial world that surrounds him. Rosamond, finally, neglects her outer self entirely, investing all her energies into her imagination, "a close network aloof and independent" (427), which provides, at least for a time, a "real romance," but which requires her to act as a lower species does, putting up an "iron resistance" (364) to anything from the outer life—including the feelings of her husband— that might impinge on her stability.

As Bichatian medicine teaches and Eliot's narrative reveals, all of these strategies ultimately must fail, for "our passions do not live apart in locked chambers" (123–24) as Rosamond assumes, nor can we keep our "intention separate from [our] desire" (516), as Bulstrode tries to, nor do we live in social isolation, as Lydgate assumes. "The life is bound into one," Eliot insists, "by a zone of dependence in growth and decay" (450), and under the strains that inevitably arise out of "the indefinable movements" of the individual's own passions and/or the "small solicitations of circumstance" impinging from without, the uneven web of ego is eventually torn.

The pathologically organic plot thus takes the shape of a descending arc, in which the individual is progressively disarticulated, as in *Madame Bovary*. Worse still, the action of decay, of deindividuation, proceeds not in heroic or romantic deeds, but in a continuous and minute process almost imperceptible to the individuals involved. As Eliot tells us, the catastrophe of romance may involve a punctual and definitive event such as a marriage or a "fatal parting," but the catastrophe in pathological realism takes place in slow motion, as it were, and within the souls of characters, like a spreading infection: "Nothing in the world more subtle than the process of their gradual change! In the beginning they inhaled it unknowingly; you or I may have sent some of our breath toward infecting them, when we uttered our conforming falsities or drew our silly conclusions: or perhaps it came with the vibrations from a woman's glance." (107)

Lydgate is the case study for this reflection, and for him, Rosamond's glance is the most virulent infectious agent, the immediate cause of their engagement. In the scene that ends with their betrothal, Eliot brilliantly draws on the metaphor of the self as web or network in order to emphasize the subtlety and unknowingness of the beginnings of Lydgate's catastrophic infection. Rosamond, we learn, has been knitting "some trivial chain-work" in order to hide her agitation at Lydgate's cold manner (he has come intending to make it clear to her that he is not seriously interested in pursuing a romance). As Lydgate rises to go, after being unable to bring himself to speak, Rosamond inadvertently drops her chain and Lydgate picks it up. When he raises his eyes he sees Rosamond on the verge of tears, and he is overcome. "He did not know where the chain went" (222), Eliot comments, but he has nevertheless been "bound" by it, and will eventually end up doing his own trivial chain-work, writing only a treatise on gout rather than forging some more important link in the chain of discovery.

As a physician, Lydgate should know better, for as we see earlier, he recognizes the importance of paying attention to the trivial chain-work of the body, "those minute processes which prepare human misery and joy" (122). His problem, as Eliot makes clear, is that he does not consistently view women from a clinical point of view, which would entail interpreting their individuality and charm by assuming that it always depends "on conditions that are not obvious" (119). Unfortunately, "that distinction of mind which belonged to his intellectual ardour," Eliot tells us, "did not penetrate his feeling and judgment about furniture, or women" (112). Rather than interpret, he tends to classify Rosamond, and rather than seeking to go beyond obvious conditions, he tends to be satisfied with the evidence of his eyes. He sees Rosamond as having

just the kind of intelligence one would desire in a woman—polished, refined, docile, lending itself to finish in all the delicacies of life, and en-
shrined in a body which expressed this with a force of demonstration that
excluded the need for other evidence. Lydgate felt sure that if ever he
married, his wife would have that feminine radiance, that distinctive
womanhood which must be classed with flowers and music, that sort of
beauty which by its very nature was virtuous, being moulded only for
pure and delicate joys. (121)

Eliot clearly wishes to denigrate the kind of classificatory intelligence Lydgate himself displays here.[44] Had he maintained his clinical
detachment when dealing with women as well as patients, he would
not have mistaken Rosamond so completely, but would have inquired
into the more hidden aspects of her character. But even if Lydgate
were able to interpret Rosamond's sighs, tears, and longing looks not
as signs but as vital signs, as symptoms, finding out the truth about her
would still be far from easy. For one thing, many of the processes that
make a character what he or she is must remain hidden, inaccessible to
an interpreter or even to the character being interpreted (just as the
processes of the organic life are hidden within the body and thus not
directly representable for either the patient or the physician). In fact,
not even the interpreter's own self is completely accessible. Eliot puts
this ontological conundrum in the form of a rhetorical question: "Who
can represent himself just as he is, even in his own reflections?" (521).

The blind spot inherent in self-reflection creates great ethical problems (how does one define hypocrisy? responsibility?), but for Eliot the
prior problem is more strictly medical, a matter of diagnosis rather
than of judgement. The self's doubleness, its inherent duplicity, ob-
structs any effort to grapple with illnesses that may be festering beneath the surface of consciousness. If this is true of Rosamond's neu-
rosis, it is equally true of the more serious ethical illness of Bulstrode,
of whom Eliot says that he suffers from a "diseased motive . . . like an
irritating agent in his blood" that he cannot repress. Bulstrode is conceived not only as a hypocrite but as a pathologically organic character, according to the analogy between mind and body described above.
Just as the body is separable into an organic life and an active life, so
the self is separable into desires and avowals, and sickness may arise in
one even while the other continues to function normally: "A man
vows, and yet will not cast away the means of breaking his vow. Is it
that he distinctly means to break it? Not at all; but the desires which
tend to break it are at work in him dimly, and make their way into his
imagination, and relax his muscles [could Eliot here perhaps be pun-

ning on "morals"?] in the very moments when he is telling himself over again the reasons for his vow" (519). Bulstrode's condition reveals, even more clearly perhaps than Rosamond's, the interconnection between diagnostic and hermeneutic limitations. Even where the self seeks to be "honest" as Mary Garth is honest, Eliot makes clear through Bulstrode that—in this particular plot at least—there exists no ideal speech situation in which what one says about oneself can directly reveal what one is truly feeling, wanting, or meaning. Not even the situation of prayer, where the interlocutor is God, can overcome this ontological condition: "Does anyone suppose that private prayer is necessarily candid—necessarily goes to the roots of action?" How much less candid, then, must the speech be between doctor and patient, or husband and wife! And how difficult it must be to establish the truth about oneself or others! If, like Rosamond, one can have "no consciousness that her action could rightly be called false" (487), to ask that she act or speak truthfully is to ask the impossible.

What characters like Rosamond and Bulstrode know of themselves they know only through an act of self-misinterpretation. Once again, Eliot emphasizes the particular medical provenance of this condition by describing it in diagnostic terms: "men and women make sad mistakes about their own symptoms, taking their vague uneasy longings sometimes for genius, sometimes for religion, and oftener still for a mighty love" (552). Thus, Rosamond's love, while genuine enough to her, is in fact symptomatic; like her counterpart Emma Bovary, she suffers an illness of *mauvaise foi* that she cannot recognize. But how then can one *avoid* misinterpreting, taking symptoms as signs? Lydgate's attempt to understand Rosamond offers the best answer Eliot can muster to this question. Only by adopting what Lydgate refers to as a "philosophy of medical evidence" (93)—a pathologist's hermeneutics of suspicion about the meaning of an individual's outward signs—does he eventually learn to survey cautiously Rosamond "as if he were looking for symptoms" (480) of a diseased motive, rather than manifestations of feminine graces.

Even if one does exercise extreme caution, however, there is still a limit to the degree of certitude one can achieve in determining motives. What Lydgate calls "pathological doubt" must remain a part of any hermeneutics based on the medical model, because motives, like the source of disease in medicine, can no longer be disentangled. Here, as usual, Lydgate's and Eliot's medical perspective is historically exact: the idea that illness develops from a localizable "lesional site" ultimately visible to the physician-anatomist gives way, with Broussais (with whom Brooke informs us Lydgate has studied!) to an idea that illness can only be physiologically localized as "inflammation." The epistemological shift accomplished by Broussais's substitution of inflammation for lesional localization has been brilliantly summed up by Foucault:

> inflammation is not a constellation of signs: it is a process that develops within a tissue. . . . In order to detect this primary, fundamental, functional disorder, the gaze must be able to detach itself from the lesional site, for it is not given at the outset, although the disease, in its original source, was always localizable; indeed, it has to locate that organic root before the lesion, by means of the functional disorders and their symptoms. It is here that symptomatology rediscovers its role, but it is a role based entirely on the local character of the pathological attack: by returning along the path of organic sympathies and influences, it must, beneath the endlessly extended network of symptoms, "induce" or "deduce" (Broussais uses both words in the same sense) the initial point of physiological disturbance. [45]

For someone attempting to induce or deduce the initial point of a moral or psychological disturbance, the interpretive process must be equally as imprecise as that implied in Broussais's symptomatology. Nineteenth-century medicine reacts to its situation by developing statistical methods to control the uncertainties of diagnosis, but such methods remain unsatisfactory substitutes for a secure predictability, and are not fully integrated into medical practice. Physicians—and in *Middlemarch*, all those, except for the Garths, who try to do good for those characters who are organized pathologically—find themselves forced to submit to the element of chance in their evaluations, despite their aversion to it. Like Lydgate, who "had said to himself that the only winning he cared for must be attained by a conscious process of high, difficult combination tending towards a beneficent result" (490), such characters as Dorothea see themselves as instruments of reason rather than as gamblers. Yet precisely because of the pressure to take therapeutic action tending toward a beneficent result, doctors and do-gooders must proceed even where the combinations are too difficult to be gauged.

In this situation, the ability to care and the desire to cure count for more than anything else. One must believe, as Dorothea does, that if character "may become diseased as our bodies do . . . then it may be rescued and healed" (538), even if one does not know how to do so. This ethical imperative comes to the fore in Lydgate's own medical experience in *Middlemarch*: it is his ability to care, his sensitivity toward the feelings of his patients, beyond his technical knowledge, that makes him such an excellent physician. Eliot strongly endorses the "twice-blessed mercy" he displays, hallowing it as the definitive quality of physicians: "Many of us looking back through life would say that the kindest man we have ever known has been a medical man, or perhaps that surgeon whose fine tact, directed by deeply informed perception, has come to us in our need with a more sublime beneficence than that of miracle-workers" (489). Yet despite Eliot's eulogy, Lydgate's own fate paradoxically seems to imply that the ability to be touched and to touch is ultimately self-sacrificing, if not self-destructive. It is this very aspect of his character that brings him and Rosamond together to begin with. In the engagement scene mentioned earlier, Lydgate's verbal reaction to Rosamond's distress is pointedly couched in the language of a physician: "What is the matter? you are distressed. Tell me—pray." His physical response is no less medical. As Eliot points out when Lydgate goes on to put his arms around Rosamond, enfolding her protectingly, "he was used to being gentle with the weak and suffering" (222). Lydgate's view of women, in other words, is shaped not only by a classifying, antiscientific mentality, but also by his specifically clinical perspective: "this rather abrupt man had much tenderness in his manners towards women, seeming to have always present in his imagination the weakness of their frames and the delicate poise of their health both in body and in mind" (474). The dénouement of the plot simply involves the gradual exposure of this underlying clinical element in Lydgate's relationship with Rosamond, the transformation of a putative husband-wife bond into one between doctor and patient—a bond, moreover, in which there is no hope for a cure. Eminently intractable, Rosamond's hysteria condemns Lydgate to an essentially custodial role: "he had chosen this fragile creature, and had taken the burthen of her life upon his arms. He must walk as he could, carrying that burthen pitifully" (586).

Although shouldering such a responsibility may be morally laudable, the bleakness of Lydgate's remaining years shows how unsatisfied Eliot is with the necessity that one be merely a physician, even a so-called "successful" one. Her rigor as an artist forces her to accept the bitter limitations, the human finitude inherent in the medical model she adopts in the Lydgate-Rosamond-Bulstrode narrative. But Eliot's social instinct is meliorist, and she cannot accept the idea, implied by Lydgate's fate, that no social progress whatsoever is possible. Flaubert, we may recall, does accept this idea as part of the price he must pay to gain the transcendent perspective of a pathological realist that he assumes in *Madame Bovary*. Eliot, in contrast, multiplies her perspectives, and hence her plots, to provide alternatives to finitude within what is putatively the same social reality.

We have already seen how the Fred Vincy-Mary Garth plot operates according to quite different principles of characterization than those of pathological realism. This plot, however, does not offer a strong alternative to the Lydgate-Rosamond plot, from which it remains very much isolated and insulated. The two kinds of characters operate in two distinct social spheres, being brought together only intermittently. And when they do meet, as in the scene discussed earlier between Rosamond and Mary, the confrontation only emphasizes their immiscibility. Another plot line, however, *does* mix, at least partially, with that of Lydgate, Rosamond, and Bulstrode: the love story involving Dorothea and Will Ladislaw. This third narrative form and these characters represent Eliot's strongest attempt to overcome the limitations of self, interpretation, and narrative possibility inherent in pathological discourse.

Will and Dorothea share many similarities as characters with their pathologized counterparts, Lydgate and Rosamond. Both sets of characters have inner lives that struggle against the unpropitious conditions of their outer lives. Lydgate and Will are both subjects for betting on whether their careers will be successful or not. It is as true of Dorothea as for Lydgate that her ardor is spent in "unheroic acts," and Eliot's generalization—"there is no creature whose inward being is so strong that it is not greatly determined by what lies outside it"—applies to Dorothea as well as to Lydgate. One could go on indefinitely, charting out the "matrix of analogies" that binds together these strands of *Middlemarch*. But Will and Dorothea differ from Lydgate and Rosamond in one crucial way: they are conceived as subject not to "growth and decay" but to development and mutation.[46] If Lydgate and Rosamond must fail because of their innate flaws, the unalterable spots of commonness in their fixed organization, their organic finitude, Will and Dorothea have at least a chance to progress because, as Will suggests to Dorothea, each of them has "a soul in which knowledge passes instantaneously into feeling, and feeling flashes back as a *new* organ of knowledge" [my emphasis] (166).

By analyzing Eliot's use of scientific rhetorics, one can show that embryological and evolutionist terms are applied almost exclusively to Will and Dorothea. It is possible, of course, for such rhetorical concentration to be merely thematic, a matter of certain metaphors being at hand for Eliot. I would argue, however, that as with the language of tissular pathology, the languages of mutation and transformation provide Eliot with a strategic vision of relations and possibilities that structure a narrative. By seeing Will and Dorothea as capable of evolving new organs, Eliot can generate certain critical shifts and tendencies in their plot, shifts and tendencies that in the end account for their relative success compared to Lydgate and Rosamond's fate.

Eliot's double standard becomes most evident if one compares the ways in which she permits Lydgate and Will, or Dorothea and Rosamond, to respond to similar situations—the hazarding of vocation by Lydgate and Will, the experience of shock for Dorothea and Rosamond. Eliot plots Lydgate's career, we recall, as a struggle against the current in which the chances of his being successful are "complicated probabilities" to be calculated on the basis of "the possible thwartings and furtherings of circumstance, all the niceties of inward balance" (111)—in other words, the reciprocally determining conditions of his outer and inner lives. Will's career prospects are similarly described in terms of a chancy gamble: he is "a bright creature, abundant in uncertain promises" (345). But whereas Lydgate's uncertainty concerns a vocation that has already been born (and which can thus be scrutinized from a medical point of view), Will's uncertainty stems from his not yet having been born as a vocational self. His inward balance has not yet taken on a finalized form, but is still gestating, and hence his chances must be given the benefit of a different, more promising kind of doubt than the pathological doubt we give Lydgate—the optimistic doubt of embryology: "We know what a masquerade all development is, and what effective shapes may be disguised in helpless embryos.—In fact, the world is full of hopeful analogies and handsome dubious eggs called possibilities" (61).

Dorothea is one of the few who accepts this embryological view of Will's possibilities. For her, where there is a will, there may be a way, even if she is not yet sure what that way *is*. "After all," she responds to Casaubon's complaint about Will's unwillingness to apply himself instrumentally to some Aristotelian end, "people may really have in them some vocation which is not quite plain to themselves, may they not? They may seem idle and weak because they are growing" (61). Perhaps. But idleness and weakness may signify illness as well as growth, and Dorothea herself fails to distinguish between the two in the case of Casaubon, whose years of research Will compares to those "pitiable instances of long incubation producing no chick" (61). "Doubtless, many an error vigorously pursued has kept the embryo of truth a-breathing," Eliot grants, but Casaubon's embryo turns out to be stillborn, despite Dorothea's hopes for him. Dorothea's mistake points to the impossibility, given the state of embryological knowledge during this period, of determining whether what appear as errors are in fact progressive or pathological, positive mutations or abortive monstrosities. Only with the emergence of genetics and biochemistry in this century does it become possible to unify the insights of embryology and pathology under the aegis of a concept of error.[47] For Dorothea, as for Eliot and her compatriots, the embryological assertion—that changes in the organization of the self do in fact involve the progressive creation of "new organs"—must be taken on faith.

Nowhere is that faith on Eliot's part more obvious than in *Middlemarch*'s climactic episode, in which she subjects Rosamond and Dorothea to the identical shock of learning (or in Dorothea's case, believing she has learned) that Will is not in love with them. Rosamond, of course, has a pathological constitution that has already been weakened by her investment of desire in an imaginary self. Her controlled self-consciousness of manner, Eliot points out, is "the expensive substitute for simplicity," so that by the time Ladislaw turns upon her to vent his rage at having had Dorothea mistake him for Rosamond's lover, her emotional reserves, like her financial reserves, have been exhausted, and her psychic economy verges on collapse. In this, as well as in the *ennui* she feels at finding her romance with her husband's image giving way to "everyday details which must be lived slowly from hour to hour, not floated through with a rapid selection of favourable aspects" (484), Rosamond strongly resembles Emma Bovary. Unsurprisingly, then, she responds to Will's destruction of her last refuge of fantasy by suffering an hysterical syndrome very much like the one Emma endures after Rodolphe puts an end to their affair. Emma, we should recall, first runs to her attic where, leaning out her window, she feels herself at the brink of suicide, "suspended, surrounded by vast space"[48] she nearly faints, but returns to the dining room, where she finally has a fit before her horrified husband's eyes. Rosamond similarly finds herself "almost losing the sense of her identity" in her now empty world: "The terrible collapse of the illusion towards which all her hope had been strained was a stroke which had too thoroughly shaken her: her little world was in ruins, and she felt herself tottering in the midst as a lonely bewildered consciousness. . . . After he was gone, Rosamond tried to get up from her seat, but fell back fainting. . . . She threw herself on the bed with her clothes on, and lay in apparent torpor" (571–72).

Unlike Charles Bovary, Lydgate is a perceptive, competent clinican, and on seeing Rosamond he immediately notices her agitation, even before her syncope strikes. Only after he asks her what is wrong does she actually break down: "Clinging to him she fell into hysterical sobbings and cries, and for the next hour he did nothing but soothe and tend her" (572). Lydgate's diagnosis—"He imagined that Dorothea had been to see her, and that all this effect on her nervous system, which evidently involved some new turning towards himself, was due to the excitement of the new impressions which that visit had raised"—comes very close to the truth Eliot wishes to convey about Rosamond's pathology, although Lydgate is oblivious of the mediating role Rosamond's imagination has played in transmitting impressions to her nervous system.

Rosamond's response to the shock she receives implies her inability to evolve. Her psychic organization, like that of Casaubon, is "inflexible," incapable of adaptation. She must be excused for this flaw, for which she cannot be held responsible; and yet, as Lydgate finds, "it was inevitable that in that excusing mood he should think of her as if she were an animal of another and feebler species" (489). If Lydgate only comes to this judgment at the end of the novel, Eliot thinks of Rosamond as a lower species throughout *Middlemarch*, describing her, as we have seen, at various times as a torpedo and a Venus's fly-trap. The bitterness and irredeemability of the struggle between Rosamond and Lydgate becomes a human parallel to the view of nature "red in tooth and claw," a nature of conflicting and fixed species without the possibility of amelioration.

But the very prevalence of such evolutionary terminology in Eliot's analysis of Rosamond implies an alternative to Rosamond's kind of organic rigidity, the existence of "a creature who entered into every one's feelings, and could take the pressure of their thought instead of urging his own with iron resistance" (364). This is Dorothea speaking of Will, but she herself is also such a creature, as shown in the novel's climactic scene in chapter eighty, where Eliot describes Dorothea's reaction to discovering Will and Rosamond together. Like Rosamond, Dorothea must deal with the consequences of "her lost woman's pride of reigning" in Will's mind. Will now appears to her, as to Rosamond, as "a changed belief exhausted of hope, a detected illusion." And like Rosamond, Dorothea falls into hysterical sobbing. But unlike Rosamond, Dorothea is "vigorous enough" to survive, and even benefit from, her shock. "It was not in Dorothea's nature," Eliot reminds us, "for longer than the duration of a paroxysm, to sit in the narrow cell of her calamity, in the besotted misery of a consciousness that only sees another's lot as an accident of its own." Her "vivid sympathetic experience returned to her now as a power," allowing her to widen her vision as a Rosamond or an Emma Bovary, faced with the same newly opened spaces, cannot. Indeed, Eliot's famous description of Dorothea's moment of recovery from her shock might stand as the exact antithesis of Flaubert's equally famous description of Emma's moment of succumbing to *her* shock. Here are the two passages, the first from *Madame Bovary*, the second from *Middlemarch*:

The dazzling sunlight burst in.

Opposite, beyond the roofs, the open country stretched as far as the eye could reach. Down below, beneath her, the village square was empty; the stones of the pavement glittered, the weathercocks on the houses stood motionless. . . . She looked about her wishing that the earth might crumble. . . . She advanced, looked at the paving-stones, saying to herself, "Jump! Jump!"

The ray of light reflected straight from below drew the weight of her body towards the abyss. The ground of the village square seemed to tilt over and climb up the walls, the floor to pitch forward like in a tossing boat. She was right at the edge, almost hanging, surrounded by vast space. The blue of the sky invaded her, the air was whirling in her hollow head; she had but to yield, to let herself be taken; and the humming of the lathe never ceased, like an angry voice calling her.[49]

It had taken long for her to come to that question, and there was light piercing into the room. She opened her curtains, and looked out towards the bit of road that lay in view, with fields beyond, outside the entrance-gates. On the road there was a man with a bundle on his back and a woman carrying her baby; in the field she could see figures moving—perhaps the shepherd with his dog. Far off in the bending sky was the pearly light; and she felt the largeness of the world and the manifold wakings of men to labour and endurance. She was a part of that involuntary, palpitating life, and could neither look out on it from her luxurious shelter as a mere spectator, nor hide her eyes in selfish complaining. (578)

The *style indirect libre* of Eliot's passage and its syntactical pacing (three consecutive parallel descriptive statements—"on the road," "in the field," "far off in the bending sky"—followed by a conjunction that links these statements to a final independent clause) are typically Flaubertian—in fact, one can find similarly constructed sentences in the passage from *Madame Bovary* quoted above. Yet Eliot here turns Flaubert's pathological vision on its head. To be "a part of that involuntary, palpitating life" is not suicidal, but regenerating, at least for those creatures strong enough to immerse themselves in it. The evolutionary self takes what would be a moment of pathology for the morbidly organic self and uses it as an occasion for creating a new normalcy, a new organization of the self.

Dorothea and Will's evolving fate mitigates but does not resolve the horror of Lydgate's submission to Rosamond's involuntary pathological life, nor does it touch upon the calm and happy life of Fred, Mary, and the Garths. *Middlemarch*'s conclusion, with its half-hopeful, half-pessimistic tone and its presentation of three distinct ends for the three plots we have discussed, represents Eliot's strained attempt to unify as a single reality all three of these divergent views of life and character. One of the marks of the greatness of *Middlemarch* as a realistic novel is the extent to which such discourses are orchestrated and their tendency to dispersion or contention muted. By comparing *Middlemarch* with *Daniel Deronda*, we can see more clearly how Eliot accomplishes this *rapprochement*. One obvious change is that by *Deronda*, Eliot has completely jettisoned the traditional organicism represented in the Garth-Fred Vincy plot, thereby revealing in a much starker way the strain between pathological and embryological-evolutionary perspectives—between the hysteric world of Gwendolen and the transformative world of Daniel. Traditional organicism, as Eliot employs it in *Middlemarch*, thus may be said to provide a kind of buffer zone between two more epistemologically sophisticated (and therefore more clearly competitive) views of reality. But a second, more subtle but perhaps more important difference separates *Middlemarch* from *Daniel Deronda*: the ethical counterweight provided by Lydgate to the optimism of the transformative perspective in *Middlemarch* can no longer be found in Eliot's later novel. In *Middlemarch*, Lydgate's clinical attitude, his devotion to those who cannot evolve, still at least helps to sustain the ideal of a social totality in which the healthy and the sick can share in the same reality. No such figure appears in *Daniel Deronda* to tend to Gwendolen's ills as Lydgate does to Rosamond's. Deronda himself, who performs this role for a part of the novel, does so uncomfortably, in the absence of a clear vocation of his own. Deronda, in fact, is a rewriting not of Lydgate, but of Will: just as Will abandons Rosamond, so Deronda abandons Gwendolen upon discovering what he must become. The medical perspective no longer inheres, even as an ethical ideal, and as a result, both life and reality itself begin to fissure. Realism, so fretfully and delicately held together by Eliot, begins to give way to other novelistic modes.

FIVE

ON THE REALISM/NATURALISM DISTINCTION

SOME ARCHAEOLOGICAL CONSIDERATIONS

THERE SEEMS TO BE general agreement among literary historians that something like a "crisis of representation" afflicts realism during the last few decades of the nineteenth century, and that modernism—understood variously as "going-beyond-representation," beginning with a text rather than an intention, or a turning inward of narrative—ultimately emerges to supplant the worn-out representational practices of Balzac, Flaubert, Eliot, Dickens, Turgenev, et al. Like all simple stories, this one has its attractions: it is easy to follow, offering only two protagonists, a dramatic break with the past, and clear winners and losers. Moreover, it points to a certain general historical pattern of change that unarguably did occur, at least in the sense that modernism and realism do constitute distinct literary practices. But as an historical narrative, it is woefully inadequate, ignoring as it does a whole range of literary practices that lived (and in some cases died) in the interim: sensation fiction, naturalism, detective fiction, science fiction, the fiction of empire, and so on. In what amounts to a case of literary critical ecmnesia, the work of writers like Collins, Zola, Conan Doyle, Verne, Kipling, Stevenson, Huysmans, and Wilde simply vanishes within this foreshortened literary-historical perspective.

Part of the problem, as I suggest in previous chapters, lies in the analytic instruments that literary critics use to define such generic terms as *realism* and *modernism*. Representation is too broad and crude a notion to adequately describe the work realists perform; one could hardly expect it to permit one to discriminate between realism and all these other literary practices that are neither quite realistic nor modernist, much less to offer an historical explanation for the evolution of so-called "transitional" genres. If, on the other hand, an analytics of discourse helps to clarify the nature and nuances of realism itself, it also might help both to specify and to account in historical terms for the differences between realism and these other genres.

The genres posing the most serious difficulties are those that seem at first glance closest to realism: naturalism and detective fiction. In each case, one can recognize at least the rudiments of realism—an eschewing of supernatural explanation, an appeal to scientific standards of truth, a reliance on empirical detail. One way to test the value of rethinking literary history in discursive terms, then, is to probe the representational practices of these two quasi-realistic genres more closely, to see if, how, and why the assumptions so central to realism— the medicalized notions of knowledge, truth, and authority—might be redeployed, subordinated to other concerns, abandoned, or criticized in these other literary forms.

A little more than kin, and less than kind, naturalism—and in particular the work of Emile Zola—has long been felt to constitute a departure, in one way or another, from the achievement of Balzac, Stendhal, Eliot, Dickens, and Flaubert. But even those literary historians of realism who most vehemently assert the distinction have found it difficult to pin down. I am thinking here of the powerful and sustained classical Marxist attack on naturalism mounted by Georg Lukács, as well as the recent effort by Fredric Jameson to renew this attack in a more up-to-date formal vocabulary. For Lukács, naturalism involves the displacement of realism's vision of "the complete human personality," "the type," by a view of man as a "lifeless average," a "grey statistical mean."[1] Jameson argues similarly that the shift from the "first great realisms" to "'high' realism and naturalism" (Jameson's quotation marks implying that, for him, such late-blooming realism actually constitutes a degeneration rather than a culmination) entails a "gradual reification of realism," although for Jameson this reification stems from "a perfected narrative apparatus" rather than a submergence of subjectivity as in Lukács.[2] Lukács's and Jameson's desire to enforce a distinction between realism and naturalism could hardly be clearer. And yet, as Jameson's conjunction linking "high" realism with naturalism and his use of the term *gradual* indicate, he has difficulty pinpointing the liminal moment when organic realism decomposes into reified naturalism. For Lukács as well, the moment when reification ceases to be a merely local condition and metastasizes through the social and literary metabolism is hazy; realism turns out to shade into naturalism, with some writers (most notoriously Flaubert) falling into a gray area that makes them particularly difficult for Lukács to categorize and evaluate.[3]

In view of these uncomfortable slippages even within the discourse of those most insistent on maintaining the distinction between realism and naturalism, it is hardly surprising that new historicist critics of the nineteenth-century novel aggressively, even exuberantly, ignore the distinction altogether. Both Mark Seltzer and D. A. Miller, for example, have offered important retellings of literary history in which what Miller calls "the very practice of novelistic representation" subsumes all generic differences only to be subsumed in its turn by the policing power that operates through it.[4] Thus, where Lukács or Jameson would claim that between Balzac or Scott and Zola or Gissing the veil of reification has fallen, Miller and Seltzer can see Balzac, Zola, Flaubert, Trollope, James, and a number of other novelists all participating in what Seltzer calls a common "fantasy of surveillance," a normalizing ideology of power that itself constitutes the essence of a "realism" or novelistic representation without clear boundaries.

This neo-Foucauldian approach, like its Marxist counterpart, thus ultimately fails to resolve the nagging question of generic limits and transformations, and for similar reasons (despite the mutual hostility of the two intellectual camps). Neither approach, given its instruments of analysis—the concept of reification on one hand and power on the other—has the means to grasp the way particular forms of scientificity or epistemic postures inform or structure texts and genres. Seltzer's and Miller's shortcomings in this regard stem from their having appropriated from Foucault only the skeletal conception that modern societies enact a general strategy of power through policing. In Foucault's work, however, this strategy is forced into visibility through a stringent analysis of concrete apparatuses of discipline—apparatuses in which such *savoirs* as medicine, criminology, architecture, and penology participate in distinctive ways. Each of these "scientific" disciplines, in Foucault, has its own integrity, its own epistemological and technical complexities. For Miller and Seltzer, in contrast, there is no need to do much reading beyond the text itself, since these various disciplines, whatever the details of the scientific discourses they employ, are all versions of one overriding process of surveillance.[5] The result is a relatively unnuanced (although politically highly charged) view of the history of fiction in general, and of realism in particular.

Lukács and Jameson, on the other hand, can hardly be said to ignore the sciences in their analysis of reification. Lukács, in particular, devotes a number of pages to scientific epistemology in his groundbreaking essay, "Reification and the Consciousness of the Proletariat." For Lukács, in fact, it is science—rather than (as one might expect) commodity fetishism, factory labor, or the logic of capital—that ultimately becomes the manifestation of capitalist consciousness, of reified "contemplation at its purest." "The formalistic conceptualisation of the specialised sciences," Lukács claims, "become [sic] for philosophy an immutably given substratum and this signals the final and despairing renunciation of every attempt to cast light on the reification that lies at the root of this formalism."[6] In his later work on the novel, Lukács's antiscientific attitude expresses itself, as we have seen, in a hatred of the statistical view of man. But, like Seltzer and Miller,

Lukács never turns to any particular science, referring only to "natural science" in general. He thus fails to appreciate the epistemological nuances among the various sciences—including the distinction discussed in chapter one between formalized and dubious sciences. Clinical medicine, the dubiously scientific discourse on which we have been focusing, is neither a statistical nor a reified science in Lukács's sense (as is implied, by the way, by his willingness to use medical terms like *metabolism* to analyze the processes of reification). The physician always confronts a patient, not just a body, so that although his or her practice entails a certain technical or reified view of illness, his or her knowledge can never be value-free, but must necessarily be in some way "human" knowledge, knowledge permeated with norms (notions of what constitutes health or morbidity). Moreover, in the period we have been considering, clinical discourse in fact fuses observations and value judgments, statistical and qualitative judgments, in a single cognitive operation of diagnosis. Unlike Lukács's stereotypical and stereotyping scientist, the clinician does not proceed by reducing quality to quantity, the human case before him or her to a mere statistic, or a life to its elements or laws. The physician's science remains a human science.

That kind of reduction, on the other hand, *is* an indispensable step in the basic sciences, including such life sciences as experimental physiology and cytology. Despite Lukács's fuzziness, then, his epistemological critique of the sciences at least suggests where one might begin to look for the conceptual roots of naturalism. Without condemning the reductive sciences out of hand as Lukács does, one can pose the same sorts of archaeological questions asked previously about clinical medicine and realism: What makes a statement readable as true or false in these various reductive sciences? What are the rules for producing knowledge in each case? And how, if at all, can these rules, presuppositions, and cognitive assumptions be said to shape naturalist fiction?

One need not look far for confirmation that a rather strong historical correlation exists between naturalism and at least one reductive science: experimental physiology, or what its founder Claude Bernard called "experimental medicine," which emerges in the 1850s. Bernard's name, of course, is familiar to literary critics from Zola's much-maligned manifesto of naturalism, "The Experimental Novel." In this essay, Zola develops at some length the analogy between Bernard's work and his own, arguing not only that the method of research and experimentation developed by Bernard is identical to Zola's, but that this method is also that of Balzac and Flaubert, indeed of realism *tout court*. For Zola, in other words, realism and naturalism, far from constituting distinct literary practices, are conflated. Both can be thought of as medical in the particular sense of Bernard's "experimental medicine." Zola would seem to contradict the argument I have been making about the medical basis of realism's distinctiveness, even as he foregrounds the importance of medicine. At this point, however, we need to examine Zola's thesis in a bit more detail, in order to see how Zola illuminates (sometimes in quite unexpected ways) the distinction between realism and naturalism that he would deny, and that I wish to reconceive on discursive grounds.

Zola begins by detaching Bernard's experimental medicine from what the novelist derides as the unscientific, merely empirical medicine that supposedly preceded it. Zola is alluding to the clinical pathologist Magendie, Bernard's erstwhile mentor, who from this polemical viewpoint embodies a putative antitheoretical bias of clinical medicine.[7] Bernard's great innovation, according to Zola, stems from one assumption: that "there is an absolute determinism in the existing conditions of natural phenomena, for the living as for the inanimate bodies" (3). Whatever one may think about the possibility of ever achieving such determinism either in science or in literary representation, one can certainly accept Zola's assessment of the novelty of Bernard's claim. To argue that the course of a disease could (even if only in theory) be predicted with absolute certainty was to break with the dominant view in clinical medicine, which, as we have seen, was not antitheoretical but did preach hermeneutic cautiousness (as the title of one of the most influential works on prognostics, Cabanis's *Du degré de certitude de la médecine*, makes evident).[8] Despite the advances made in statistical analysis by Louis, and the discovery by Bichat and his followers that the course of an illness could be retrospectively determined in a postmortem, clinicians of the period remained wary about claiming that medicine could establish laws having predictive power. "In pathology," the eminent pathologist Paget typically reminded his students during this period, "we must admit the existence of many rules or laws the seeming exceptions to which are more numerous than the plain examples of them."[9]

Why, then, is Bernard so sanguine? Because, Zola explains, he has perfected an experimental method that supposedly does away with the hazards of personality and of haphazard observation that infect most medical practice. The experimental method "recognizes no authority but that of facts, and it frees itself from personal authority" (44). This is not to say that Bernard believes in the empiricist dogma that was associated within clinical medicine in the 1830s with Magendie's name—which claims that truth can be found only through observation pure and simple.[10] Bernard is not a Lockeian who understands because he sees; rather he is one who "must see, understand, invent" (12). Medical cognition as Bernard defines it absolutely requires invention or hypothesis. The experimental method, however, requires something more than observation of facts or the use of hypothesis and imagination, although both emphases are crucial. Bernard's genius, as Zola understands it, lies rather in his having forged these elements into a method by treating them as strictly distinct moments in a dialectical process leading toward truth. In this discursive framework, the scientist begins with imagination, feeling, invention, and hypothesis. But once having formulated his hypothesis, he must abandon all preconceptions (indeed, all conceptions) to observe what happens in his experiment. As Bernard puts it in a passage quoted approvingly by Zola: "Observation should be an exact representation of nature"; the scientist "listens to nature and he writes under its dictation" (7).

One need not be a Derridean to recognize in Bernard's last formulation a naïve attitude toward language (and subjectivity), a belief in the photographic potential of signifiers to make present their signifieds, or of writing to translate unproblematically the spoken. My interest here, however, is less in the possible inadequacies of Bernard's philosophy of representation (or Zola's, for that matter) than in the implications for literature posed by Zola's annexing of Bernard's method. For Zola, Bernard's determinism applies equally well to the passions as to the processes of physiology. "If the experimental method leads to the knowledge of physical life," Zola postulates, "it should also lead to the knowledge of the passionate and intellectual life" (2), so that eventually "a like determinism will govern the stones of the roadway and the brain of man" (17). Zola's analogical claims here have long been ridiculed (although they are not different in kind, only in intensity and public dissemination, from Flaubert's assertion that art and science eventually would merge into one practice, or Eliot's notion that the novel can chart time's experiments on man), but in attacking the validity of the analogy, many critics seem to have missed its peculiar relevance for Zola's practice as a naturalist. The important analogy is not the putatively spurious one between passions and physical processes, but between Bernard's *method* and Zola's. Like the experimenter with his object, the novelist, Zola asserts, seeks to ascertain the laws of passion, its "mechanism" (12), through a series of cognitive steps that strictly divide the various faculties: first, the novelist imagines what he thinks will happen to the passion given certain conditions for its operation; then he records what he sees under these conditions.

That second step, to be sure, is a vexed one, since a writer can never actually set up an experimental milieu into which he or she places a passion. The writer imagines both the passion and its milieu, to some extent, and thus never gets beyond hypothesis. But the impossibility of actually mimicking Bernard's scientific procedures does not prevent Zola from trying to sustain the Bernardian disjunction between hypothesis and observation. Thus, he deliberately begins his compositional work by hypothesizing about the possible effects of heredity and environment on a single passion, and then uses his narrative as the equivalent of an experiment to demonstrate the mechanism he has imagined. In their inevitability and tendentiousness, their almost obsessive grinding down of the self into its merely corporeal stuff, Zola's narratives of course fail in every way to live up to Bernard's strictures concerning the objectivity of the experimenter. The lugubrious determinism of Zola's plots stems from his investment in his own hypothesis; they are closer to myths than to experiments. But if Zola's conscious adaptation of experimental medicine is flawed, he does manage to preserve the fundamental distinction between hypothesis and observation as discrete *moments*—not in the compositional undertaking as a whole, which Naomi Schor has brilliantly elucidated as a process of mythmaking—but in the more local exercise of his prose style.[11] The most salient feature of Zola's writing is the interpolation, within an almost delirious mythicizing narration, of paragraphs, sentences, or sometimes merely phrases, in which the reader is offered a dossier-like recording of details—details originally recorded in notebook after notebook of observations Zola made while on field trips researching his books. Both these features of Zola's practice of novelistic representation—his mythmaking and his pure observation—need to be accounted for together, as elements in a single discursive phenomenon. One can begin to do this by recognizing in Zola's shifting between narration and description the novelistic equivalent of the conceptual segregation of hypothesis from observation in Bernard's experimental method.

The relation between narration and description, of course, has been recognized as an important one for distinguishing between realism and naturalism ever since Lukács's *Erzählen oder Beschrieben?* appeared in 1936. For Lukács, however, as the title of his book indicates, the issue was starkly posed as an alternative between narrating or describing, rather than as an analysis of how these two literary elements might be combined. Description in itself is for Lukács a symptom of reification: the naturalists—and Zola most egregiously, to Lukács's mind—replace "portrayals by mere descriptions—supposedly scientific, and brilliant in detail—of things and thing-like relationships," while the realists emphasize narration. As I have tried to show, this view of Zola is inaccurate, since both theoretically and practically, Zola makes room for narration as well as for description. To retain the idea that realism differs fundamentally from naturalism, one must establish this difference not on the basis of the relative presence or absence of one or the other literary element, but on the basis of the conceptual assumptions that govern the way these elements are used in realistic as opposed to naturalistic novels. I have tried to show in previous chapters that in realism, description and narration (as well as a number of other elements of fiction) are medicalized: a detail in Flaubert or Eliot needs to be taken not as a pure observation but as an incipient symptom, within a narrative procedure that aims not at confirming an hypothesis but at elaborating a diagnosis. Zola's procedures—at least for the two basic formal features we have examined—stem not from medicine but from biochemistry, and the biochemical paradigm helps structure a literary form in which narration and description must function independently if the truth is to be told.

The source of that truth, on the other hand, remains the body, and it would be wrong to conclude from Zola's differing epistemological roots (in Bernard rather than Bichat) that his writing fails to grasp the reality of the same object—the pathogical body—as does realism. In fact, as the end of *Nana* shows, Zola's individual bodies quite often are profoundly fleshed out through the pathologies that run through them, and he certainly sees himself as the successor to Balzac as an analyst of the pathology of the social body. But that embodied reality itself, and not only the forms in which the embodied self is described or narrated, differs unmistakably from the reality of the tissular body found in the realistic novel, just as Bernard's sense of the processes of life differs from Bichat's. Neither Balzac, nor Flaubert, nor Eliot would have been capable of depicting the body as Zola does, for instance, in this example from *Germinal*:

> Thus passed a day, two days. They had been at the bottom six days. The water had stopped at their knees, neither rising nor falling, and their legs seemed to be melting away in this icy bath. They could certainly keep them out for an hour or so, but their position then became so uncomfortable that they were twisted by horrible cramps, and were obliged to let their feet fall in again. Every ten minutes they hoisted themselves back by a jerk on the slippery rock. The fractures of the coal struck into their spines, and they felt at the back of their necks a fixed intense pain, through having to keep constantly bent in order to avoid striking their heads. (389)

It might seem almost obscene to compare this passage with Eliot's delicate description of the various sensations Dorothea feels as she sits in seeming torpor all night long during her crisis. Clearly enough, Zola's is a description that Eliot would be incapable of deeming writable—not only because she would never write about the actual conditions of work for the working class, but because her way of conceptualizing the human body—whether working-class or bourgeois—implies that a meaningful analysis of its working must respond to its internal complexity—its consensus of delicate strands of sensibility—and its consequent responsiveness to slight stimuli. For Zola, the stimuli are impossible to miss: the body is crushed, frozen, bent, broken, twisted. Moreover, the body's mode of response to stimuli has been simplified, from sensibility to reflex-like sensations (hunger, cramps, pain), as in more pleasurable circumstances from desire to passion. And as the conclusion of *Nana* makes painfully clear, the same simplification of the body's elements and processes governs Zola's representation of the body politic.

The discursive conditions making this more violent and elemental incorporation of meaning possible stem at least in part from Bernard, whose vivisectional experiments (for example, draining the gastric juices from the stomach of a living dog to analyze digestion independently from the body) encourage the notion that the organized body should be disintegrated into its processes—that instead of observing Bichatian tissue and its inflammation, one ought to study (and even reconstitute experimentally) the *milieu intérieur* of blood and fluids and the discrete functions (i.e., carbohydrate metabolism) operating in it. This is not to say, of course, that Zola's corporeality is not also inflected by any number of other postclinical discourses on the body, including those of degeneration, social Darwinism, and hygienism, as well as a range of medicolegal discourses.[12] To situate Zola fully, one would have to map the cultural field of scientific rationalities of his time, in order to grasp the politics of knowledge in which Zola's fiction, as well as his criticism, participates. That would be a valuable undertaking, although one beyond the scope of this book. My aim here is more modest: to clarify the nature of the displacement of one genre (realism) by another (naturalism) by correlating it with the displacement of one form of scientific thought (that of clinical medicine) by another (that of experimental medicine).

Clinical medicine, however, provided realism not only with an epistemology and a set of assumptions about the body, but also with an ethos, a sense of professional authority and responsibility. Zola, in turn, developed a full-blown literary and intellectual persona of the writer-as-scientist. Again, it would be beyond the scope of this book but well worth studying in some detail the conditions of literary work and the strategies of professionalization that might have driven Zola to invent this persona. Here I can only suggest briefly an archaeological explanation for how and why the ethos of naturalism differs from the ethos of realism. Bernard's experimental medicine offers both a different epistemology and a different sense of where knowledge of the body is to be found, both of which structure Zola's writing. But it is the ethos of the experimentalist, rather than the intricacies of his cognition, that probably most strongly attracts Zola to Bernard, and that also may explain why experimental medicine, rather than any other of those postclinical discourses on the body, becomes paradigmatic for Zola. For, unlike those other sciences, which focus on heredity or environment, Bernard's experimental medicine directly and seemingly brutally invades the body and hence requires an extraordinary ethical defense of its operations, a defense quite different, in turn, from the appeal to charismatic tact we found in psychiatric discourse and in Balzac or Dickens, or from the indifference to public perception we found in clinical discourse and in Flaubert, or from the resigned acceptance of a finally primarily caring and feeling role for the physician or writer in Eliot. For Bernard, and for Zola as well, the scientist can neither ignore public opinion nor claim that he is a man of compassion. If the practitioner of experimental medicine is not to be regarded as a moral monster, he must acknowledge the brutality of his work, while denying his own libidinal investment in it: the experimental physiologist "is a man of science, absorbed by the scientific idea which he pursues: he no longer hears the cry of animals, he no longer sees the blood that flows, he sees only his idea and perceives only organisms concealing problems which he intends to solve."[13] Such tough-minded aggressiveness gave Zola a model, I believe, for precisely the attitude that he most wanted to develop so as to carve out a niche for himself in the literary field—inheriting the scientistic, antisentimental posture of the Flaubertian realist, without devolving either into the indifference of the specialist or the posturing for posturing's sake of the aestheticist.[14]

Much of the aura with which both Zola and Bernard in their own ways tried to invest themselves has faded, as has the scientific authority of the ideas they claimed to be pursuing. One nowadays reads Bernard to savor the myth of scientific practice he so charmingly purveys, as one reads Zola for his myths. But once one understands naturalism not as a myth, nor even as a (reified) ideology, but as a cognitive practice that stipulates at once an object of knowledge (the elementary functions of the body as flesh), a set of rules for elaborating knowledge (the rigid demarcation between hypothesis and observation, narration and description), and a knowing subject (the experimentalist), we may better grasp the intensity of the will to truth that runs through those myths and the historical specificity of naturalist thought.

SIX

FROM DIAGNOSIS TO DEDUCTION

SHERLOCK HOLMES AND THE PERVERSION

OF REALISM

IF NATURALISM eagerly (some would say, all too eagerly) insists on being read in the context supplied by the sciences of its time, and in so doing establishes both its affinity with and its distance from realism as a genre, the classical detective story would seem at first glance to transcend context—whether historical or generic—altogether. Even though detective fiction seems more directly concerned with questions of knowledge than any other genre, there is nothing discursive or even fundamentally historical, it would appear, about the way knowledge is generated in this genre. As it has been theorized, the detective story seems a "form without ideological content" (to quote Jameson) in which not a clinical, or embryological, or Darwinian scientific discourse, but something like a pure rationality, a *logic*, can be analyzed.[1] The nature of that logic, to be sure, remains highly debatable. Jacques Lacan, for example, reads Poe's "The Purloined Letter" as an allegory of the logic of the signifier, a logic of the unconscious that permits (indeed, requires) nonidentity and contradiction.[2] For the narrative theorist Peter Brooks, on the other hand, Conan Doyle's "The Musgrave Ritual" offers "an allegory of plot" that illustrates an equally bizarre "double logic" operating in all narratives.[3] As one might expect, philosophers present more normative as well as more precise models of the logic in detective fiction, although even here disagreements persist, with each philosophical tradition narcissistically seeing the image of its own favored idea of logic mirrored in what the detective does. Thus Bertrand Russell, in his classic essay, "Descriptions," suggests that detective fiction offers a logical positivist form of knowledge.[4] More recently, Umberto Eco, Thomas Sebeok, and other semioticians have argued that detective stories illustrate the quite different philosophical logic of Peircean abduction; game theorists like Hintikka, in turn, have taken the same stories as exemplifying the logic of game theory.[5] But whatever the disagreements over the shape detective logic takes, there is no disagreement about the claim that the genre of the detective story represents an apotheosis of the logical.

For the literary historian interested in studying genres as historical phenomena, the ahistorical and even antitextual bias of theories of detective fiction seems both extreme and frustrating—extreme because it reduces to rock-hard clarity the thick atmosphere that lurks in so many detective stories, frustrating because logic, although a form of knowledge, is not historically precise in the way discourses are. But in isolating the logic in detective fiction from all textual and contextual implications as the transcendental essence of the genre, the narratologists, psychoanalysts, and semioticians can claim to be merely obeying an imperative inscribed within the fiction itself (or at least within its most spectacular and central instance): the imperative to recognize what Sherlock Holmes calls "the light of pure reason"[6] shining through the narrative's murky complexities. As Holmes admonishes Watson, "logic is rare. Therefore it is upon the logic rather than upon the crime that you should dwell. You have degraded what should have been a course of lectures into a series of tales."[7] Ideally, Holmes implies, one ought to be able to reconstitute those lectures, that logic, in abstraction from the story or tale. That, indeed, is the *telos* of the theorists as well.

But as Holmes's last sentence recognizes, such a telos is not identical to the detective story. The tale does not get subsumed by the lecture on logic that may be contained in it. And so a different, degraded lecture may and does persist despite Holmes's best efforts, a reading experience grounded in what Holmes describes as the "sensational" aspects of his cases. The contextual reference is, at one level, to the crime literature of the novel of sensation—to Braddon, LeFanu, and Collins—as well as to the sensationalist journalism of the 1880s and 1890s, and Watson elsewhere tells us that Holmes possesses an "immense" knowledge of this literature. As D. A. Miller has shown, however, one should understand the sensational first and foremost as referring to something more immediately textual—to the palpable somatic effects of shock, confusion, surprise, confirmation, jubilation, and craving for more produced when one reads the detective story as most of its faithful readers do (as opposed to what Barthes calls the "pensive" effects one enjoys in reading realistic novels).[8] Detective fiction yields not only purely abstract knowledge, but something like carnal knowledge as well. It can be thought of, then, as enacting not only a logic but also an erotics.

An erotics, to be sure, that is disavowed by narrative theorists, as well as by Holmes himself. But any complete analysis of the genre must account not only for the logic inherent in detection, but for the well-nigh addictive pleasures (or at least sensations) inherent in detecting—and in reading about detecting. Logic and sensation, moreover, must be understood as coexisting and interacting within the same narrative space. But what could the pure, austere logic of the detective story possibly have to do with the "degraded" pleasures of the text it disavows? To pose this question is already to begin to rehistoricize and retextualize detective logic, to see that logic as embedded, or embodied, in a particular narrative activity within which logic functions not as a key to Truth with a capital T, but as a technique used to generate the pleasure peculiar to the genre of detective fiction. Rather than a set of principles divorced from the empirical world, a thing in itself, one can treat detection as a cognitive practice that works, like clinical thinking in realism, to constitute both objects of knowledge and a certain way of telling truths about those objects. Clinical thinking was governed by two kinds of assumptions: first, epistemic ones that led the clinician or the clinical realist to define his or her object as an embodied person, an organic, potentially pathological amalgamation of tissues and sensibilities; second, hermeneutic ones in the form of diagnostic guidelines that helped the clinician or novelist to recognize and generate some statements as clinical while excluding other statements as unscientific. For detective fiction, similarly, one thus needs to ask the same general sorts of questions. First, what assumptions enable the detective to transform people into objects of knowledge to be identified? And what presuppositions about making sense of clues come to be accepted as appropriate to detective reasoning while others (most often those used by Watson) are excluded as nonlogical?

One needs, in other words, to excavate the archaeological ground of detective logic. Doing so will make it easier to determine how that logic has displaced the clinical thinking that dominated the realistic novel (but that, I shall suggest, continues to function in a subordinate yet vital position within the detective story itself). And by studying the interaction of these distinct instrumentalities of thought, one may also then be able to fulfill the promise of Barthes's claim that "the body of bliss is also my historical subject"[9]—to account in historical terms for the peculiarly (peculiar because it involves sensation, and peculiar in the sensations it involves) sensational effects that detection can produce in the detected, the detective, and the reader—effects that themselves are being given a scientific, even medical, status at the very moment when the detective story comes into its own as a genre: the moment of Holmes.[10]

Traces of Individuality

Whether Holmes's method is inductive, deductive, or abductive, one thing is clear. That method always has the same aim: identification or designation. Holmes's logic, whatever its internal structure, always formulates definite descriptions—Bertrand Russell's term for propositions about what Russell calls "the so-and-so" (usually but not necessarily the agent of a crime or scandal). In "The Boscombe Valley Mystery," for instance, Holmes offers us a catalog of definite descriptions, all predicated of the same subject, as the narration's syntax makes explicit:

> "And the murderer?"
> "Is a tall man, left-handed, limps with the right leg, wears thick-soled shooting-boots and a grey cloak, smokes Indian cigars, uses a cigar-holder, and carries a blunt penknife in his pocket." ("Boscombe," 213)

The efforts, by Russell and his antagonists, to develop or refute a propositional logic grounded in these sorts of descriptions need not concern us here. What matters archaeologically about these descriptions is not if they contain information in themselves, but how they function strategically to help, as Holmes puts it, to "reconstruct the man" (*Hound of the Baskervilles*, 669). Or to quote Russell's more rigorous formulation: "In a detective story, propositions about 'the man who did the deed' are accumulated, in the hope that ultimately they will suffice to demonstrate that it was A who did the deed."[11]

Insofar as its object is what both Holmes and Russell call a man, detective logic can be thought of as a branch of the humanities, if not a human science. One could probably go on from here to try to place the detective story's conception of man within the general conceptual milieu of nineteenth-century liberal humanism, that classical individualism promoted by Mill, whose ideal of autonomous personhood still holds true for many people. But as Poe's gorilla indicates, *man* or *person* does not quite capture what it is that the definite descriptions of a detective story ultimately help to designate. The object of detective logic, one might say, is not really a person at all—people, after all, are not reconstructed. The personal identity of the detective's quarry, in fact, seems to be irrelevant to the detective, who often identifies beings who do not exist as persons at all, as in "A Case of Identity," where a bridegroom disappears, only to be revealed ultimately to have been the would-be bride's father in disguise, or the

"Adventure of the Noble Bachelor," where it is the bride of whom Holmes must conclude, "there is not, and there never has been, any such person" (296).

The nonexistence of such persons as Hosmer Angel and Lady St. Simon may seem like an outrageous ploy on the part of the detective story writer, a cheap trick more akin to the strained use of doubles in a sensation novel or Gothic, Jekyll-and-Hyde style fantasies than to a fiction that prides itself on its rigorous scientificity and realism (in the general sense). But the use of nonexistent persons in certain of the Holmes stories is only an extreme instance of an archaeological necessity of detective logic: the need to take individuals rather than persons as objects of narrative knowledge. Like sensation fiction and late-Victorian gothic, the detective story developed by Conan Doyle thus diverges from the realistic novel, insofar as realism's medicalized emphasis on the deterministic finality of the material self retained as its fundamental aim the analysis of what Elaine Scarry has called "embodied persons."[12] In the detective story, although truth about the self is still at stake, the object of knowledge is no longer the pathologically embodied person of realism, but what one might call the individuated body.

This distinction between embodied persons and individuated bodies is inscribed in the detective story's narrative hierarchy, between Holmes's method and Watson's. Watson's point of view is simply that of a now enfeebled realism. He describes and interprets in ways that Auerbach and Lukács would call Balzacian, in fact. When analyzing a person, he garners plenty of information, describing the body in sometimes sensitive detail, but the discourse into which his observations are cast is characterized by qualitative, indefinite descriptions, usually converging in what Auerbach calls in Balzac the "atmospheric" evocation of a substantial, qualitative totality or "type" (to use Lukács's word): a body whose traits somehow convey the metaphysical essence or peculiarity of a person. Take, for instance, Watson's inspection of Mr. Jabez Wilson, in which Watson actually sets out "after the fashion of my companion to read the indications which might be presented by his dress or appearance." What Watson notes is that

> our visitor bore every mark of being an average commonplace British
> tradesman, pompous and slow. He wore rather baggy grey shepherds'
> check trousers, a not over-clean black frock-coat, unbuttoned in the
> front, a drab waistcoat with a heavy brassy Albert chain, and a square
> pierced bit of metal dangling down as an ornament. A frayed top-hat,
> and a faded brown overcoat with a wrinkled velvet collar lay upon a chair

beside him. Altogether, look as I would, there was nothing remarkable about the man save his blazing red head, and the expression of extreme chagrin and discontent upon his features. ("Red-Headed League," 177)

As it turns out, the one peculiarity Watson does note—that blazing red head—is precisely the relevant one (because of its very irrelevance!) in the case of the Red-Headed League. What counts archaeologically, however, is that for Watson all the indications or marks are to be read "altogether"; like the details he offers us about the King of Bohemia in "Scandal in Bohemia," these details convey a single synthetic "impression" of Jabez Wilson's "character," an impression "suggested," as the King's is, "by his whole appearance."

For Holmes, on the other hand, who seeks to establish the individuated body's identity rather than the embodied person's character, there is no need to sum up details about the body in a synthetic whole that would express the person. The body the detective studies is not an organized totality of qualities woven biologically into a person, a "vivid aggregate" in Herbert Spencer's sense (which is also the sense of the body in pathological realism), but a corpus of isolated, discrete elements, a congeries or consilience of particulars (including the particular "traces of . . . individuality"[13] left on the material world by parts or extensions of the body—the foot, the elbow, the finger). In some stories, the body is literally offered to Holmes in bits and pieces—a pair of severed ears here, an engineer's thumb there. But these, again, are only extreme instances of a general condition of the body under Holmes's gaze: a surveillance that, like that of a cubist painter, analytically decomposes the material body in order to reconstruct the private eye's object: the individualized man.

If the body's integrity as a living totality is not respected by Holmes, the body parts he chooses to isolate do not get much respect themselves. For one thing, Holmes is willing, nay, eager to stare at parts and products of the body that Watson discreetly ignores. The first comment Holmes makes in the *Adventures*, for example, is that Watson has gained seven and a half pounds, and he goes on to point out that the doctor reeks of iodoform and that he has a bulge (in his hat). But it is not only looking that distinguishes Holmes; it is the way he looks at the body. Rather than qualities of living flesh whose significance needs to be measured against one's sense of the person as a whole, the detective sees each embarrassing, peculiar detail as a particular that must be defined in unambiguous terms. What matters is not that Watson has gotten fatter, but that the weight gain can be quantified; not that Watson stinks, but that he smells of iodoform rather than perfume. For the detective, it is the shoes rather than the man who stands in them that signify, and if a person's leg is wooden, all the better for the analyst seeking to identify his individuality.

The reduction of human qualities to quantities, of course, precisely describes what Lukács called reification, although for Lukács what was being turned into a calculable thing was not a person's body so much as his interiority or subjectivity, his intentions and emotions. I have spoken as if Holmes disregarded this dimension of the self, but of course he subjects intention and emotion to the same procedure of reduction and reconstruction that he applies to physical traces. As Watson tells us at the beginning of the *Adventures*, "the softer passions"—and the harder ones as well, one might add—are not ignored or denied existence by Holmes, but they are dealt with by him not as qualities of the self but only as instruments "for drawing the veil from men's motives and actions" ("Bohemia," 161). Thus, for example, if a father does not want his stepdaughter to marry ("A Case of Identity"), the potentially Jamesian entanglement of the father's and daughter's feelings is irrelevant; what matters is only that the father have a motive that sets his body in motion in a particular way. If Colonel Barclay ("The Crooked Man") unexpectedly comes face-to-face after many years with a rival for his wife's affections whom he thought he had long ago done away with, and if this unexpected confrontation occurs just after the Colonel has had a shouting match with his wife, the potentially Hardyesque quality of his consternation, horror, guilt, or anxiety goes unrepresented; what matters is only what the emotion does to the body (the shock kills the Colonel). If a stout man with a weird smile on his face offers to pay a woman an exorbitant fee if she will wear a certain dress and sit in front of him ("The Copper Beeches"), the woman may wonder about the reasons for his conduct, but those reasons never take on the psychological depth of a compulsion or perversion, only those of a "fad"; although Holmes may mutter that "no sister of his should ever have accepted such a situation" (323), he ultimately finds that the stout man is driven by reasons that are purely pecuniary, not voyeuristic. If a man suffers an attack of brain fever following the theft of a treaty he feels responsible for ("The Naval Treaty"), his inner torment, the complexity of his sensibility in this condition, is irrelevant; what counts, again, is only the effect his disturbance has on his body, which is to place it in a sickbed in the very room where the treaty has been hidden.

This catalog would seem to force one to the verge of rejecting detective fiction, as does Edmund Wilson most notoriously, for its crudity of characterization compared to the realistic novel, its simplistic and simplifying reliance on "flat" rather than "round" characters, on motive rather than motivation. Certainly calling what happens in the detective story "reification" invites this sort of sour attitude. A Marxist might suggest, however, that in categorizing the essence of detection as reification, one is grounding one's distaste for its methods in a critique of historical conditions. If detective fiction, far from offering what Chesterton called "the romance of contemporary life," actually offers only the ersatz totality of a reified rationality, at least Conan Doyle cannot be held responsible for this deplorable feature of his work. For reification is a general phenomenon of the era of high capitalism, not something Conan Doyle, any more than Flaubert or Zola or Dreiser or Crane (all of whom have been called novelists of reification), could have successfully resisted in any case.

A more refined Marxist analysis would go on to stipulate that although the detective story may represent itself as a form of knowledge, as a logical activity, it is better understood as promoting a form of false consciousness—that is, as an ideological activity. Like other ideological mechanisms under capitalism, the argument might go, the ideology of detection is naturalized, its ideological status disavowed: Holmesian "deduction," and the detective story itself, poses itself as the end of ideology, as a demystified and demystifying alternative to dogmatic forms of knowledge, obsolete belief systems that need to be remorselessly critiqued in the interests of reason. The literary equivalents to such superseded dogmas, Fredric Jameson has suggested, are the remains, under capitalism, of inherited narrative paradigms such as folktales, legends, myths, and rituals. Unsurprisingly, these residual genres and the symbolic mode of thought they represent pop up repeatedly in the Sherlock Holmes stories: the devil-ridden parish in "The Devil's Foot," the Musgrave ritual, the Sussex vampire, and of course, the legendary hound of the Baskervilles, to name only a few. The only thing more certain than the invocation of such archaic forms is the ruthlessness with which Holmes will estrange us from the narrative explanations they imply.

Archaic narrative forms like these, however, do more than offer a conveniently irrational background against which the triumphant rationality of modern narrative can stand out. As Jameson has brilliantly argued (drawing on Ernst Bloch's political philosophy of utopia), these irrational literary elements also signify—beyond and in spite of their negation by reason—a utopian impulse that in the modern period has been driven underground by reification. But if literary texts in modernity thus bear within them a political unconscious, that unconscious must differ from genre to genre, period to period. Where and how the utopian impulse becomes visible must be genre-specific. One might well ask what becomes of this utopian impulse in the detec-

tive story, where, far more stringently than in realism, sensation fiction, or naturalism, *every* symbolic explanation must be refuted, demoted from the status of knowledge to that of mere superstition.

One of the few refuges for the utopian, symbolic impulse in the
Sherlock Holmes stories is on the margins of narrative, in quirky descriptive excesses that do little or nothing to move the plot along to its
rational dénouement. Take, for instance, this description of the Grim-
pen Mire, the wonderfully named bog where Holmes's prey hides in
The Hound of the Baskervilles: "Rank reeds and lush, slimy water-plants
sent an odour of decay and a heavy miasmatic vapour into our faces,
while a false step plunged us more than once thigh-deep into the dark,
quivering mire, which shook for yards in soft undulations around our
feet. Its tenacious grip plucked at our heels as we walked, and when we
sank into it it was as if some malignant hand was tugging us down into
those obscene depths, so grim and purposeful was the clutch in which
it held us" (759–60). This description seems, for want of a better word,
peculiar, especially in a detective story. The sort of knowledge it transmits (or at least acquaints us with) is anomalous and fragmentary, neither fused into narrative form as overt mythos nor demystified as an
indefinite description by logic (as for instance Pip's similar description
of hands reaching up from the graveyard soil to pull him down is
demystified as a childhood fantasy), but potently suggestive nonetheless. In such passages, it is as if the very stringency with which the
detective story represses the irrational has paradoxically facilitated
the emergence of an entirely different textual phenomenon from either realism or detective fiction. It will require a Freud, however, to
give discursive status to these sorts of passages, by seeing them as containing a distinct kind of knowledge (the symbolic knowledge of sexual
anxiety and desire) that can be made sense of only within the distinctive narrative form of the Freudian case study.[14]

The detective story, on the other hand, never fleshes out the sexual
anxieties and desires that it projects onto the landscape in the passage
quoted above. Instead, in a telling and typical sublimation, Watson
reconfigures these anxieties and desires so that they can comfortably
be represented as hermeneutic tensions connected to the mystery
Holmes sets out to solve: "So there is one of our small mysteries
cleared up. It is something to have touched bottom anywhere in this
bog in which we are floundering" (720). Watson's displacement recon-
tains the potentially explosive libidinal forces that lurked in his earlier
description, offering in compensation the more prudish satisfaction
provided by the sensation of "touching bottom."

Analyzing detection as reification (whether of persons or utopian
impulses) thus helps somewhat to show how watching the detective

could provide a certain sort of pleasure, and to historicize the cognitive activity called detection. But the analytics of reification can only take one so far, for reification is too general, too ontological, an historical phenomena to account for the differences between detective stories and other roughly coeval narrative forms. Naturalism, sensation fiction, modernism, even Flaubertian realism, have all been described as "reified," yet they incite radically different emotional responses in and make quite distinct intellectual demands upon their readers.

Where the ideological analysis of detective reasoning errs is in jumping prematurely from Holmes's method out to a sociohistorical context (itself woefully underarticulated and global) that supposedly determines that way of reasoning. The first, most immediate context for detective reasoning, to repeat a point made earlier, is the detective story itself. To remain true to the spirit of Jameson's battle cry, "Always historicize!" then, one needs to proceed tentatively to try to grasp just how detection works, without reducing that work to an instance of a general mode of production. So far, we have defined detecting's intellectual technology: the presuppositions that enable the detective to take for granted both his object (the embodied person treated as an individuated body) and the kinds of statements that are permitted about that object (definite descriptions and designations or identifications). Now it is necessary to define the genealogy of such intellectual work, the relations and effects of power that detecting produces through its friction against or synergy with other discourses. I have already suggested that in the Holmes stories, detection poses itself directly against the discourse of embodied personhood that Watson continually reinvokes. One way to get at the power involved in detective fiction, then, would be to ask what happens to the detected person when a detective like Holmes succeeds in identifying his or her individuality, "the given which," says Barthes, "makes my body separate from other bodies and appropriates its sufferings or its pleasure."[15]

Invasive Procedures

From the detected person's viewpoint, identification separates one's body not so much from other bodies as from one's own self-possession. It involves an invasion of privacy by the private eye, an invasion that appropriates a veritable *frisson* of humiliation from the detected person. Holmes's clients, for instance, almost always undergo a sort of humiliation ritual when they first meet the detective, a ritual in which they discover that they have exposed themselves in ways they never dreamed possible. The King of Bohemia's reaction to being taken by surprise, having his sovereignty violated, so to speak, is typical: "The man sprang from his chair, and paced up and down the room in uncontrollable agitation. Then, with a gesture of desperation, he tore the mask from his face and hurled it upon the ground" ("Scandal," 165). Other victims are said to have given "a violent start, and looked up, with fear and astonishment" ("Identity," 192), or to have turned "white to his lips" (199). Perhaps the funniest response belongs to Neville St. Clair, a gentleman who impersonates a beggar until Holmes forces him to "cut a more respectable figure" by rubbing his face with a wet sponge while St. Clair sleeps. We are told that the poor fellow sat up, "rubbing his eyes, and staring about him with sleepy bewilderment. Then suddenly realizing his exposure, he broke into a scream, and threw himself down with his face to the pillow" ("The Man With the Twisted Lip," 242).

Not merely indifferent but actively hostile to persons, detection exposes and unnerves them, destroying the sovereignty, autonomy, dignity, and respectability that they believe makes them more than mere bodies. The violence inflicted is so extreme that Conan Doyle feels the need to defend the detective's prerogative by having Holmes argue—like Claude Bernard or Zola—that any brutality is accidental, an unfortunate by-product of the science of detection. Sometimes Holmes even apologizes for the pain he causes, as for instance after he ignores Watson's sensibilities to deduce the unhappy life history of Watson's brother from that dead brother's pocket-watch. "Viewing the matter as an abstract problem," Holmes admits, "I had forgotten how personal and painful a thing it might be to you" ("Sign of Four," 93). But there *is* something "personal and painful" involved in almost every act of detection he undertakes. It is as if this kind of pain, far from being secondary or gratuitous, were a fundamental requirement in the detective story. What possible discursive point or economy—what cultural logic—could be served, however, by the recurrent inflicting of such pain?

The most reassuring way to understand Holmes's attacks on persons, his invasion and violation of their privacy, is as efforts to meet a pressing cultural or social need: the necessity of restoring confidence in the class order of bourgeois, respectable England, an order threatened not by Holmes's violence but by *parvenus* who pose as gentlemen. The Holmes stories thus seem to offer what Stephen Knight calls "the anxious enactment of a class's suspicions of its own kind."[16] In a late-Victorian culture where the middle class is swelling, the detective allays petit bourgeois suspicions that middle-class identity is not actually an identity at all, by unmasking interlopers.

According to this explanation, the detective exerts a purely negative power: he identifies in order to exclude, and by excluding he shores up a concept of personal identity and a social order that already exists. But there are some problems with such a functionalist explanation, the most serious of which is that Holmes violates the privacy of respectable clients as well as criminals. To make sense of this, one needs to rethink the nature of power along lines suggested by Foucault. Power, Foucault suggests, does not always exclude or repress; in some forms, it actually produces or brings to light that on which it works. One might well think of detection not as a means of repression but as an instrument of discipline.

At the very least, the similarities between Holmes's power and the disciplinary power Foucault has studied are striking. Like discipline, detection operates in the name of the law but is in fact independent of the law (Holmes is not a police detective but a private investigator, and as he points out, "a fair proportion" of the cases he involves himself in "do not treat of crime, in its legal sense, at all" ["The Copper Beeches," 317]). Like discipline, which takes the family as one of its privileged loci of penetration, Holmes's detection again and again exposes problems within families. Finally (and most pertinently), like discipline, Holmes's detection works directly upon the bodies of people, thereby interpellating such people as "dangerous individuals" to be disqualified as juridical subjects, removed from the category of persons.[17]

More than simply an analogy links detection with discipline, however. Conan Doyle explicitly affiliates Holmes's method with a range of disciplinary parasciences—what Foucault calls individualizing discourses—that arise during the 1880s and 1890s. To completely historicize detective fiction, then, one would have to describe this intellectual context in some detail, in order to show how developments both within and between the sciences make detective logic and thereby detective fiction thinkable. Here I would only emphasize that the fate of clinical medicine is crucially important. As described in my chapter on *Middlemarch*, a new epistemological hierarchy takes shape during the latter part of the century, so that clinical medicine, once queen of the human sciences, becomes subordinated as a form of knowledge to the more exact sciences of bacteriology, chemistry, and microscopic anatomy. One signal of this shift is the reduced status of the general practitioner, compared to the specialist who has access to these other sciences.[18] Within clinical medicine itself, the same period witnesses the hardening, in clinical diagnostics, of the distinction between symptoms (verbal indications given by patients) and signs ("objectively" observed), a split that spurs the emergence of semiology as a discipline distinct from symptomatology[19] and permits specialists like Conan Doyle's Dr. Selby to "forget the patient in his symptom"[20] just as Holmes is able to forget the personal in his deductions.

In view of this double shift, it becomes clear why realism should be represented in the detective story by Watson, a not particularly successful general practitioner, rather than by some other character. Watson's diagnostic point of view is subordinated to Holmes's deductive point of view ("Knowledge of Chemistry.—Profound, . . . Knowledge of Anatomy.—Accurate, but unsystematic"[21]) just as clinical medicine's knowledge is culturally subordinated to that of the more exact, basic, or specialized sciences in the last quarter of the nineteenth century. The medical connection, of course, is not only sociologically accurate but biographically overdetermined, just as it was for Flaubert and Eliot. One could easily imagine an *Idiot of the Family*-style study that would focus in detail on how Conan Doyle's personal medical situation gives rise to his project as a novelist. I would only point out here that Conan Doyle was a subordinate and marginal, respectable yet poverty-stricken clinical practitioner, so typical that M. Jeanne Peterson used his semiautobiographical *Stark Munro Letters* to document the dreary condition of the general practitioner in Victorian England. Unlike, say, Charles Bovary, Conan Doyle felt enormous *ressentiment* as a subordinated professional, although this emerged not in active attacks on his superiors (ressentiment never does) but rather in the nightmarish quality of the medical tales he compiled in *Round the Red Lamp*. But in the detective story that resentment is sublimated into adulation. It is well known that Conan Doyle modeled Holmes on Joseph Bell, his redoubtable anatomy professor in medical school, of whom Doyle wrote that "if he were a detective, he would surely reduce this fascinating but unorganized business to something nearer an exact science."[22] Tellingly, Bell differs from the clinical anatomists that Flaubert and Eliot take as paragons, insofar as he subordinates clinical medicine as a science to bacteriology. "The greatest stride that has been made of late years in preventive and diagnostic medicine," Bell claims, "consists in the recognition and differentiation by bacteriological research of those minute organisms that disseminate cholera and fever, tubercle and anthrax. The importance of the infinitely little is incalculable." This is a microscopic rather than tissular anatomy.

Bell makes the comments above in the midst of a review of Conan Doyle's work. Their aim is to associate Holmes's method with his own postclinical diagnostic medicine, understood as a science of particularities equivalent to those other more notorious ones of the fin de siècle that suppose, as Bell puts it, that "racial peculiarities, hereditary tricks of manner, accent, occupation or the want of it, education, environment of all kinds, by their little trivial impressions gradually mould or carve the individual, and leave finger marks or chisel scores which the expert can recognize."[23] But more than these other sciences of the body, Bell's anatomy enjoys authority as a science, so that it is above all with "something of the air of a clinical professor expounding to his class" (1. 637) that Holmes teaches that "deduction is, or ought to be, an exact science" (1. 611).

Detective reasoning, of course, is no more an exact science of the body than are fingerprinting, Lombrosian criminal anthropology, or Bertillonage. Like them, detection differs from formalized scientific thinking in not having as its object the goal of constituting an organon of knowledge, a unified field of concepts.[24] If the emblem for such scientific totality is a medical or scientific dictionary (as in *Madame Bovary*) or an entry on "Anatomy" in an encyclopedia (as in *Middlemarch*), the emblem for Holmesian knowledge is his index or his *Continental Gazeteer*—eclectic collections where entries are related to each other by nothing more than alphabetical propinquity, as Irene Adler's biography is "sandwiched in between that of a Hebrew rabbi and that of a staff-commander who had written a monograph upon the deep-sea fishes" ("Scandal in Bohemia," 165). The index, like that other Holmesian repository of wisdom, the monograph, represents such a loose intellectual order of things that one is tempted to say that there is no form of knowledge, no intellectual system here at all, only a jumbled collection of facts, something like Borges's Chinese encyclopedia. Indeed, one can easily imagine (and Holmesian fanatics—including Borges himself—have) how such entries as the one mentioned above might give rise to a Borgesian fabulation, a mode of antiknowledge or counterdiscourse reintegrating this heteroglot material: in which, say, the Hebrew rabbi's biography might turn out to involve a Jonas-like encounter with the deep-sea fish of which the staff-commander has written. But if detective reasoning has an extremely low epistemological profile, that is not so that it can give rise to fantasy, but so that it can penetrate more easily and completely into everyday life. In the allied technologies of identification emerging at the same time, this bent toward total application is very clear. Bertillon, for instance, proposes an "Infinite Extension of the Classification" system he invented originally to identify criminals.[25] Similarly, Francis Galton, who invents fingerprinting analysis to help police keep track of criminals in India, recognizes early on that "in civil as well as in criminal cases, the need of some such system is shown to be greatly felt."[26] This extension could be thought of as innocuous, even as socially beneficial, if the discourse being applied were clinical, and the cases pathologies (as in the realistic novel). One might even welcome the medicalization of everyday life, as we seem to in our hyper-health-conscious society. But detection is not a healing art, and for this science to arrogate for itself the panoptic point of view of Holmes's *Continental Gazeteer*, treating everyone as a potential case, is far more ominous, opening up what D. A. Miller, in a related context, calls "the fearful prospect of an absolute surveillance under which everything would be known, incriminated, policed."[27]

Perverse Professionalism and the
Erotics of Identification

But is the prospect really so fearful? Certainly for those who are detected, exposed, fingered and sometimes pinched by the detective, it is painful to contemplate. But for the detective—and by extension, although with some modifications, for the detective story's readers—identification, humiliating as it is to its victim, yields a dividend of pleasure, the kind of pleasure that, Foucault reminds us, "comes of exercising a power that questions, monitors, watches, spies, searches out, palpates, brings to light."[28]

Of course this pleasure must be disavowed, given that it is linked to the pain of others. Hence the repeated signals in the Holmes stories that the detective, after all, is a professional seeking knowledge, not pleasure—a figure who is, in Stephen Knight's words, "unperturbable yet comprehending," curious rather than avid, disinterested rather than aroused, a "most perfect reasoning and observing machine" ("Scandal in Bohemia," 161). Detection, Holmes insists, is "an impersonal thing—a thing beyond myself"; [29] if he gets any pleasure from it at all, he tells us, it is that of "the work itself, the pleasure of finding a field for my peculiar powers."[30] But these professional alibis do not explain the virulence of Holmes's curiosity, which even Dr. Bell recognizes as "insatiable, almost inhuman,"[31] and which, Doyle writes, "transformed [Holmes] when he was hot upon . . . a scent" so that "his nostrils seemed to dilate with a purely animal lust for the chase"; elsewhere Watson adds that when Holmes's curiosity is engaged "his eyes kindled and a slight flush sprang into his thin cheeks."[32] There can be little doubt, in view of descriptions like these, that for Holmes identification constitutes the closest thing he has to an erotic experience—or rather, for Holmes detecting *is* an erotic experience.

The erotics of identification, however, is—to use a word that seems unavoidable when talking about detection—peculiar, if not pathological (in the same sense that Hans Blumenberg describes modern scientific curiosity in general as "the endogenous pathology of the cognitive appetite of reason itself"). For what kind of pleasure depends upon the intellectualized inflicting of pain on others, if not sadistic pleasure? At certain moments in the stories, Holmes's sadistic side is quite explicitly portrayed: at the end of "A Case of Identity," for instance, where Holmes first tells James Windibank that he deserves punishment, then says, "it is not part of my duties to my client, but here's a hunting-crop handy, and I think I shall just treat myself to—" ("Adventures," 201). More often, the sadism inheres in the mere act of looking rather than any immediate physical coercion. "I will get her to show me," Holmes says of Irene Adler, and if, as Watson protests, "she will refuse," Holmes can assure the doctor as one man to another that "she will not be able to." Roland Barthes has compared the logic of narrative with that of a striptease; perhaps the more appropriate comparison, for Holmes's detective logic and narrative, would be to a rape.

For anyone who continues to value the autonomy of embodied persons, as I myself do and as the clinician Watson does as well, that is no way to treat a lady, and Irene is one of the lucky few to take revenge on Holmes—with Watson's sympathy—for his having "taken advantage of" her against her will ("Adventures," 173). Part of the resonance of the title given her adventure, "A Scandal in Bohemia," lies in the logical scandal she causes within Holmes's "Bohemian soul" by avenging herself.[33] But what needs to be stressed here is that Holmes's detective reasoning, looked at in this way, is *already* something scandalous—far more scandalous than, say, Lydgate's "spots of commonness" in *Middlemarch*, or Benassis's secret past in *Le Médecin de campagne*, or Larivière's disdain in *Madame Bovary*, each of which are also tied to the (clinical) reasoning they use, and that the realistic novel also uses. Holmes's cruelty presents a scandal that, as I have said, the narrative tries to disavow by making him out to be a pure professional, like Dr. Jekyll.[34] Yet that cruelty, and the coldly aggressive subjectivity it indicates, resurface again and again. Only by hinting in a number of ways that the detective himself is rather peculiar or, to use the euphemism Holmes lovers have come to prefer, "eccentric," does Conan Doyle keep the scandal under control. In fact, Conan Doyle invokes a panoply of what in the 1880s were quite recently invented categories of deviant individuality to try to identify Holmes for his readers: the detective has a "Bohemian soul"; he is, most notoriously, a cocaine addict; he is an aesthete who carries a "pocket Petrarch" ("Boscombe Valley Mystery," 207), quotes the Persian author Hafiz, as well as Flaubert—in French!—and suffers from "ennui" ("Red-Headed

League," 190); he is a decadent, whose lodgings Oscar Wilde would have envied, and who like Wilde has a penchant for flowers and aphorisms.[35]

But Holmes is neither an aesthete, nor a decadent, nor a homosexual, nor a sadist—to return to the category of deviancy I find most accurate, and that like these other denominations of the self first becomes thinkable, first enters into discourse, during the last quarter of the century (Krafft-Ebing's *Psychopathia sexualis*, published in 1888, reaches its fifth edition in translation by 1892).[36] Just how Holmes ought to be categorized, just what kind of person one should take him for, remains unsettled, the one enduring mystery that makes these stories more than mere logical exercises. It is a question, on the other hand, that Watson, the reader's surrogate in these adventures, hardly ever raises seriously and directly, despite dropping all these hints, and fascinated though he is by the detective. Why should this be so? What prevents Watson from identifying Holmes as a dangerous individual?

One answer might be that some sort of homosocial desire binds the two men, some love that dare not speak its name but that leads Watson, in the very first scene of the first "Adventure," to speak in quasi-libidinal terms of their relationship. "My marriage," he writes, "had drifted us away from each other. My own complete happiness, and the home-centred interests which rise up around the man who first finds himself master of his own establishment, were sufficient to absorb all my attention ("Scandal in Bohemia," 161). That normative heterosexual, middle-class cathexis (which absorbs Lydgate and Charles Bovary, and is characteristic of clinical realism) turns out here to be extremely fragile. Watson's attention is easily diverted: "As I passed the well-remembered door, which must always be associated in my mind with my wooing, . . . I was seized with a keen desire to see Holmes again" ("Scandal in Bohemia," 162).

One need not reduce this argument to the absurd, as Rex Stout does in his infamous essay, "Watson Was a Woman," to recognize something more than mere friendship in the Holmes/Watson relationship. But homosocial desire is a rather amorphous category, crying out for more specification. Just as Flaubert's impassivity, Balzac's vocational intensity, Eliot's tentativeness, and Zola's tough-mindedness can be linked to the values of the specific kind of scientific thought on which they rely, so Watson's (and by extension, Conan Doyle's) particular subjectivity can be linked to the values of detective thinking. What is Watson's position in the power game that Holmes plays? The answer is obvious: if Holmes is an intellectual sadist, Watson is an intellectual masochist. He himself admits, "I was always oppressed with a sense of my own stupidity in my dealings with Sherlock Holmes" ("Red-

Headed League," 185), and one sees him as Holmes's most handy victim, submitting to embarrassment time and again. Moreover, although Watson emphasizes that "there was something in [Holmes's] masterly grasp of a situation, and his keen, incisive reasoning, which made it a pleasure to me to study his system of work, and to follow the quick, subtle methods by which he disentangled the most inextricable mysteries" ("Scandal in Bohemia," 167), when Watson tries to emulate Holmes, he finds it painful: "I cudgelled my brains" ("Boscombe Valley Mystery," 209) is the way he puts it, in fact.

Why would anyone want to be on the receiving end of such a cudgelling or such embarrassment as Watson suffers at the hands of Holmes? How much more pleasant it would be simply to admire the detective's way of reasoning, to take that detective reasoning in its cleaned-up form as *the* form of knowledge—logic—and as the only form of knowledge, that the detective narrative conveys! And yet, like Watson, readers of detective fiction permit—even require—that the detective place them in a submissive position. From the detective story one demands a pleasure that comes only in the wake of the anxiety and humiliation of not being able to reason things out for oneself.

Such pleasure, however, is itself historically determined. It becomes possible as a regular, generic experience only when a new mode of professional subordination emerges: a subordination based in turn on a reconfiguring of the human sciences. Only when the clinician has been demoted does a science of identification, a logic of detection, become authoritative enough to serve as a model for fiction. To say this is not by any means to argue for a crude homology between clinical medicine and realism on one hand, individualizing sciences and detective fiction on the other. On the contrary, it is to stress an element of continuity. Detective fiction *depends* on clinical medicine and realism to provide embodied persons, without whom it would have no one to identify and consequently no sadomasochistic pleasure to incite. The detective story, in other words, should be understood neither as a genre that purifies a logic of narrative logic inherent but muddied in realism, nor as a genre that breaks with realism, but as a genre that turns realism to perverse ends.

SEVEN

THE PATHOLOGICAL PERSPECTIVE

CLINICAL REALISM'S DECLINE

AND THE EMERGENCE OF

MODERNIST COUNTER-DISCOURSE

AS THE EMERGENCE of pararealistic genres like naturalism and detective fiction indicates, the tensions within pathological realism, already evident in *Middlemarch*, do not abate but intensify as the century draws to a close, ultimately imperiling the enterprise of realism as such. Early on, Edmond Duranty, writing in the magazine *Réalisme*, had defined that enterprise's object as "the frank and complete expression of individualities, . . . the exact, complete, sincere reproduction of the social milieu and the epoch in which one lives."[1] Duranty's terms have become standard ones for understanding realism, as well as for understanding the crisis of reproduction or representation that realism suffers. But if one looks a bit more closely at the textual basis for these terms, both realism and its crisis take on a quite different cast. For Balzac, Flaubert, and Eliot, the terms *comprehension*, *concrete*, *individual*, and *sincere* bear connotations that can be described without exaggeration as medical. Comprehending social totality, in the realistic novel, means defining that totality not only as a milieu (with the biological overtones that word implies), but as a *pathological* milieu. Capturing the concrete realistically means maintaining faith that details will prove to be "both particular and typical"[2] in the same way that medical diagnosis assumes that signs and symptoms will resolve into cases of disease. The individual, in turn, is defined in realistic fiction as a pathologically embodied person whose limits and potentialities stem from the limits and potentialities—death and growth—imposed by organic finitude. Finally, realism's sincerity is analogous to the disinterested benevolence claimed by the medical profession.

For medicine to function effectively as a sort of master code or discursive template for the realistic novelist, however, its truthfulness as a science and its ethical attractiveness must be affirmable. As Eliot's work shows, however, sustaining the first of these conditions—medicine's truth-value—becomes more and more problematic as new sciences arise that offer truths seemingly irreconcilable with those of illness and death. Cell theory threatens to replace the medical vision of life's concrete basis as organizable tissue with a much more chaotic vision of what Eliot describes as "involuntary palpitating life"; embryology and evolutionary theory, in turn, challenge the clinical vision of individual development as bound to the finitude of organic embodiment and of death, proposing instead to see development as essentially open-ended, unpredictable, atelic. And as Zola's and Conan Doyle's work shows, medicine itself becomes more experimental and specialized, deterministic and logically absolute in a manner that is foreign, even condescending, to clinical medicine.

The second of the conditions for clinical medicine's hegemony as the grounding discourse for realism—the ethical authority ascribed to medicine as a vocation—becomes equally problematic as the century draws to a close. From the time of Balzac to that of Eliot, it is possible to regard the medical man as the epitome of a professional class whose interests are progressive. As a figure whose labor seems neither reified nor exploitative, and as one who has succeeded during this period in establishing his work at a distance from the havoc of the marketplace, the physician of this era seems to point the way toward a professional utopia, a place where knowledge and power might be united and turned to beneficent social action. Professionals in general, and doctors in particular, do in fact vigorously participate in many of the reformist and even revolutionary political activities of the first two-thirds of the century, taking on their identity as a class in apparent opposition to the bourgeoisie and to laissez-faire capitalism.[3] With what M. S. Larson has described as "the consolidation of professionalism" toward the end of the century, however, it becomes increasingly clear that despite their differences, the professional class and the bourgeoisie are not radical antagonists.[4] Capitalism manages to co-opt professionalism without much difficulty. Indeed, in a strange twist, the physician, who stood for an alternative to marketplace individualism in the earlier period of unbridled free enterprise capitalism, now can take on almost the opposite role, standing as the epitome of liberal individualism in an era of emerging corporate and international capitalism. From being a focus of protest against the bourgeoisie, the professional—and specifically, the medical man—is transformed, both in himself and in the public imagination, into the ideal bourgeois, the cultured yet self-made man par excellence.

This double shift in the status of medicine—from an authoritative science to an auxiliary one, and from a progressive to a subordinate social praxis—has important cultural ramifications, including a new wave of antagonism against medicine and medical professionals. George Bernard Shaw's *The Doctor's Dilemma* and Stevenson's *The Strange Case of Dr. Jekyll and Mr. Hyde* are the most noteworthy literary products of this antagonism. My concern here, however, is with an issue not directly relevant to Shaw or Stevenson: that of how the decline of medical authority affects the fortunes of the realistic novel. I am not arguing for a direct cause-and-effect relationship between medicine and realism, of course. Changes in cultural values or in the hierarchy of the sciences will cause shifts in literary forms, but any such shift must involve a number of mediating factors. Nevertheless, given the strong correlation between realism and a certain medical perspective, it seems reasonable to try to understand in a general sense how what happens to the novel after Eliot is tied to the decline of medical authority. One thing seems clear to begin with: for self-conscious novelists writing after Eliot, realism becomes a more difficult literary mode to uphold, insofar as the decline in medical authority translates into a decline in literary authority at both the stylistic and the ideological levels. In stylistic matters, the realistic novelist claims literary authority based on the verisimilitude, the truth-to-life, of his or her characterizations. Now, however, those who continue to lay claim to this power find themselves attacked (as Arnold Bennett is by Virginia Woolf) for using conventions no longer vitally true to the real, conventions that lead to the creation of characters who are *merely* "cases."[5] The late realist faces a similar problem with his ideology of form: if he continues to identify his literary authority with that of the physician, he must perforce give up the claim that such professional authority is socially progressive or at least critical—precisely the claim that prompted earlier critical realists like Balzac, Flaubert, and Eliot to identify with the physician to begin with. The professional realist (again, Bennett is a salient example) has by this time been assimilated to the bourgeoisie, as the professional physician has been assimilated, and the political intensity of his prose is accordingly clouded, his diagnostic criticism of social ills is muffled, and his ability to project a healthier alternative is undermined.

To describe this development of stylistic and ideological troubles within realism is not to imply that realistic novels written after 1880 are second-rate or even that they must be ideologically nugatory. But it does mean that even the best of the late realists find themselves caught up in a situation where their options are limited. One of the few ways of stemming this degradation is to adjust the horizon of realism, from that of a given social totality to that of an isolated pathological world that can then be examined and analyzed from an authoritative medical perspective. Such is Thomas Mann's strategy in *The Magic*

Mountain, a novel that can be seen as a kind of polar cousin to Balzac's *Le Médecin de campagne*. Both novels are masterpieces of realism that are set in isolation from a society that they nevertheless represent at a distance. But although Balzac's isolation is the prerequisite for the flowering of a therapeutic utopia where a healthy social totality might be situated, Mann's isolation can do no more than diagnose the social totality as ontologically sick. If Balzac makes his community an asylum, Mann makes his sanitorium the world.

Part of Mann's greatness as a realist stems from the lucidity with which he accepts the necessity for retrenchment, and the profundity with which he analyzes his microcosm. Like his predecessors, Mann crams his novel with an almost encyclopedic profusion of concrete details. Such details may concern ideas more often than material objects or objects of desire, but they raise the same ultimate questions about their significance that are raised when one reads Flaubert or Eliot. And perhaps even more rigorously than either of these two novelists, Mann broaches the central question dealt with in the realistic novel: the question of what it means to be a mortal individual, an embodied person whose body is diseased. Unlike Eliot, who takes account of competing scientific views of life only with misgivings and by isolating them in different narratives, Mann firmly subordinates these other nonindividual views of life to the medical perspective. Hans Castorp's question, "What then was life?" requires knowing cell biology, embryology, comparative anatomy, and evolutionary theory, and Mann takes us through the explanations offered by these sciences. But Hans tellingly concludes his research by musing over a volume of pathological anatomy, where the Bichatian dictum, "Disease was a perverse, a dissolute form of life," suggests a clinical answer to his metaphysical question: "And life? Life itself? Was it perhaps only an infection, a sickening of matter? Was that which one might call the original procreation of matter only a disease, a growth produced by morbid stimulation of the immaterial?"[6] This clinical view of life is the most true, the most appropriate to Hans's subjective condition, his morbid enthrallment with Clavdia Chauchat. In fact, the chapter concludes with Hans dozing off over his last speculation and dreaming of Clavdia. One accepts Hans as a realistic character, Mann seems to imply, insofar as one recognizes the primacy of the medical perspective.

Most other late realists, unfortunately, do not adjust as well as Mann to the loss of stylistic and ideological power in realism that accompanies the decline of clinical medicine. These novelists in effect are left behind by historical change, appearing in retrospect as merely repeating the same literary gestures as their more illustrious predecessors, gestures that in an altered situation appear increasingly unsatisfying in either aesthetic or ideological terms. A. J. Cronin's *The Citadel* (1937), for example, follows Eliot in examining the problems of professional vocation through the story of a scientifically informed, reform-minded country doctor, Andrew Manson, whose travails greatly resemble those of Lydgate. Cronin's plot, however, evades dealing with the very dilemmas that Eliot most strongly emphasizes: the limits of medical/realist knowledge and the contradiction between vocation and social structures. Nor does Cronin reflect these dilemmas in his own style. Like Eliot, and like most realists, Cronin does at times share his doctor's vocabulary, and clearly also shares the doctor's values. But unlike Eliot with Lydgate, Cronin never interrogates or doubts the certainty of Manson's knowledge or its eventual triumph. Manson, in fact, stakes his future on the latest scientific breakthroughs against the wisdom of the medical establishment, and nonetheless is in the end exonerated by his colleagues, in stark contrast to Lydgate; and although Cronin does explore the problems of juggling marriage and vocation, as Eliot does, he ends by simply killing off Manson's wife in order to guarantee the purity of the doctor's vocation, rather than accepting the dilemma as Eliot does in condemning Lydgate to Rosamond's company. The clinician triumphs, but it is a hollow triumph, and the realism that represents it is hollow as well.

Arnold Bennett is a far more self-conscious novelist than is Cronin, both stylistically and ideologically. Indeed, one could make a case (as Frank Kermode has done) for including Bennett in the first rank of the literary artists of his time.[7] Yet, like Cronin, Bennett ultimately fails to cope lucidly with the issues raised in realism by the decline of medicine as a grounding discourse. His confusion comes through in particularly interesting ways in *Riceyman Steps*, published in 1923 after Bennett's reputation had long been established by such popular successes as *The Old Wives' Tale* and *Clayhanger*. As the most accomplished of the late realists, Bennett, by the 1920s, became the target of the slings and arrows not only of Woolf but of a number of other important writers and critics (among them Lawrence, Pound, Wyndham Lewis, and Henry James) who pointed out the inadequacies of his realism. With *Riceyman Steps*, Bennett explicitly set out to write a novel that would pass muster with this elite reading public, securing his reputation as not only a best-seller but also a great novelist. To this end, he imported many individual techniques ascribable to those very writers who had criticized him, to such an extent that he could boast that the Conrad manner "is after all my own."[8] But these techniques—the most obvious of which is that of symbolism, used in describing such things as the railroad and the wedding cake—do not dominate Bennett's work; they do not function, in other words, as principles that govern the narrative pattern and the presentation of character, as, for example, stream-of-consciousness functions in Joyce's work.[9] Rather, what Kermode calls Bennett's "metaphysical substructure" remains realist, bound to the old conceptions of character, truth, and narrative authority whose forms I have been attempting to define as medical.

A closer look at *Riceyman Steps* reveals that Bennett in fact marshals techniques from the two main paradigms of realism, the early medical realism of Balzac and Dickens and the mature pathological realism of Eliot and Flaubert. Although Bennett does not quite succeed in synthesizing these modes, he does manage to deploy the two sets of techniques in a marvelously economical way, allocating each set to a different pair of characters and thereby creating a double plot. The central plot concerns Henry Earlforward and Violet Arb, both of whom are conceived as pathologically realistic characters, assumed to possess hidden, complicated inner lives that have been infected by diseased desires. Henry suffers from a "secret passion" for money that fights within him against his love for Violet (95), while Violet in her turn is debilitated by her "thwarted desire" for Henry and by the "dangerous secret" of his hoarding that she must herself repress (166). Given such characters, Bennett then orients himself as the pathological realist typically does, writing (and asking the reader to read) from the ironic perspective of "an experienced and cautious observer of mankind" (1) who gets at the secret of Henry's and Violet's characters not by directly connecting signifier to signified, but by indicating the implications of what is not said or even known to the characters themselves, by treating their marks of character as symptoms. And, as usual in pathological realism, Bennett's plot itself grounds this hermeneutics of indirection, guaranteeing the meaning of these symptoms by gradually revealing their context as that of diseased character, of an "internal trouble" (284) that slowly perturbs and finally kills both Henry and Violet.

Joe and Elsie, in contrast, survive, and they do so, in large part, because they have been conceived in different terms, as Balzacian/Dickensian types. For such characters, like the Garths in *Middlemarch*, interiority is not an issue for interpretation—not because they have no inner life, no secrets to conceal (Elsie's secret, as Bennett reminds us, is Joe, whom she is sheltering), but because the inside is transparently evident to the outside, at least for the narrator. As in Balzac and Dickens, the signs of character are legible in Elsie's face, which blushes and shines with the "instinctive goodness" (205), the "honest love" within her. Moreover, the plot in which Elsie and Joe participate is structured, like the typical early realist plot, around a particularly conceived problem of illness and treatment. Illness, in this paradigm, does not reside within the characters themselves (as does Henry's and Violet's cancer) but impinges upon them from the outside. Joe suffers from two illnesses—malaria and shell shock—both of which Bennett regards as environmentally caused sicknesses, in spite of the fact that Freud had already pointed out the complex internal dynamics of war trauma. Bennett takes little interest in the narrative possibilities inherent in Joe's psychological ills, for he conceives of him, as of Elsie, as essentially healthy. The only treatment necessary for such ills is the old-fashioned treatment recommended by Balzac and Dickens—tender loving care, supervised by a charismatic, caring physician and administered in a reconstituted facsimile of the family.

Between the two kinds of realism in Bennett's novel, there is as little interaction as there is communication between Joe or Elsie and the Earlforwards, for whom Elsie works as a maid. Each set of characters lives in its own interpretive universe, as becomes clear at those moments when Elsie shares with her employers what should be common experiences but that the narrator reveals to be incommensurable. Elsie, for example, is totally unconscious of the workings of currency, a topic that is Henry Earlforward's ruling passion, so that when he reads about the Belgian franc falling "in sympathy," she wonders "how its performances could be actuated by such a feeling as sympathy" (161). If Henry is sustained by his belief in "the magic gold," Elsie finds "the magic of her belief" in marriage (111). It is primarily in those cases where the opposition between Elsie's and Henry's ways of seeing are highlighted by the narrator that the novel in fact comes closest to iconoclastically transcending the interpretive possibilities of realism altogether. In these instances, an object—the wedding cake, the wedding shoe, or even Henry's illness—assumes the status of an enigma, promising a meaning that is not exhausted by the interpretations provided for it. These are the moments in the text that come closest to modernism, but they are not sustainable by Bennett. The logic of the two plots proceeds inexorably to the doubly clichéd conclusion of the Earlforward's extinction (Henry's death scene is particularly redolent of Zola) and Elsie's and Joe's redemption into a happy family.

The demand for such a happy ending, of course, came from Bennett's mass readership, who ignored the Earlforward plot, focusing entirely on Elsie's sentimental story. The public's enthusiasm for Elsie, in fact, eventually compelled Bennett to write a sequel detailing her further adventures, but he himself found the taste for such a character and such an ending rather vulgar: "As if the sympathetic quality of Elsie," Bennett writes, "has anything whatever to do with the quality of the book!" Bennett's exasperation stemmed from his desire for an audience that would transcend the emerging opposition between the best-seller-reading public and the elite interested in quality but hostile to realism. *Riceyman Steps* provides a kind of allegory of this reader-reception problem for the late realist, with the distinct reading publics represented in the structure of Henry Earlforward's bookshop, described early in the novel:

> The shop had one window in King's Cross Road, but the entrance, with another window, was in Riceyman Steps. The King's Cross Road window held only cheap editions, in their paper jackets, of popular modern novels, such as those of Ethel M. Dell, Charles Garvice, Zane Grey, Florence Barclay, Nat Gould, and Gene Stratton Porter. The side window was set out with old books, first editions, illustrated editions, and complete library editions in calf or morocco of renowned and serious writers, whose works, indispensable to the collections of self-respecting book-gentlemen (as distinguished from bookmen), have passed through decades of criticism into the impregnable paradise of eternal esteem. The side window was bound to attract the attention of collectors or bibliomaniacs. It seemed strangely, even fatally, out of place in that dingy and sordid neighbourhood where existence was a dangerous and difficult adventure in almost frantic quest of food, drink and shelter, where the immense majority of the population read nothing but sporting prognostications and results, and, on Sunday mornings, accounts of bloody crimes and juicy sexual irregularities. (4)

The shifts in tone throughout this passage reveal Bennett's ambivalence about both of his possible audiences. For the readers of "cheap editions" of "popular modern novels," whose taste inclines them toward journalistic sensationalism, Bennett's repugnance is clear. Yet he also seems to grant a certain authenticity, and hence a certain value, to this untutored aesthetic, which is grounded in the realities of life in "a neighbourhood where existence was a dangerous and difficult adventure." The other reading public, that audience of "self-respecting book-gentlemen" interested only in first editions of "serious writers," similarly seems at first the intelligent, discerning, and favored class of readers whom Bennett would hope to please. This group, however, is subjected to criticism in turn: they are less gentlemen than "collectors and bibliomaniacs," and Bennett sarcastically rebukes their aesthetic timidity, their unwillingness to read any book that has not "passed through decades of criticism into the impregnable paradise of eternal esteem."

This concern for the audience of realism was expressed, to be sure, by realists long before Bennett. One thinks of Balzac's hope that duchesses and scullery maids will read his novels; of Flaubert's deliberate attempt to write a novel that could be read stupidly as a novel of adultery or intelligently as a therapeutically antagonistic analysis of bourgeois ways of reading; of Eliot's attempts to educate her audiences so as to forge a single "we," a cultured readership. But for these earlier novelists, despite their differing attitudes toward the reading public, the problem of audience could resolve itself in the same way, through the mediation of a third class of readers, a class whose vision of the real could in some way be thought of as commensurate with the realist's vision. Balzac's Benassis, Flaubert's Larivière, and Eliot's Lydgate all stand as figures, within their novelists' fictions, of the implied ideal reader for that novelist, their positions with respect to other characters indicating the novelists' positions with respect to their own reading publics. Bennett, like his predecessors, turns to a physician, Dr. Raste, as a mediating figure representing the novelist's hoped-for public. In the novel as a whole, Raste stands between the two plots, treating both Henry and Joe; he is in fact indispensable to the logic of the narrative, for it is his hiring of Elsie that makes it possible for her to marry Joe at last, concluding the action of the novel. But Raste's mediating status has been implied from the very beginning of the novel. We first see Dr. Raste when he enters Earlforward's bookshop immediately after Bennett has given us the description quoted earlier. If that description established the division of the reading public into mere collectors and avid but uneducated mass-market readers, Bennett's description of Raste makes it clear that the doctor transcends these classifications. He is clearly not a member of the lower classes, but he cannot be pigeonholed as a bourgeois reader either: he has the air "neither of a bookman nor of a member of the upper-middle class" (5). He is, rather, a professional man, come to buy a copy of Shakespeare for his daughter.

For Bennett, Raste's daughter—and more generally, the professional class that has consolidated its social position, begun to reproduce itself and claim its share of culture—represents his best hope. But he can only sustain this hope by ignoring the increasingly manifest contradictions within professionalism itself, the necessary reification inherent in professional service, and the equally necessary assumption of a humanitarian impulse behind the professional mask. In Raste, this split comes through as an opposition between public and private selves, between his attitude as "the doctor exclusively" (264) and his attitude as a doting father. As a doctor, he must become, like Henry Earlforward, an individualist who is secretive, "impenetrable": "the secrets of the night were locked up in that trimly dressed bosom" (264), Bennett tells us, using a metaphor that applies to Henry and to Violet as well. With his daughter, on the other hand, he becomes a different person—loving, giving, caring. It is this difference that makes it possible for Bennett to end the novel as he does, with what from a professional physician's view must seem to be "a very strange episode, upsetting as it did all optimistic theories about the reasonableness of human nature and the influence of logic over the springs of conduct."

Presumably Bennett would have us recognize the novel's closure not as strange but as organic. The ending of the novel, however, is strange, its Dickensian solution (Dr. Raste taking Elsie and Joe into the home to please his daughter) at odds with the pathological inflections of Henry's death in the previous chapter. Bennett concludes that "No one knew quite where he was" (317), but in the final analysis the reader himself comes to feel that it is Bennett as a novelist who does not quite know where his characters are, what textual world they inhabit—the pathological world of Henry and Violet or the traditional organic world of Joe and Elsie.

I do not mean to imply that Bennett's incoherency results from sloppiness or a failure of technical skills. On the contrary, one need only read the opening paragraph of *Riceyman Steps*, with its marvelously economical introduction of details soon to prove significant of Henry's miserliness (we are told only that he goes hatless in autumn and that he is near-sighted but does not own eye-glasses), to recognize what Frank Kermode calls Bennett's "efficiency." What I *am* suggesting is that even Bennett's devotion to efficiency is less than totally gripping, because the efficiency is of a kind that serves an idea whose time has passed—the idea that realism and the clinical medicine that supports it are the most true and progressive forms of cultural and social practice.

Anticlinical Modernisms

If late realists cling to concepts of efficiency, truth, and ethics as these are defined through the analogy with medicine (efficiency as a diagnosis of the organically embodied person, truth as pathology, ethics as professional vocation), and if Zola and Conan Doyle, in different ways, demote without quite abandoning such clinically coded notions, modernist novelists take as their point of departure the pointed rejection, or at least the critique, of these very notions. Literary modernism, admittedly, is a vastly complicated phenomenon, in which the forms of this rejection, the emphases of this critique, and the alternatives offered must be specified in each instance through close readings. Obviously, I cannot hope to do this here. Instead, I shall try to sketch out a few of the major ways in which modernist novelists go about displacing realism either by inverting the medical perspective or by turning to discourses other than medicine for ideas of efficiency, truth, or ethics.

One species of modernism, exemplified in the work of Joyce and Woolf, may be characterized by its technical innovation, its challenging of the realistic novelist's claim to the efficiency of his or her representation of reality. In realistic fiction, a wide variety of techniques of characterization and description certainly conveys information very efficiently, but this efficiency (as in a medical case study) is always defined in relation to the embodied person. The novelist, in other words, assumes, to begin with, that the self is an organization of sensibility grounded in space and time, hemmed in by his or her empirical nature and finitude; techniques must be marshaled and deployed to give significance to these ontological conditions. In the Joycean/Woolfian mode of modernism, on the other hand, the embodied person is no longer the fundamental organized entity from which the novelist begins.[10] This does not mean that the novelist has been freed from the constraints of characterization into a world of scattershot techniques. Rather, it means that the self can now be thought of as a fiction (and not necessarily as the supreme fiction), structured by systems of order (and hence meaning) beyond those of the organized body. Such systems may be mythical, psychoanalytic, linguistic, or even textual, but they all allow for a much denser and, in abstract terms, more efficient narrative, in which significance is largely independent of character.[11]

The abandonment of the embodied person as the constitutive element of fiction has other ramifications as well. For one thing, the concepts that provided the self with what Heidegger calls being-in-the-world—the categories of empiricity and time—must be redefined. In the realistic novel, the empirical, as we have seen, is a matter of detail, objects, and physicalities that exist to be incorporated through sensation into the sensibility of character as well as to disintegrate that sensibility and character. In Flaubert's work, for example, an umbrella, an article of clothing, or an apricot may have no intrinsic meaning but can illuminate character by being taken as meaningful and then withdrawn. If in Flaubert's novels "the separate fragments of reality lie before us in all their hardness, brokenness and isolation," as Lukács puts it,[12] this negation of organic wholeness, because it is understood as pathological, still permits us to reconstitute an organized character. In the work of modernists like Joyce, by contrast, the empirical no longer is shaped by a dialectic of organization and disintegration, and hence never lies before the reader as distinct fragments that one could take as the disintegrated elements of an embodied person; rather, the empirical itself has been dissolved into elements of language, technique, or sheer perception (as Woolf indicates with her famous image of atoms randomly falling on the mind).[13]

The concept of time is similarly transformed. In realism, as we have seen, the temporality of the novel follows the temporality of the individual life. If medicine presumes that the fundamental characteristic of pathologized time is that it is bounded by death, the realistic novelists with whom I have dealt take this finitude as a point of closure for organizing their stories. Death, of course, has held this value for narrative at least since Scheherazade used stories to ward off a death sentence. Balzac's, Flaubert's, and Eliot's conception of death is specifically clinical, however, not simply a limit external to life, but a constitutive part of it. They assume, with Bichat, that life is the set of functions that resists death, and hence that lives can be understood as temporal ordeals culminating in death.[14] Illness, the medical term for this ordeal, has its own paces, its tempo of crisis, recovery, relapse, acceleration, or recurrence, which realistic narratives focusing on the pathologically embodied individual will necessarily imitate. The temporality of illness, moreover, must be measured in a double dimension, for, according to clinical medicine, the individual lives two lives simultaneously and thus can die a series of partial deaths. The temporal complexities of the *homo duplex*, as we have seen, play themselves out not only in Bichat but in Flaubert and Eliot as well. In abandoning the clinically embodied self as the fundamental principle of narrative, modernism does not necessarily abandon the idea that, as Nietzsche puts it, "Man is the sick animal." But jettisoning the clinical perspective on this sickness does require the modernist to uncouple the temporality of his fiction from that of pathology. The temporal principle of the novel can no longer be the ordeal of an embodied self resisting mortality. Instead, modernism—or at least that species of modernism represented by Joyce and his followers—bases its narrative on a different temporal a priori: that of repetition (and its corollary, chance). The structure of a life is grounded not in organic change but in an eternal return, the uncanny, or the vagaries of chance. One finds Bloom repeating Ulysses, as other characters repeat Oedipus, or else one meets characters who are caught in a Prufrockian temporality of undirected contingency in which there is "time for you and time for me, / And time yet for a hundred indecisions, / And for a hundred visions and revisions, / Before the taking of a toast and tea."

By defining realism in medical terms, as a discourse that finds significance in and through the pathologically embodied person, one thus can distinguish a certain kind of modernism from realism by the stress this modernism places on semantic efficiency and by the abandonment of the clinically embodied individual such a technical emphasis entails. This is not the only way in which modernism can be distinguished from realism, however. A second kind of modernism may be identified, a literary style less directly concerned with stretching the technical boundaries of the novel beyond the embodied person; in fact, in this second type of modernism, as in the realistic novels we have discussed, not only is the body significant, but meaning is inextricably bound to illness. What then marks off the writing of Dostoevsky, Proust, Franz Jung, and Gide from the realistic writing of Balzac, Flaubert, or Eliot? The analysis of realism in medical terms, once again, is helpful here: this modernism differs from realism in the intensity with which it questions the truth-value of the distinction between the pathological and the normal. In the realistic novels of Balzac, Flaubert, and Eliot, this normal/pathological distinction serves a heuristic end. It permits the narrator to distinguish himself from his characters as a physician from his patients, and to make sense of them from a position of relative certainty as to what counts as significant. The celebrated distance and omniscience of the realist narrator is precisely the distance that separates those who are sick from those who recognize what sickness is. In the second kind of modernism I have in mind, on the other hand, the pathological perspective becomes the dominant one—it is the narrator himself who is sick, from Dostoevsky's Underground Man ("I am a sick man" are his first words) to Gide's immoralist to Proust's Marcel. Not only is the writing subject now the sick subject, but the pathological perspective may even be cultivated for its own sake, as one can see by comparing Proust's attitude toward odors and the involuntary irruptions of memory they cause with Flaubert's attitude toward the same condition in *Madame Bovary*. Proust luxuriates in the process; Flaubert diagnoses it (even though he personally has first to experience it) through Emma's fits.[15]

Kafka pushes to its extreme this inversion of the distinction between medical perspective and pathology bequeathed by all those realists who claimed to be writing as physicians. Kafka has long been recognized as a master at conveying abnormal, indeed ultimately estranged, perspectives like that of Gregor Samsa in *The Metamorphosis*. For the reader of realistic novels used to defining pathology in opposition to the medical perspective, however, an even more radical case of estrangement—that of the medical perspective itself—occurs in one of the very few stories Kafka published during his lifetime, "A Country Doctor." Kafka's country doctor could not be more different from Balzac's, Flaubert's, or Eliot's country doctors. He speaks directly to us, but as if in a nightmare, telling a story in which seemingly realistic details and events mix with other details and events whose significance is clearly symbolic, registering the physician's own anxieties and desires. Take for example this moment, when the doctor examines his patient:

> In his right side, near the hip, was an open wound as big as the palm of my hand. Rose-red, in many variations of shade, dark in the hollows, lighter at the edges, softly granulated, with irregular clots of blood, open as a surface mine to the daylight. That was how it looked from a distance. But on closer inspection there was another complication. I could not help a low whistle of surprise. Worms, as thick and as long as my little finger, themselves rose-red and blood-spotted as well, were wriggling from their fastness in the interior of the wound toward the light, with small white heads and many little legs. Poor boy, you were past helping. I had discovered your great wound; this blossom in your side was destroying you.[16]

The first few sentences, with their beautifully nuanced descriptive power, their almost aesthetic attention to the qualities of the pathological, remind one of the best of nineteenth-century clinical writing. They also call to mind the kind of scrupulous treatment of detail found in the description of illness in many realistic novels, for example in Flaubert's description of croup in *L'Education Sentimentale*. But almost immediately this masterful perception is superseded by another perception, equally intense yet pointing not to the real, objective wound but toward complicated sexual feelings within the doctor himself (later, the doctor even finds himself forced to undress and lie in bed with his patient!). There is thus, in Kafka, no norm, no standard of truth against which the pathological could be opposed, distanced, controlled. As in Gottfried Benn's novella *Gehirne*, which also features as hero a "physician who could not endure the real world, who could not grasp reality anymore," Kafka's physician himself is sick, and narrative takes form as the exposure of what Peter Hohendahl calls "the loss of reality" without any hope for amelioration.[17]

If Joycean modernism focuses its challenge to realism on the issue of the narrative efficiency of the embodied person, and if Kafkaesque modernism challenges realism on the issue of the opposition between truth and pathology (making the pathological perspective the truly real perspective), a third kind of modernism must also be differentiated. In this modernism, of which Conrad can serve as exemplar, the point of attack is neither the embodied self nor the the authority of the pathological viewpoint, but rather the professional ethos, the vocational impulse that I have argued sustains both realism and medicine. One becomes a doctor, as one becomes a realist, because one believes that practicing medicine or writing is finally a pure act, benevolent and divorced from oppressive forms of power. Balzac, Flaubert, and

Eliot all sustain this idealization of vocation and link it to medicine—
Balzac through the presentation of an ideal medical figure of vocation, Eliot through Lydgate at the start of his career, and Flaubert
through his almost anchoritic devotion to technique conceived in
medical terms.

In sharp contrast, Conrad assumes, to begin with, that the vocational impulse—whether medical or not—colludes with the most base
and powerful material interests. The classical exposition of this principle comes in *Heart of Darkness*, where Kurtz's civilizing mission goes
hand in hand with the exercise of an imperialist will to power. It would
be easy enough to dismiss Kurtz as a sick individual: his particular way
of acting could be described as excessive, a perversion of ideals and
practices that remain valuable. This particular professional may have
gone wrong, one might argue, but professionalism, insofar as it har-
bors a therapeutic value system, an ideal of improvement, can be
saved. As Marlow puts it: "what redeems [imperialist conquest] is the
idea only . . . not a sentimental pretense but an idea; and an unselfish
belief in the idea." Or, if the idea of improvement appears bankrupt,
one can fall back on the professional assumption that technique at
least is valuable in itself, without reference to the context of its application. What saves one then, Marlow again anticipates, "is efficiency—
the devotion to efficiency."[18]

These arguments may have held for the realists. Balzac certainly
asserts the redemptive features of his art, its capacity to heal society,
while Flaubert finds salvation in devotion to efficiency. For Conrad,
however, any such arguments about having a calling appear as mere
rationalizations. Vocation can no longer be depended upon to legitimate the power of either the hero or the novelist. It is not surprising,
then, that the figure of the physician, so often a type of vocation in the
work of the realists, degenerates in *Heart of Darkness* into a minor figure who examines Marlow before the latter leaves for Africa, and
whose ludicrous scientific pretensions are admittedly parasitic on the
imperialist enterprise: "I have a little theory," the company doctor
tells Marlow, "which you Messieurs who go out there must help me to
prove. This is my share in the advantages my country shall reap from
the possession of such a magnificent dependency. The mere wealth I
leave to others" (38). Medicine appears as an intellectually bankrupt
search for knowledge, devoid even of the trappings of idealism that
inspired Balzac or Eliot's physicians (and the novelists themselves).
Moreover, Conrad denies to medicine not only its ideals but its technical power, its ability to pierce into the soul to get at the inner truth
about the patient (as Flaubert's Dr. Larivière is said to be able to do).
The theory of Conrad's doctor turns out to be a remnant of the by-

gone days of phrenology: he measures with calipers the crania of those who will go to Africa, not to do a before-and-after comparison (he never sees those who come back), but in order to classify those crazy enough to go in the first place. He is intelligent enough to recognize that "the changes take place inside," but his art, unlike Conrad's, stops where the inner darkness and real (modernist) significance begins.

Disembodied Realism: James's *Wings of the Dove*

From this excruciatingly compressed survey of modernist fiction, I hope I have at least begun to demonstrate how defining realism's pathological basis might enable one to analyze modernism as the precise antithesis of realism's medical premises (rather than as an attack, say, on representation in a general sense). But such generic discriminations, although useful (and, I would suggest, indispensable in practice), may leave some readers with the uneasy feeling that a great number of important novels considered "realist" or "modernist" do not fit snugly into either of the categories as I have theorized them.

One response to this objection has already been put forward in my introductory chapter, where I suggest that any discussion of genre inevitably must generalize from a limited set of data, whether the genre in question be scientific or literary. The question then becomes, which and how many cases adequately represent a genre? Here an important difference arises between literary critics interested in genre and their scientific counterparts. The biologist studies strains, or in some instances individual cases, under the assumption that they statistically represent the genre or species in which they are grouped. If a literary critic were to follow the statistical imperative, one would expect to define realism by studying novelists whose style was statistically the most commonplace. Yet despite the efforts of some critics (most prominently, Michel Riffaterre) to theorize genre by focusing on the most banal examples possible, no important genre study of realism has proceeded in this way. On the contrary, the most respected works on realism as a genre—by such critics as Ian Watt, Donald Fanger, Harry Levin, George Levine, and Fredric Jameson—have dealt intensively with a small number of canonical figures, as I have done here. The assumption under which these critics work, and which I share, is that writers like Flaubert, Balzac, George Eliot, Dickens, Trollope, Dostoevsky, or Gissing are representative and original, exemplary and transformative with respect to questions of genre. They initiate, perfect, bring to the fore, or turn to new uses a characteristic of realism (whether a new technique, a new kind of character, a new thematic emphasis, or a new point of view) that then becomes part of the repertory of later realists or modernists. To say this, of course, is to leave open the question of whether there might not exist other realisms, even coeval with the pathological realism I have identified. One might well construct an alternative tradition running through, say, Gaskell or Tressell or Gissing, dependent on different premises and insisting on a different kind of authority than that found in pathological realism.

I have tried to show how three central figures in the realistic tradition may be understood in terms of their dependence on medical ideas and ideals, a dependence that takes different forms in each instance, but that fundamentally links these writers to a single genre while separating them from their naturalist and detective fiction stepchildren and their modernist successors. But, once again, one might ask, what of writers who fall between the cracks, who cannot easily be categorized as either realistic or modernist? To show that the methodology I have employed is supple enough to handle such tough cases, I have thought it appropriate to conclude this chapter by briefly considering a work by a novelist who is usually considered one of the most important transitional figures between realism and modernism: Henry James. My concern in discussing James is not to join the longstanding debate over his status as a member of one or the other camp; the definitions of realism at stake in such discussions do not in any case coincide with mine, and to pick apart the differences between realist and modernist Jamesians would be a dangerous as well as a tedious matter.[19] Rather, I want to show how James, in one of his greatest novels, repeats the gestures of his realist predecessors—their technical, epistemic, and ethical procedures—while at the same time subtly transposing into a different register realism's medicalized notions of the embodied person, pathological truth, and detached yet empathic authority.

Viewed in the light of the novels and issues I have been considering, *Wings of the Dove* might appear to be a kind of *summa*, a grand recapitulation of themes, tropes, techniques, and stylistic orientations found in the work of the three earlier realists I have discussed. This is perhaps most evident in the way in which James sets up the doctor : patient relationship in the novel. From Balzac (and from Dickens as well), James derives the image of the physician as an omniscient yet benevolent figure. Sir Luke Strett, like Benassis and Physician before him, possesses a knowledge of the real transcending the "merely professional" (148)—a knowledge indissociable from feeling.[20] Strett's effectiveness, we are told, "wasn't on a system or any basis of intimate knowledge; it was just by being a man of the world and by knowing life, by feeling the real, that Sir Luke did [Merton] good" (350). His defining characteristic, in short, is the same as that of Dickens's and Balzac's doctors: he is a "genius" of tact and sympathy (148).

At the same time, however, Sir Luke also shares a characteristic with Flaubert's physician, who inhabits a different medical (and realist) universe from that of Dickens's and Balzac's doctors: Strett, like Larivière, is inscrutable. Of all the central characters concerned with Milly, he is the only one never seen from within, never permitted to give us his side of the story, never allowed to confess (as, for example, Balzac's Dr. Benassis does). Moreover, like Larivière's medical knowledge in *Madame Bovary*, Strett's knowledge about Milly remains virtual, never becoming available to the other characters in the novel. And, as is true for Flaubert, this hermeneutic hierarchy ranging the physician's way of knowing against that of the other characters allegorizes the interpretative relation between the novelist and his characters. The assumption that Milly can be understood, albeit in a medical form inaccessible to the characters, enables James, like Flaubert before him, to analyze the bourgeois imagination as pathological, as sick consciousness.

Eliot, finally, contributes to Jamesian realism the epistemic emphasis, in James's analysis of what Virginia Fowler calls the "malady of self,"[21] upon the relational quality of that pathologized self, the sense that human identity is organized within and as part of a network both imaginary and social. Given this assumption, the study of what James calls his "case" must extend beyond the individual consciousness to include the consciousness of others, insofar as these others are involved in the network that gives one an identity. James, like Eliot and Flaubert before him, therefore conceives of character (in his preface to *The Portrait of a Lady*) in physiological terms, as a "germ" to begin with—a germ that develops through relations that, universally considered, stop nowhere, but that pragmatically are subjected to the constraints of organic form. Relations may go on infinitely, but every germ faces innate limits on its individual growth and change. Indeed, it is this very finitude of mortality that makes narrative closure (and the revelation of the truth about Milly or Lydgate or Dorothea or Emma Bovary) possible in James as in Eliot or Flaubert, even as the two novelists gesture toward the life and relations that continue to proliferate beyond the novel's term.

Far from turning against the clinical configurations of realism in *Wings of the Dove*, then, James remains extraordinarily faithful to them. In equating his authority with that of an ethical physician, in equating knowledge of character with technical knowledge of relations of sensibility, in equating the very possibility of knowing with the mortality of the self (to the extent that what is "interesting" for James means what is pathological), James's attitude matches that of his predecessors. And yet, something has changed in the discourse on illness in James's novel. Within the overall system whose outline remains the same, the ontological status of the self has shifted in a slight but crucial way. In Balzac's, Flaubert's, and Eliot's medical realism, the self is bound to the corporeal, to what Valéry beautifully defines as "the instantaneous 'sphere' of exteriority that encloses us in its 'instant,' and whose transformations and invariables—extinctions also, and harmonies and dissonances of presence etc. etc.—play the fundamental role of reference."[22] Consciousness in realism always inhabits a body that serves as an empirical grounding-point, the site at which death occurs and the truth emerges, like the inky fluid spewing forth from Emma's mouth after she has killed herself. In Milly's case, as well as in Emma's, death is the precondition for our knowledge. Yet James never shows us Milly's body, only the "remembrance" she leaves to Merton. The Jamesian self, in short, has been disembodied. This should not be taken as implying that James's fiction categorically denies the self any empirical existence; James is in no sense a solipsist or a textualist of the Joycean kind. Rather, in the absence of the body, James redefines the self purely as a consciousness of relations and impressions. We may thus speak of an empiricity of the impression in James, analogous to the empiricity of the physical in his predecessors. Where they rely on referential details to inform character, he relies on verbal nuances; the care that Flaubert might devote to description, James devotes to qualification.

This shift, slight as it may seem, ultimately alters the tenor, if not the fundamental structures, of medical realism. To begin with, the act of living must now be understood in terms of the accrual and disposition of impressions. To live, in James's world, is not so much to experience what Jameson calls the resistance of the real, but to move in a milieu of impressions, to be impressed and to make an impression upon others. As James himself puts it: "If experience consists of impressions, it may be said that impressions *are* experience, just as (have we not seen it?) they are the very air we breathe."[23] Edmund Wilson, for one, found such a "psychological atmosphere" bad for his respiration; James' later novels, he complained, are filled with "the Jamesian gas instead of with detail and background."[24] Wilson did not appreciate, however, that this sublimation of detail into impression does not affect the *nature* of the life James's characters possess, only its quality. Life in James, as in his predecessors, still demands a projective, incorporative, urgent engagement with the empirical. In other words, for James character consists of more than a passive collecting of impressions (just as character for Balzac, Flaubert, or Eliot consists of more than a statistical registration of details). It involves in its essence what James in the preface to *Wings of the Dove* refers to as an ordeal of consciousness, a struggle to realize one's passion, as Kate presumes Milly to have "realised her passion," through finding it answered in the impressions one receives. A synthesis of will and mere impressions, the realized character represents the successful transformation of instinct into a system of selfhood, through a process that consists simultaneously of externalizing desire and internalizing impressions.

This idea of life as a struggle for self-realization and against collapse is analogous to the Bichatian view of life as resistance to death. But James, dealing with impressions in the absence of the body, finds a more convenient model for characterization not in the medical idea of organic development or degeneration per se, but rather in fictive or poetic activity. To live fully requires what James describes in Kate Croy as a "talent for life," an innate strength of will combined with the intelligence to be able to control impressions. Kate indeed is like a strong poet, grappling in her personal life with the poetic problems of tradition and originality, and resolving them brilliantly. As Merton comments, "she didn't give their tradition up; she but made of it something new" (397), finding in herself "a difference for the differing time." "You're different and different—and then you're different again," he points out elsewhere. And this difference, this constant newness, is the very root of the realization of aesthetic character: "The women one meets—what are they but books one has already read? You're a whole library of the unknown, the uncut" (220).

The creation of a real self, however, is more than a poetic problem in James, requiring resources other than Kate's ability to give the impression of a "smooth superficiality." James's conception of realization requires not only that one manipulate impressions but also that one create a *true* self in the process—a self in which impressions carry with them the depth of will or feeling from which they have been created. Those characters who lack moral depth—Mrs. Lowder, Mr. Croy, Lord Mark—have lost sight of the distinction between truth and impression. Mrs. Lowder, for example, is willing to lie, "and lie well . . . when, as sometimes will happen, there's nothing else so good" (249). Lord Mark's ability to produce "an effect without his being in any traceable way a cause" likewise denies the crucial assumption, for James, that true feeling hovers behind (or within, or around) the impressions one gives. Kate's father shows the ultimate extension of Kate's attitude toward impressions: he dresses impeccably, is always presentable, and yet "there was no truth in him." By this attitude, Mr.

Croy and other characters like him dehumanize themselves. One cannot even begin to think of them as humanly vulnerable, for they deny the very interiority necessary to the realistic self. In nineteenth-century realism that interiority entails the potential to be ill; unsurprisingly, then, characters like Mr. Croy cannot even be thought of as sick. As Kate says of her father: "He might be ill, and it might suit you to know it, but no contact with him, for this, would ever be straight enough. Just so, he might die, but Kate fairly wondered on what evidence of his own she would someday have to believe it" (23).

For such characters, the real itself exists as nothing more than impressions. They are able, like Lord Mark, to hint "at the propriety rather, in his interest, of some cutting down, some dressing up, of the offensive real." This attitude, Milly recognizes, is not only detestable, but murderous—"it simply kills me"—because it denies the value of a depth of feeling, of passion or will, beyond but bound to impressions. Lord Mark is willing to settle for the accoutrements, without the interiority, of Milly's self; indeed, her value, for him, consists only in her money.

And yet Mark's costuming finally is only an extreme version of Milly's own way of dealing with the offensive real. Milly, however, is at least not morally culpable, for she does not deny the necessity for truth in feeling. She is, rather, sick, her malady consisting in a weakness of her own will, a weakness that calls into question for her as for others the "truth about the girl's own conception of her validity" (262–63). Incapable of generating out of her inner resources "a healing and uplifting passion," "a force that should sweep [Milly and any lover] both away," Milly instead relies upon the impressions with which she surrounds herself to provide her with the "motive" (125) for a fictive identity. In a quite physical sense, she does this by moving to a Venetian palazzo that "with all its romance and art and history—had set up round her a whirlwind of suggestion that never dropped for an hour" (280). Unfortunately, the palazzo is not reality, only a "museum": it lacks truth because it has been purchased not by an expense of spirit but only by an expense of money, and it can only provide a pseudo-identity at best.

To see money as performing the function that passion should perform, as Milly does, is to deny the fundamental hierarchy of medical realism, in which life (and death) is the measure for what is most real and true, in order to participate in what she recognizes to be "experiments tried with the truth that consisted, at the worst, but in practising on one's self." This experimenting with truth, it should be emphasized, is the antithesis of what her doctor has ordered: "Sir Luke hadn't said to her 'Pay enough money and leave the rest to *me*'—which was distinctly what Eugenio did say. Sir Luke had appeared indeed to speak of purchase and payment, but in reference to a different sort of cash. Those were amounts not to be named nor reckoned, and such moreover as she wasn't sure of having at her command" (264).

Milly's experimenting with the truth, in fact, is not a sign of strong will (as, for instance, Lord Henry Wotton's self-experimentation in *Dorian Gray* is) but a symptom of her pathological lack of will, of what Bichat refers to as "force vitale" or "élan." The retreat to the palazzo is only the physical enactment of this symptomatic experimenting, which also takes place at the psychological level in Milly's romancing. Given her need for impressions of passion to prop up her own lack of will, she discovers in romance the ideal aesthetic mode, ideal precisely because it is not *too* true. In romance, that is to say, wishes come true only because the impressions given are granted a sort of immanent meaningfulness. The unspoken in romance presupposes an "inner truth" (296), a depth to impressions, "a felt intensity" (273) that—like Milly's own inner resources of feeling—is not to be named.

To sustain romance thus would seem to entail nothing more than a certain "diplomacy" (a key word in *Wings of the Dove*), an acceptance that "things were understood without saying" (282), as Merton believes to be the case between himself and Kate, and as becomes the case for a time between himself and Milly. Milly's romance depends on this unspokenness, for it provides her with the illusion of a depth of feeling; and it is this illusion that takes the place of her own will. It is easy enough to read Milly as a sheer victim of others, but she herself participates in the conspiracy of silence by not sharing the truth of her illness with anyone. The "beautiful little eloquence involved in Milly's avoidances" sustains the romance just as surely as Kate's and Densher's avoidances.

Yet, as Milly, Kate, and Densher all learn, diplomacy, romance, and avoidance can only delay, by covering over, the revelation of a fatal deficit of will. The truth about Milly can only be withheld for so long by "the expensive vagueness made up of smiles and silences and beautiful fictions and priceless arrangements. . . . 'The mere aesthetic instinct of mankind—!' . . . from which the specified had been chased" (347). The specified is mortality, and in evading it for the sake of keeping Milly's romance viable, Kate and Densher are forced inevitably to squander their own "essential wealth of life" (220). The phrasing here is itself symptomatic: the very distinction between the value of wealth and life, the sense of what is truly essential, has been collapsed under the pressures of aesthetic evasion.

As truthfulness becomes increasingly irrelevant (indeed, there comes to be a positive need "not to be too true" [401]), the romantic self then comes to be seen as "embodied poetry," as Milly in her pearls appears to Merton and Kate. But this aestheticized body has no depth, for the codes that should provide this depth are no longer ordered hierarchically on the basis of the truth they have to tell about the self. They have taken on a purely serial form: "Milly . . . happened at the moment to notice them, and she sent across toward them in response all the candour of her smile, the lustre of her pearls, the value of her life, the essence of her wealth" (310). The repeated parallel constructions and oddly assorted modifiers in this sentence reveal how, for Merton and Kate at least, life, wealth, pearls, and smile have become virtually interchangeable.

Critics who wish to push James into the modernist camp tend to focus on the scene above as revealing James's modernist sensibility. But James, although he does give us a glimpse of something approaching modernist technique, remains a realist, in the sense that the ultimately real truth for him—"the truth that was the truest about Milly"—is finally confirmed as grounded in the individual matter of life and death. In *Wings of the Dove*, it is Dr. Strett who represents the assertion of the existence of that real truth, as an alternative to seriality. Among all the characters, only Strett "knew what mattered and what didn't; he distinguished between the essence and the shell" (351). It is to Strett's method of distinguishing, his way of knowing, that we must now turn, to see how it constitutes a negation of romance and an affirmation of the kind of realism that I have been discussing in this book.

Strett's superiority to other characters is manifested in his attitude toward Milly's malady of self, her lack of the will to go beyond romance to realize her passion. He attempts neither to manipulate Milly as if she were passive nor to subdue her in any sort of direct way by forcing her brutally to face life head-on. Rather, he acts almost as a psychoanalyst might: "the great grave charming man knew, had known at once, that [Milly's version of her condition as being a matter of life and death] was romantic, and in that measure allowed for it" (146). This allowance requires a "listening stillness, strained into pauses and waits," an absolute impassivity (like that of Flaubert's Larivière, or for that matter like that of Flaubert himself) that allows for "clean truths" about his patients to emerge in distinct forms. For Milly, waiting in Strett's office, just such a clean truth does emerge for her, even in his absence. Looking at the mementoes left by his previous patients, she immediately begins to imagine what she can contribute to the office, but then, in a moment of insight, catches herself in the act: "This was precisely an instance of what she felt he knew of her before he had done with her: that she was secretly romancing at that rate, in the midst of so much else that was more urgent, all over the place" (146).

Their subsequent interview consists of Milly talking "while he waited—waited again as if with his reasons for letting her, for almost making her, talk" (147). His reasons are to allow Milly's pathological romancing to surface, so that it may be seen not as an act of free will but as unreasonable: "as he simply met [Milly's] spontaneity in a manner to show that he had often had it from young persons of her race, and that he was familiar even with the possibilities of their familiarity, she felt her freedom rendered vain by his silence, and she immediately tried to think of the most reasonable thing she could say" (149–50).

The illusion of freedom having been dissipated, Strett can proceed with his subtle treatment. His therapy, as seen through the shifts within Milly's consciousness as she reacts to it, consists of allowing her imaginatively "to reverse for her their characters of patient and physician": "What was he in fact but patient, what was she but physician, from the moment she embraced once for all the necessity, adopted once for all the policy, of saving him alarms about her subtlety? She would leave the subtlety to him. He would enjoy his use of it, and she herself, no doubt, would in time enjoy his enjoyment" (254). Milly of course is herself being somewhat oversubtle. In fact, Strett's curative strategy is precisely to let Milly use her subtlety for her own good, to enable her to turn her imagination into an imagination of health:

> She went so far as to imagine that the inward success of these reflexions flushed her for the minute, to his eyes, with a certain bloom, a comparative appearance of health; and what verily next occurred was that he gave colour to the presumption. . . . Since such was his penetration, therefore, why shouldn't she gracefully, in recognition of it, accept the new circumstance, the one he was clearly wanting to congratulate her on, as a sufficient cause? If one nursed a cause tenderly enough it might produce an effect; and this, to begin with, would be a way of nursing. (254)

To treat character in this way, by transforming it at the level of will rather than of impression, of cause rather than effect, is what makes Strett's medical approach superior, both ethically and therapeutically, to that of those who misleadingly offer Milly romantic impressions.

Milly's response to Strett reveals both the superiority of his view of her and her inability finally to take advantage of his treatment. Her immediate reaction to their meeting, James tells us, consists in a

> sense, at the last, that she had gained above all an impression. The impression . . . was neither more nor less than that she might make, of a sudden, in quite another world, another straight friend, and a friend who would moreover be, wonderfully, the most appointed, the most thoroughly adjusted of the whole collection, inasmuch as he would somehow

wear the character scientifically, ponderably, proveably—not just loosely and sociably. . . . She might find she had interested him even beyond her intention, find she was in fact launched in some current that would lose itself in the sea of science. (142–43)

Strett in fact *is* straight, as his name indicates, but Milly in her illness interprets this straightness merely as an impression, interpreting it in a romantic, "might find" way by invoking the possibility (but always predicated as existing in quite another world) of something in her physician akin to passion, a vital force by which she might be swept away "beyond her intention" and hence vivified.

In the last analysis, Milly, despite her wish for a friend, cannot go beyond her impressions to see Strett as a human being like herself; even when she looks him straight in the face, she sees not him but it, not a person but an object and a relation that is itself reified: "what it would show her would be what was good, what was best for her. She had established, in other words, in this time-saving way, a relation with it; and the relation was the special trophy that, for the hour, she bore off" (143).

Milly is to be disappointed in these hopes about Strett's ability to aid her, for rather than romantically showing her what is good for her, the doctor offers only the simple advice to live. In the moments immediately following her visit, the doctor's gnomic prescription briefly seems to have been efficacious. As Milly registers it, Strett has at least momentarily made a mixture of her consciousness—"a strange mixture that tasted at one and the same time of what she had lost and what had been given her. It was wonderful to her, while she took her random course, that these quantities felt so equal: she had been treated—hadn't she?—as if it were in her power to live; and yet one wasn't treated so—was one?—unless it had come up, quite as much, that one might die" (152). Yet Milly does not permit this Bichatian revelation to transform her consciousness, does not abandon romance in favor of life, does not come to a realistic recognition that her mortality is the ground of her significance as a person; rather, she directly falls back into the pathological activity of metaphorizing and romancing her own mortal condition:

The beauty of the bloom had gone from the small old sense of safety— that was distinct: she had left it behind her there for ever. But the beauty of the idea of a great adventure, a big dim experiment or struggle in which she might more responsibly than ever before take a hand, had been offered her instead. It was as if she had had to pluck off her breast, to throw away, some friendly ornament, a familiar flower, a little old jewel, that was part of her daily dress; and to take up and shoulder as a

substitute some queer defensive weapon, a musket, a spear, a battle-axe—
conducive possibly in a higher degree to a striking appearance, but de-
manding all the effort of the military posture. (152)

In conceiving of her condition in terms of an adventure, an experiment in appearances, Milly has already given in to the conditions of
romance. The crux of the matter is that Milly cannot accept Strett's
dictum that she can live if she wills to do so: "It was perhaps superfi-
cially more striking that one could live if one would; but it was more
appealing, insinuating, irresistible in short, that one would live if one
could" (156). To disobey doctor's orders by conceiving conditions as
being more determining than self-will is to continue romancing, and
Milly thus seals her fate.

Milly's peculiar pathos is that she fails to recognize that in turning
to romance she is denying her own real, the complexities and potential
freedoms inherent in her own medical determinism. Indeed, she mistakenly feels that in accepting the power death has over her she is
participating, at long last, in something real. To highlight this delusion, James has Milly, following her visit to Strett, enter the park to
observe the life around her. This kind of confrontation with the real
is familiar to us from *Middlemarch*, where Dorothea, similarly jolted
out of her romantic view of things, looks out her window at the "involuntary, palpitating life" in what I have earlier described as an invigo-
rating recognition of the real (see chapter five). We need to recall,
however, that Dorothea's revelation stems from her acknowledging
that the real consists of "the manifold wakings of men to labour and
endurance"—she sees "a man with a bundle on his back and a woman
carrying her baby; in the field she could see figures moving—perhaps
the shepherd with his dog."[25] Milly, in stark contrast, can see no such
figures, because she imagines no such necessary labor, no such expenditure of energy, in what *she* takes to be "the real thing":

> the real thing was to be quite away from the pompous roads, well within
> the centre and on the stretches of shabby grass. Here were benches and
> smutty sheep; here were idle lads at games of ball, with their cries mild in
> the thick air; here were wanderers anxious and tired like herself; here
> doubtless were hundreds of others just in the same box. Their box, their
> great common anxiety, what was it, in this grim breathing-space, but the
> practical question of life? They could live if they would; that is, like her-
> self, they had been told so: she saw them all about her, on seats, digesting
> the information, recognising it again as something in a slightly different
> shape familiar enough, the blessed old truth that they would live if they
> could. All she thus shared with them made her wish to sit in their com-
> pany. (153)

Milly refuses to answer "the practical question of life" practically and actively for herself, preferring the "idle" romantic answer that she is a dove and that life is a box. She flies away in the end, leaving only her wings—that is, the money and the letter in which she expresses her intention. This final act has been read as an example of what Conrad calls in James the "emergence from miracle, through an energetic act of renunciation."[26] This seems to me exactly the opposite of the case. Milly's act is the inevitable consequence, rather than the renunciation, of romancing—the ultimately romantic act. The specified is chased from this act just as it has been all along, not only by Milly, who substitutes her legacy for her embodied self, but also by Merton and Kate, who refuse to read the letter. The letter, if read, might perhaps have specified Milly's intention, making her romance real for Merton by providing him with "the turn she would have given her act." He recognizes, although too late, that this kind of specification, the turn of the subject, has been permanently lost, and it strikes him as what it in fact is: "the sacrifice of something sentient and throbbing, something that, for the spiritual ear, might have been audible as a faint far wail." Life itself has been sacrificed to romance.

The specified in *Wings of the Dove* finally comes to rest, as it must in the realistic novel, not in the character who dies, but in the physician who knows what death signifies, whose very domain of discourse is that of the sentient and throbbing body. Dr. Strett has no wings, but he has the real—"the truth about Milly" that Merton sees "perched on his shoulders." And it is the physician's "splendid economy" of medical knowledge rather than Milly's extravagant flightiness that James endorses, and that makes James, despite the near-total sublimation of the medicalized body in his prose, a realist in essence.

EPILOGUE

TOWARD A NEW HISTORICIST METHODOLOGY

A CENTRAL CONCERN of this book has been to show: first, how clinical medicine constitutes a certain systematic view of, and way of talking about, its object—the pathologically embodied person; and second, how, and with what consequences both for aesthetics and ideology, novelists imitate this medical praxis as they go about their work. My premise is that the disclaimers of scientific clinicians and literary realists notwithstanding, neither line of work is occupied with a simple act of transcription or prescription, and neither looks at reality with an innocent eye. Both diagnosis and description, prognosis and plotting, involve not only what Donald Fanger, speaking of Balzac, calls a "principled deformation of reality,"[1] but its principled *formation*. To see with a medical eye means invoking, however tacitly, a complicated system of techniques, conceptual configurations, presuppositions, and protocols of interpretation that enable one to take signs as symptoms and thereby to impose a particular order on reality. It is this discursive system of clinical pre-scriptions, and its deployment through medical and literary fields, that I have tried to elucidate. Beyond that, however, the results of the present detailed study of this particular literary/discursive nexus have a number of implications for the more general question of how one can situate literature in history.

The first is that the history relevant to literature includes the history of science, that the sciences are a cultural phenomenon providing part of the cultural basis for literature just as other kinds of intellectual activity do. This is not a very daring suggestion, to be sure. In thinking of medicine in particular as a culturally implicated rather than purely scientific practice, I am by no means alone. But the archaeological method I have used to analyze the cultural resonance of this practice distinguishes my book in several ways from other recent cultural studies focusing on medicine. These works include fascinating discussions of such medical topics as menstruation, the use of chloroform, the etiology of hysteria, and the symptomatology of degeneration, as well as critiques of the egregious bias against women enforced not only by particular medical men like Acton, Maudsley, or Weir Mitchell, but by the medical profession as a whole.[2] Above all, the criticism of these topics has emphasized medicine's participation in ideology, focusing attention on the operational presence within the medical context of gender, class, or racial oppositions—oppressive ideological differences that medical ideas reinforce or restabilize as pathologized stereotypes.[3] An archaeological analysis, on the other hand, although not denying the existence and salience of cultural axes such as male/female or white/black in medical thought, cuts through that thought in a different way. Archaeology seeks to identify in medical (or any other) discourse a set of cognitive assumptions that have their own consistency, a consistency irreducible to that of a stereotyping or scapegoating mechanism, and irreducible as well to the axes along which such mechanisms move.[4]

One way to reconcile archaeological and ideological methods would be to seek an axis of discrimination as pervasive as gender, race, or class, but peculiarly the province of archaeological criticism. In the archaeology of medicine, such an axis might be that of "pathology," because the production of medical statements does the work, above all, of differentiating the healthy from the sick. But the notion of an axis of oppositions, which seems appropriate for the ideological analysis of race, gender, and class, does not quite capture the way in which medical thought carves up conceptual space. Although pathology certainly entails a distinction between the normal and the abnormal, the rhetoric of pathology does not divide already given subjects from each other (separating black from white, men from women, bourgeois from proletariat) so much as it generates a profusion of pathologized persons within and across all these groups. To reduce pathology to difference (to paraphrase the title of Sander Gilman's important book on that topic) is to risk obscuring the complexity of this intellectual operation and the enormous dispersion of historically specific categories of self it yields. For example, one can certainly analyze hysteria in ideological terms as a misogynistic medical concept, as feminist critics as diverse as Cixous and Ehrenreich have done; but as I point out in my reading of *Madame Bovary*, hysteria may also be understood as a condition to which not only women but men as well are susceptible, and which signifies a more wide-ranging medicalization of the embodied person (and not only of the embodied woman) that is occurring both within Flaubert's novel and within his culture.[5] The particular medical discourse that defines the hystericized feminine body also brings into focus not only hysterics, but monomaniacs, cretins, club-footed men, and many other pathologized individuals; and this is accomplished not through a monolithic mechanism of repression (patriarchal, capitalist, racist, and so on) working along a single axis, but through a nuanced, multiply-directed variety of diagnostic, etiological, and nosological techniques.

These techniques, we have seen, are orchestrated and given consistency, translated into knowledge, by a medical rhetoric whose quasi-poetic quality we risk overlooking as well, if we focus merely on the stereotyping of race, class, and gender identities. That artistic capacity is perhaps more clearly displayed in medical statements less blunt or controversial than those that invite criticism from the sharpness of their stereotypes. Take for example the following textbook description, by a physician whom the medical historian M. Jeanne Peterson has argued was far more representative of Victorian medicine than Acton, Maudsley, Lallemand, or the other usual names mentioned by critics.[6] The physician is Sir James Paget; the description is that of a brain tumor:

> The material composing these cancers (when not disordered by the effects of haemorrhage, inflammation, or other disease) is a peculiar, soft, close-textured substance, having very little toughness, easily crushed and spread-out by compression with the fingers. It is very often truly brain-like, most like foetal brain, or like adult brain partially decomposed and crushed. Many specimens, however, are much softer than brain; and many, though of nearly the consistence of brain, are unlike it, being grumous, pulpy, shreddy, or spongy, like a placenta, with fine soft filaments. Very few have a distinct appearance of fibrous or other regular structure.
>
> In colour, the material may be white, but most commonly, when the cancer is fresh, it is light grey (like the greyness of the retina after death.) The tint is usually clear; it is in many cases suffused with pale pink or lilac, or with a deeper purple; and in nearly all, is variegated with effused blood and full blood-vessels, whose unequal abundance in different parts of the tumour produces a disorderly mottled appearance. Masses of bright yellow or ochrey substance also, like tubercle, are often found in or between the lobes, as if compressed by them, while withering and drying in the midst of their growth.
>
> When pressed or scraped, the soft medullary cancers yield abundant "cancer-juice," a milky or cream-like, or some other turbid, material, oozing or welling-up from their pressed mass. There is no better rough test for the diagnosis of medullary cancers than this is; and the substance thus yielded is generally diffusible in water, making it uniformly turbid, not floating in coarse shreds or fragments.[7]

Paget's description depends less on the gender, race, or class of the patient than on a semiology of symptomatic signs and a heuristics capable of moving from description to more or less certain assessment, both working within an overall narrative framework that enables Paget to place this description, a few pages later, within "the probable history, or, as I would call it, the life, of the morbid material in the blood, and in the tissues" (363). These elements, among others, restrict the range of what Paget finds significant and impose a terminology on his perception, so that one can recognize Paget's as medical language; yet the same elements also make possible an astonishingly concrete and subtle statement whose vocabulary exceeds in richness and semantic range even that of Zola's postmortem description of Nana at the end of that novel.

I have tried to uncover the implicit principles of pathological discourse that give Paget's and other clinicians' prose its distinctive quality. To do so has required disinterring long-obsolete medical textbooks and diagnostic manuals (where presuppositions elsewhere taken for granted may be more plainly exposed), as well as such standard works of nineteenth-century medical philosophy as Bichat's *Physiological Researches on Life and Death* and Cabanis's *On the Degree of Certitude in Medicine*. The methodological point to be stressed here, however, is that medicine's discursive presuppositions, like those of any discourse, cannot be dissociated from its language. But language here must be construed to include Paget's writing as well as Acton's or Maudsley's or Krafft-Ebing's. Medical presuppositions may be signaled by the straightforward, lugubrious use of a terminology or by the stereotypes (of the hysteric, or the consumptive, or the homosexual, for instance) that such terminology may encourage. But on the other hand, such presuppositions may lurk in a far from obviously "medical" detail or qualification, in the tacit sense implied by the choice of an adjective or metaphor, in Paget's need (and ability) to specify the tint and texture of his tumor. In fact, the excessive obviousness of stereotyping may obscure the more fundamental and dominant presuppositions at work in a discourse.

Because of its complexity, any effort to interpret the way medical discourse works in fiction will involve something different from identifying the conventional thematics of an illness or the moral meaning of a character's affliction. Defining a character as *normal* already implies a pathologist's perspective. One thus must take account of the presence of medical terminology in a text—whether or not such language refers to a character. But taking account means not merely noting that literary language amalgamates medical jargon among a plurality of others in benign dialogism; it means, rather, addressing several difficult questions concerning the use of this jargon. What particular segment of medical language is being incorporated into the novel? Is the appropriation sporadic and superficial, focused perhaps on a single character or situation, or used as only one analogical framework among many? Or is the vocabulary used in a regular and systematic way, invoked in detail for a range of characters or situations? And how wide is this range? What other terminologies can be said to abut or obstruct medical terminology, determining its range of applicability? Does the novel contain a set of terms betraying an underlying conceptual framework within which, say, Rosamond's hysteria in *Middlemarch* might be related to Casaubon's fatty degeneration of the heart? Or does the novelist appropriate the terminology of one disease in detail while referring to another disease in the way a layperson might? How dense is the semantic web woven by medical terms in any one instance? It is one thing for a novelist to describe a character as hysterical; it is another to invoke, as Flaubert does, an array of diagnostically precise symptoms such as gagging, vertigo, and syncope. One may suspect that the language in the latter case is what might be called "discursively functional": that is, meaningful in a way that requires some understanding of medicine's cognitive presuppositions.[8]

Beyond explicit terminological reference, however, medical discourse may structure a novel in a number of other more important ways. It may help shape a novel's causal structure by providing an etiological framework for understanding causes, even where pathogenic features are not explicitly marked (as with the bad air that swirls through so many of Dickens's novels). It may help shape a novel's mode of characterization by providing a model for the internal structure of the individual (a fine network of tissues in Flaubert; a consensus of sensibilities in Eliot and James; or a bundle of nerves in Collins). Finally, it may help determine which everyday details a novelist includes in his or her descriptions, by according a certain diagnostic status to detailed observation. Just as categories of gender can, as Eve Sedgwick puts it, "have a structuring force for axes of cultural discrimination whose thematic subject isn't explicitly gendered at all," operating even in something as innocuous as the description of a landscape, so categories of pathology can operate in a text even where neither doctors nor patients nor medical terms are centrally present.[9]

The shape of a commitment to medical categories differs, to be sure, from one novelist to another, so that there is no single answer to these questions. Balzac, we have seen, relies on a different medical paradigm—both a different, although overlapping, terminology and a distinct set of concepts—from that invoked by Flaubert and Eliot. The latter novelists in turn differ markedly in the ways they choose to incorporate the medical viewpoint in their novels: where Flaubert reserves it almost exclusively for himself as narrator, Eliot shares it with one of her characters. To take such variations as a sign that medical discourse is irrelevant to what makes realism realism would not only be wrong, but would miss the point of archaeological analysis, which is to permit one to account for differences within a genre without reducing such differences to an essential identity. In this particular case, the shifting literary status and function of medical discourse can help one to discover fresh nuances in individual writers, within the identifiably common project of realism.

In this work, I have treated medicine almost as a species of literature, and certainly as an art, a set of techniques that the doctor uses to represent illness. To reduce medicine in this way to a solely interpretive or artistic activity, however, would oversimplify matters as much as if one were to go to the other extreme and ignore altogether the aesthetic qualities of the medical experience. For if medicine is literature, an art for knowledge's sake, it is a literature far more obviously embedded in history than most. Clinicians in practicing medicine diagnose and treat not simply diseases but patients; more generally, they work within a social and not merely intellectual field. I have therefore felt compelled to discuss medicine not only as a pure art aimed at representing an object of knowledge, at bringing disease into discourse, but also—like every discourse (and this is the methodologically significant point)—as a socially potent attempt to grasp, shape, and ultimately control a relationship among human beings, an act involving both authority and a special kind of power. Any historicist interpretation of medical discourse in the novel must confront not only the poetic but also the political aspect of the medical art: the issue of what makes us follow the doctor's orders.

Medical authority is an extremely complex subject, all the more so because, unlike some other forms of social power (patriarchal, political, religious, or ideological authority, for example), the physician's dominance is tied directly to an intellectual, putatively rational practice that makes it seem uncontestable, less an act of coercion than simply what needs to be done. I found it useful, as a first step, to differentiate two dimensions in which medical authority is both exercised and contested.

The first might be called an epistemic dimension, wherein medicine demands to be thought of as a discrete science (rather than an art made up of interpretive techniques). I do not presume that medicine either is, or is not, "really" a science; that is a question for philosophers of science to ponder. Instead, I examine how medicine defines itself as a pursuit of truth, an epistemological imperative, in a way that (it hopes) at once legitimates it *as* science and marks it off as a unique science, distinct from others. Medicine's most basic distinguishing feature as a form of knowledge, as Georges Canguilhem has pointed out, is its insistence that one can make true statements (or alternatively, statements that can be falsified) about what is normal and what pathological.[10] Clinical medicine, in turn, can be specified by its additional prerequisite that the normal and the pathological be understood as conditions of the body as *organism* (rather than, say, as mechanism or structure). What Flaubert calls "le coup d'oeuil medical de la vie,"[11] the medical view of life, would include, under this rubric, not merely doctors, but also poets, novelists, philosophers, and political theorists—in short, anyone who has accepted the normal/pathological distinction and the principle of "organization" as the starting point for elaborate theories, narratives, social prescriptions, and cultural programs directed toward the body individual or politic. This definition of doctoring can accommodate Sir Thomas Browne and Georg Lukács, Max Nordau and Emile Zola, Florence Nightingale and Elizabeth Gaskell, as well as medical practitioners in the narrower sense.[12] The normal/pathological axis authorizes a capacity for intervention eagerly asserted and exerted by many in the larger culture.

As Lydgate's fate in *Middlemarch* indicates, however, such epistemic prestige cannot be simply taken for granted. Neither total nor necessarily even stable, it is only as secure as the distinction between normal and pathological that enables it. Insofar as this distinction is blurred, challenged, or ignored, medicine's status as a science—as a discourse capable of yielding truth—becomes questionable, and the authority of the medical wanes. To examine the epistemic dimension of medicine thus means to uncover an historical field of struggle where medical authority defends itself against what Edward Said, in a different context, has called molestation.[13]

The word *molestation*—unlike, say, *oppression* or *subversion*—registers two important differences between the epistemic politics associated with pathology and the ideological politics associated with race, gender, or class. First, the struggle in the politics of knowledge is not about overturning or liberating so much as it is about bothering and displacing one form of authority with another. Second, the direction from which quarrels will erupt and struggles will be waged is not given in advance. Thus the distinction between health and sickness may come under attack from nonscientists, particularly when doctors seek to extend their purview to include social relationships other than the doctor-patient one and thereby trespass on the turf of other social authorities. When nineteenth-century physicians push for the establishment of specializations in such fields as "legal" and "political" medicine, for example, they meet with stiff resistance—not from the "deviants" whom they wish to medicalize, but from those who find it more appropriate or advantageous to perceive deviants as criminals rather than as patients, deviancy as an offense rather than as a social pathology. In this view an individual would be an adulteress or sinner rather than an hysteric, a thief rather than a monomaniac. In our own time, a similar battle is being fought around the AIDS epidemic. Civil libertarians and homophobes, as well as those labeled as diseased, each seek to challenge the prerogative of public health officials to deal with the disease according to medical criteria. Through the negotiations, compromises, and alliances that follow from such extramural conflicts between medical and nonscientific authorities, limits are set to the normal/pathological distinction's validity, and hence to the range of medicine's epistemic force.

From *within* the domain of the sciences, on the other hand, clinical medicine's authority also is molested during the period considered in *Vital Signs*, through challenges to the pertinency of the very ideas that permitted physicians of the time to define their work as scientific. Cytology and experimental physiology subvert the medical notion that the body can be understood as an organic confederation of tissues; embryology and evolutionary theory call into question the stability of norms; Virchow and Pasteur, with their postulates that it is the cell that becomes sick and the germ that transmits disease, undermine the truth-value of a pathology of tissues. As these new sciences rise to prominence in the latter half of the nineteenth century, the scientific authority of clinical medicine declines concomitantly, with measurable consequences, I have argued, for the authority of the realistic imagination.

The authority enjoyed by clinicians in their heyday, however, goes beyond that countenanced in the truth they advocate about matters of life and death. Here I refer to a second dimension of medical authority, an authority not epistemic but ideological—or more precisely, professional. Beginning roughly at the time of the French Revolution, clinical medicine increasingly stands out during the Victorian period as a centrally important social activity, insofar as it comes to represent—more unabashedly than almost any other form of work—the values of the rapidly rising professional class. As one of the first and most spectacularly successful instances of a modern occupation winning its way to professional status and social prestige, clinical medicine cannot be analyzed only as an art, nor as an orientation toward questions of truth, a would-be science competing with other sciences for authority. It also must be considered as a form of social activism: an ethos or self-image designed to help establish and sustain the clinician in a position of cultural and economic authority. I have found it useful to employ M. S. Larson's notion of a professional project to identify this mobilizing and legitimacy-seeking aspect of medical practice.[14] Without examining medicine as a project one cannot possibly understand the peculiar blending of scientific paradigms with political, philosophical and imaginative initiatives so characteristic of the golden age of the clinic (a period roughly corresponding to the heyday of the realistic novel).

This is not to say, of course, that a doctor's desire for what Andrew Abbott calls "jurisdiction"[15] unilaterally determines the concepts and measures of treatment he promotes, or that the idea of an organic norm merely serves as a cover for some sort of conspiracy to improve the social standing of doctors. The relationship between knowledge and human interests, in medicine at least, is not one of superstructure simply reinforcing a social base. In fact, a physician's interests typically will be directed not only toward personal or class advancement, but also toward increasing the store of medical knowledge on one hand, and defending medicine's scientific truth on the other. Medicine's will to power is not identical to its will to truth—which in turn is irreducible to its will to knowledge. Each of these three aspects of medical practice—ideological, epistemic, and discursive—has its own complexities, which an effective historical analysis should respect.

The broader methodological point here is that medical practice is no different in essence from other social practices: they too must exhibit ideological, epistemic, and discursive characteristics. The ideologies they promote in their practitioners may be feudal or bureaucratic rather than professional; the truth they try to tell may be transcendental or commonsensical or logical rather than pathological or even scientific; the discursive assumptions they rely upon may take signs as symbols or data or wonders rather than symptoms. And of course social practices can also be understood in many other ways: with reference to class conformation, gender differentiation, mode of production, functional utility, the general economy of power. The special claim of archaeology is not to somehow trump these other approaches but to open up problematics—about the nature of authority, the politics of truth, the presuppositions of statements—that other historical methods evade.

As I have indicated, professionalism is, like scientificity, a mode of authority. The term *authority*, in turn, suggests an analogy between medical and literary empowerment, an analogy that complements the one drawn in this book between the arts of medicine and fiction. If medicine does in fact provide such authors as Balzac, Flaubert, and Conan Doyle with a clinical point of view, a model for mimesis, it also provides the same writers with a model (or several possible models depending on the historical fortunes of medicine) of scientific and professional authority. There is little doubt that such models were required, given the strong, sometimes even hyperbolic, claims (implicit as well as overt) that realism makes for its truth-value and literary status. From Balzac's feverish sales pitch claim that "All is true!" in *Père Goriot*, to Flaubert's prophecy that science and literature would eventually merge, to Eliot's self-confident and ironic definition of (bad) authorship as "a vocation which is understood to turn foolish thinking into funds," the author's authority and its need to be grounded in a socially legitimated form of rationality are a constant concern.[16] The claims realists make about the truthfulness and social utility of their genre are of the same ilk as those raised by doctors, and the similarity has encouraged me to try, in *Vital Signs*, to plumb the depths of this analogy.

But some daunting methodological stumbling blocks lay in the way of ascribing any such epistemic and ethical characteristics to literature. The critical task involved in identifying a literary point of view or technique as somehow medical was relatively straightforward, at least in principle: one correlated specific elements of medical and fictional practices (for instance, the etiological assumptions made by Bichat with the causal assumptions about character development made by Flaubert). How literary *authority* could be shown to take on a medical cast, on the other hand, was far from obvious. Such authority cannot be identified from the sorts of statements mentioned in the previous paragraphs, which tell us only to which authority the realists aspired, not the authority conveyed by their texts. How, then, can one establish an epistemic orientation and an ideological intention in the work of a writer, without falling into biographical criticism with its attendant dangers? To what literary structures, what levels of narrative or elements of fiction do these dimensions of authority pertain?

To address these issues, I had to recognize that unlike medical technique and in common with all other forms of social authority, medical authority has an irreducibly oppositional and competitive aspect that it tries to mask. Given the vexed condition of medical authority, those elements of fiction most likely to register this molested authority will be those that themselves negotiate oppositions. I am thinking in particular of narrative, which modern literary theorists have taken to be reducible to a structural process devoted to organizing and mediating between sets of oppositions. Put more simply, the idea is that plot arises as an effort to resolve (or at least to manage) what would otherwise survive as an unbearable, unthinkable antinomy or contradiction—whether between characters, social types, moral categories, class aspirations, or even "ideologemes."[17]

With this schema, I could begin to sketch out the ways in which medical authority manifests itself in literature at the level of plot-generating oppositions. In the case of epistemic authority, the narrative possibilities were particularly rich. A novelist might, for example, identify the challenge to doctors from without by other purveyors of truth (lawyers, priests, or simply the unenlightened) as the problem he or she wished to write about, the subject of his narrative. The plot then would deal with a reform-minded physician—Lydgate in Eliot's *Middlemarch*, Benassis in Balzac's *A Country Doctor*, Wycherley in Reade's *Hard Cash*—struggling against stupidity, venality, and backwardness to establish his truth. Medical authority in this instance functions as an explicit theme taken up by the novelist, a theme projecting an allegory not of a disavowed power but of the novelist's own sense of authority—utopian in Balzac, tempered in Eliot, socially militant in Reade.

But even without a physician-character typifying medical authority, some narratives still can stake a claim to such authority. Insofar as a narrative is realistic, it necessarily presumes some truthfulness (and therefore some authority) not only in what it represents but in the view it takes of what it represents. To ground this truthfulness, the realist must be committed not to some general notion of truth or common sense, but to some particular epistemic trope: the normal/pathological opposition of medicine; or the juridical distinction between innocence and criminality; or the contractual distinction between marriage and adultery; or the journalistic distinction between fact and fiction.[18] Each of these is a "constituent model" for its discourse.[19] For our purposes, however, what is of interest is that each model implies certain narrative possibilities, presupposes that certain consequences will follow from a given situation, functions in short as a principle of narration.[20] Thus, for example, a narrative structured according to the constituent model of contract and transgression—as in the classical novel of adultery analyzed by Tony Tanner—will confirm the truth of that model by showing how the transgressor is ineluctably punished. For medicine, where the governing epistemological framework is that of organic norm and pathological deviation, the corresponding narrative construal can take two forms: either an explicit contrast between healthy and sick characters (or communities, as in *The Country Doctor*), or a case study of a single character who is predicated as ill. In either case, however, the novelist circumscribes the sphere of actions, making all experiences subject to the grounding experiences of health, illness, and death. The novelist's authority, in turn, depends upon the hegemony of his or her epistemic model—upon our willingness to accept this range of possibilities, this sphere of actions, as in some way more true to life, more authoritatively realistic, than any other way of imagining the real (for instance, as an experience of manners, of desire, or of language).

These are two general ways, then, to locate literary authority: in thematizations of the struggle for the truth, and in the narrative possibilities the author chooses to realize. But if authority never escapes molestation, then, as Said has suggested, molestation must also accompany any literary effort to establish the authority of the real. As pointed out above, when epistemic authority is projected as a theme—that is, a hero or heroine fighting to establish a truth also subscribed to by the novelist—the harassment, refusal, co-optation, or even destruction of such "figures of capable imagination" (to borrow Emerson's phrase) must be part of the story. But a deeper vulnerability must attach to these heroes, as to the novelist who imagines them: the chance that such figures, and the novelist as well, might be incapable of gaining a reader's assent to their would-be authority. The struggles of a Lydgate or Doctor Pascal are agonistic, and a kind of melodrama of truth is played out in such instances.

When a writer's epistemic authority takes shape not as theme but through the choice of a narrative-generating epistemic trope, showing how such authority could be challenged or opposed within the novel is a bit trickier. It is difficult to imagine how the authority of a plot could be traduced or molested. But a novel may consist of more than one plot; moreover, even a single plot may be viewed in more than one way, with each view granted a certain authority. *Middlemarch*, as we have seen, offers at least three discrete kinds of plot, only one of which is organized along normal/pathological lines, while *Madame Bovary* consists of a single plot readable as the story either of a sick woman or of an adulteress. Several different kinds of truth, even several different realities, may thus coexist within a single fiction in conditions of adjacency, imbrication, or even outright hostility between or within narrative strands. Bakhtin was the first to point out and study the presence of competing discourses, heteroglossia, in the novel, and one could probably do worse than to borrow from his terminology to describe *Middlemarch* as an example of "discursive divergence" and *Madame Bovary* as a case of "discursive subordination." Bakhtin himself, unfortunately, was hamstrung by his extreme polemical hostility toward realism, dismissing it rather abruptly, and not very usefully, as a monologic form dominated by a single authoritative, even authoritarian, discourse. Consequently, he never really investigated the anxieties of authority that haunt realist fiction's claims to truth, and which *Vital Signs* has traced in some detail.[21]

But what of that other dimension of authority, the ideological dimension where what is at stake is not the truth claimed by an author but the ideals and values he or she projects through and beyond this claim? For clinical medicine, such ideals and values amounted to something like an ethos of professionalism. The methodological problem, then, was to determine whether realism projects a professional ethos of its own, and if so, where this ethos manifests itself in the novel.

An ethos is first and foremost a conception of the active, practical good, a notion of what orients, inspires, or shapes a person's attitude toward work, giving him or her "character." Not surprisingly, then, professionalism will often be represented fictionally in a particular character who embodies or aspires to the professional ideal. Such a hero appears not only as one who seeks the truth, but as one who acts as an agent of the truth, turning objectivity and disinterestedness to the passionate pursuit of the good as he or she sees it. An accurate sense of the truth is of course a necessary precondition—one could not take seriously a would-be professional hero who was a dilettante (like Frédéric Moreau in *Sentimental Education*) or a neophyte (like Lucien de Rubempré in *Lost Illusions*)—but the professional vocation and its vicissitudes have a narrative valence distinct from that of the struggle for epistemic authority.

The professional hero, to be sure, need not be a doctor: Dickens's inventor, Daniel Doyce, and Eliot's managing agent, Caleb Garth, come to mind as nonmedical professional heroes. But the tangentiality of these figures, and the predominance of doctors in such roles, reflects the degree to which professionalism in the nineteenth century finds its archetype in clinical medicine. To say this, however, is only to point to one prominent source of the raw material—the ethos—that a novelist appropriates from his or her culture, not to describe how that ethos is worked into a story. The doctor's vocation may be given quasi-religious status (as in Balzac) or function as a quieter ideal (as with Woodcourt in *Bleak House*); alternatively, and more interesting, the novelist may emplot vocation so as to evaluate its legitimacy. What seems to be a genuine calling may be simply an ideological, self-serving veneer, unworthy of the authority it claims. A number of realist novels thus consist at least in part in a sort of trial-by-fire in which a physician finds his or her vocational impulse tested. The fate of that impulse—its discrediting or confirmation, its degradation to a mere work ethic or its elevation to special moral status and authority—registers each author's sense of the cultural potency of medicine.

The author, however, may well have a vocational impulse and a desire for professional authority in his or her own right, a will to professional power distinct from (although articulated in relation to) the aspirations of the professional hero represented in the author's novels. This impulse can cause a novelist to apotheosize professionalism as an ideal against which various characters are found more or less wanting. Or it can lead a novelist to use certain literary procedures—showing rather than telling, omniscient narration, irony of a specific sort—in the belief that they mark literature as a profession rather than, say, a craft or a spontaneous overflow of powerful feelings. To some extent, these intentions and expectations are broached within the novels themselves, in self-reflexive narratorial commentary. But authors conceptualize their missions far more often in correspondence, notebooks, and critical essays—places where they can tell not only what they are trying to show in their fiction but also why they are trying to show it. I have not shrunk from violating the taboo against biographical criticism by looking closely at these materials to gain a better sense, not of the meaning of the novels in themselves, but of the aims that are included within and projected through the novels.

Those aims, to be sure, need not be articulated as a calling, nor need they be professional aims. Moreover, even where a writer sets him- or herself up as a professional, one has to carefully specify the ideological parameters of this notion of professionalism. Trollope and Bennett, for instance, seem to derive their sense of themselves as "professional writers" from white-collar workers: their sense of labor and mission is far more regularized and muted than that of Balzac or Flaubert, for whom writing, in differing ways, constitutes a form of social activism. The guiding ethos of realistic novelists, I have tried to show, is a peculiarly medical professionalism, in which the labor of writing is thought of as both transcending the cash nexus and doing a good that is therapeutic.

Medical authority (like that of any social practice) thus can be both manifest and latent in fiction, present as subject or as authorial intention. But this double inscription in turn raises a further methodological problem: how can the authority claimed by a realist be correlated with the authority represented in the novelist's fiction? If there are complex relations between discourses in the novel, as Bakhtin has suggested, equally complex (and for the most part untheorized) relations obtain between the discourse of the novelist and discourses in the novel.[22] One can imagine, for instance, a novelist who asserts the evaluative power of the opposition between sickness and health (and the professional authority that goes along with this power) without ever introducing a doctor into his or her story as a major figure; *Little Dorrit* or *Hard Times* or *Shirley* include few or no physicians, yet the sickness in these novels, and the utopian valorizing of the sickroom and nursing as responses to the painful real, imply a medical attitude toward social problems. One might describe medicine here as a "discursive latency" within the literary text. In a more insidious version of this, a writer might introduce into his or her novel a doctor who knows nothing (Charles Bovary in *Madame Bovary*) or at least nothing worth knowing (as with the merely clever and cruel Dr. Sloper in *Washington*

Square). In such cases, the physician seems to negate medical claims to epistemic or moral authority, but in fact is set up as a kind of impotent antitype against which the realist's own quasi-medical power can be measured. This chiasmatic distribution of authority corresponds to what I have called "discursive sublation."

The labels we attach to these phenomena, however, are of less interest than the linkage they suggest between the representation of authority in the novel and the representation of authority through the novel. For the most part, this linkage is in fact remarkably overt. When physicians do appear in realistic and quasi-realistic novels, they tend to act as surrogates for the novelist. Balzac's Benassis and Bianchon, Eliot's Lydgate, James's Sir Luke Strett, Flaubert's Larivière, Conan Doyle's Watson, Zola's Pascal, all share to a greater or lesser extent the same vision and values as their creators. The vicissitudes, strengths, triumphs, and failures of these characters as social authorities thus can be understood as versions of these authors' own struggles for authority.

The ultimate methodological question, of course, is how to conceptualize medicine's coherence as a single overall practice, an effective totality combining intellectual operations, ideas, and ideals. There should be no illusion about the contingency of any such fused medical totality. Clinical medicine did not exist in the eighteenth century and no longer exists today in the nineteenth-century sense. Doctors no longer perceive disease through the grid of a tissue-based symptomatology; they no longer recognize the pathological as a function of the organized body so much as of cells; they less and less embody the virtues and authority of professionalism. But even within the relatively restricted period under consideration, medical practice is far from monolithic. At different moments within different national cultures, its profile varies. In Balzac's France, as we have seen, doctors stress their professional authority, while in Flaubert's they exploit and elaborate medical techniques confidently and without much fanfare, and in Eliot's England they defend medicine's scientificity against onslaughts.

Why bother to point out such nuances of a social practice in a book whose main concern is with literature rather than with sociology or history? One reason is that historical accuracy and specification are values in themselves. Another is that these disparate emphases help one to begin to elaborate something that has been sorely lacking within new historicist work on the novel: a methodology capable of explaining what causes a writer to appropriate the discourses he or she does. Rather than merely noting homologies between a social and a literary practice, or "swerving" insouciantly between literary and cultural phenomena, one can begin to see social practices as offering various transient strategic possibilities that novelists exploit.[23] Adopting a particular medical paradigm available in France only during the 1820s and 1830s, I have argued, enables Balzac to assert his professional authority more forcefully, while for Flaubert writing clinically means both imitating and demonstrating the immense technical powers inherent in the art of diagnosis. For Eliot, writing at a third moment and in a different national milieu, the vulnerability of medical science permits her to worry over the equally vulnerable epistemological authority of her own fiction.

All three realists, on the other hand, take their medicine whole, so that there is the tightest possible connection between, say, Flaubert's stylistic reliance on Bichat's clinical methods of diagnosis and his strictly impersonal, epistemologically untroubled authority. Similarly, Eliot's doubts about the capacity for truth of that same Bichatian paradigm correspond to her doubts about the authority of professional vocation—doubts that she shared with many doctors in England during the 1860s. But this extraordinarily deep homology does not mean that literary and medical practice are identical. Obviously, novels are not case studies, and it is precisely the richness and variety of discourses within the novel, its exorbitant inclusiveness of points of view, that one ought to protect against reductivism. As I have stressed, the competition between medical and other discourses is an essential feature of realism. But that competition should not be hypostasized in turn as an Auerbachian mixing of styles or Bakhtinian dialogism. It stems from the novelist's alignment with one or another discourse, a choice that determines the horizon and geography of discourses within the novel. In the case of novels and novelists most associated with realism—Balzac, Flaubert, Eliot, James—the determining, structurally generative discourse seems, again and again, to be medical.[24]

Paradoxically, then, focusing attention upon a single discourse in a novel, far from impoverishing the literary work, actually enables one to account for the particular nature of its richness. And this methodological dictum is true not only of individual novels but of the genre they articulate. From an archaeological viewpoint, the critical realism associated with Balzac, Flaubert, Eliot, and James appears not as a loose baggy monster of a category, but as a tightly knit literary-historical phenomenon, a weaving and reweaving of the same discursive texture. What is more, the warps and knots within this textured literary history—the twisting of realism into such pararealistic forms as detective fiction, sensation fiction, and naturalism; the more radical transformation of realism into modernism—also appear more clearly. Archaeology permits us to draw sharper generic distinctions because change is understood not linearly (as the abandonment of "represen-tational" for "language-conscious" fiction, or a switch from "objective" to "subjective" writing) but genealogically, as the eroding or displacing of one mode of authority by others and the consequent redistribution of discourses. Thus, rather than an abrupt shift from realism to mod-ernism, or realism to naturalism—if, like Lukács, one draws the line there—one marks a series of displacements in the (still functional) medical point of view, each shift accounting for the emergence of a distinct pararealistic form. Modernism, in turn, can be understood as a literary practice that rigorously inverts the medical premises be-queathed by the realistic novel. The particulars here are, however, less important than the methodological advantage they are intended to illustrate for making better sense of the understructured field of liter-ary history.

NOTES

PREFACE

1. D. A. Miller, *The Novel and the Police* (Berkeley and Los Angeles: University of California Press, 1988), 2.

2. As Theodore Zeldin points out, the French medical profession's "rise to power in the state is one of the striking features of the [nineteenth] century" (*France, 1848–1945, vol. 1: Ambition, Love, and Politics* [Oxford: Clarendon Press, 1973], 22). On the history of the professionalization of medicine in nineteenth-century France, see Michel Foucault, *Naissance de la clinique* (Paris: Presses universitaires de France, 1963; English translation as *The Birth of the Clinic* [New York: Vintage, 1975]); Jacques Léonard, *La Médecine entre les pouvoirs et les savoirs* (Paris: Aubier-Montaigne, 1981); Matthew Ramsey, *Professional and Popular Medicine in France, 1770–1830* (Cambridge: Cambridge University Press, 1988); and Jan Goldstein, *Console and Classify* (Cambridge: Cambridge University Press, 1987). On English medicine as an emergent profession during the nineteenth century, see M. Jeanne Peterson, *The Medical Profession in Mid-Victorian London* (Berkeley and Los Angeles: University of California Press, 1978), and Ivan Waddington, *The Medical Profession in the Industrial Revolution* (Dublin: Gill and Macmillan, 1984). For a sociological account synthesizing the French and English experiences, see M. S. Larson, *The Rise of Professionalism* (Berkeley and Los Angeles: University of California Press, 1977), chaps. 9 and 10.

3. I am not suggesting, however, that the history of the novel either reduces to or merely reflects the history of medicine as a profession. The reversing of expected chronological order in my treating Flaubert before Balzac is intended to emphasize that the connections between medicine and realism are epistemological and discursive in a way that is irreducible to (although bound up in) the dynamics of professionalization.

4. Cf. Richard Shryock, "American Indifference to Basic Science during the Nineteenth Century," *Archives Internationales d'Histoire des Sciences* 28, no. 5 (1948–1949): 3–18; reprinted in B. Barber and W. Wirsch, eds., *The Sociology of Science* (New York: Free Press, 1962), 98–110.

CHAPTER ONE

1. Choderlos de Laclos, *Les Liaisons Dangereuses*, trans. Richard Aldington (New York: Signet, 1962), 380.

2. On the idea of the outside, see Gilles Deleuze, *Foucault* (Minneapolis: University of Minnesota Press, 1988), 70–93.

3. The reliance on gout as a literary disease in eighteenth-century fiction (as opposed to tuberculosis in nineteenth-century fiction and cancer in modernism) exemplifies this emphasis on disease as an ongoing condition of being rather than a confrontation with mortality. Cf. Susan Sontag, *Illness as Meta-*

phor (New York: Farrar, Straus and Giroux, 1978); Lawrence Rothfield, "Gout as Metaphor," in *Art, History, and Antiquity of Rheumatic Diseases* (Brussels: Elsevier and The Erasmus Foundation, 1987): 68–71.

4. René Girard, *Deceit, Desire and the Novel*, trans. Yvonne Frecerro (Baltimore, Md.: Johns Hopkins University Press, 1965), 149. On the relation between the temporalities of disease and fiction, see Joel Fineman, "The History of the Anecdote," in H. Aram Veeser, ed., *The New Historicism* (New York: Routledge, 1989), 49–76.

5. Ian Watt, *The Rise of the Novel* (Berkeley and Los Angeles: University of California Press, 1977), 32–35.

6. Georg Lukács, *The Historical Novel*, trans. Hannah Mitchell and Stanley Mitchell (Lincoln: University of Nebraska Press, 1983), 19.

7. Harry Levin, *The Gates of Horn* (New York: Oxford University Press, 1963), 3.

8. Emile Zola, *Nana*, trans. George Holden (New York: Penguin, 1972), 470.

9. For a brilliant discussion of this shift from what Foucault calls the "episteme" of the eighteenth century to that of the nineteenth century, see his *The Order of Things* (New York: Pantheon, 1970); for Kant's conception of the role of science, see Ernst Cassirer, *The Problem of Knowledge*, trans. William Woglom and Charles Hendel (New Haven, Conn.: Yale University Press, 1950), chap. 1. In his later work, Foucault redefines the shift in question as involving not only intellectual discourses but systems of power/knowledge. More specifically, he argues that a juridically defined social framework gives way to a modern order in which extralegal discourses supersede the mechanisms of the law, with the "contractual" subject giving way to the "normalized" (or conversely, pathologized) subject defined by the sciences of man—sciences dominated in the first half of the nineteenth century, I would argue, by clinical medicine. Foucault himself makes the argument that the rise of the novel correlates with the rise of legal power. See "The Life of Infamous Men," in *Michel Foucault: Power, Truth, Strategy*, ed. M. Morris and P. Patton (Sydney: Feral, 1979), 76–91. For readings of eighteenth-century fiction as bound to a juridical model of truth, see John Bender, *Imagining the Penitentiary* (Chicago: University of Chicago Press, 1987); and John Zomchick, *The Public Conscience in the Private Sphere* (Cambridge: Cambridge University Press, forthcoming).

10. On Collins's appropriation of an extraordinarily diverse range of psychological ideas and the formal effects of deploying these ideas in his fiction, see Jenny Bourne Taylor, *In the Secret Theatre of Home* (London: Routledge, 1988).

11. According to Hans Eichner, nineteenth-century romantic philosophy had very little impact on the so-called "hard" sciences: "The real scientists of the last two hundred years—those who, with their helpmates the engineers, created the world we now live in—took no notice of Romantic theory and carried on in the spirit of Copernicus, Harvey, Newton, and even La Mettrie." Cf. "The Rise of Modern Science and the Genesis of Romanticism," *PMLA* 97, no. 1 (January 1982): 8–30. Although Eichner's notion of the historicity of science is imprecise, and he does not differentiate between various kinds of

science, he does recognize the relative autonomy of scientific from philosophical discourse during the period that concerns us.

12. Cf. Michel Foucault, *L'Archéologie du savoir* (Paris: Gallimard, 1969), 157; English translation as *The Archaeology of Knowledge*, trans. A. M. Sheridan Smith (New York: Pantheon, 1972).

13. On the correlation of modernist and postmodernist textual practices with twentieth-century physics, see N. Katherine Hayles, *The Cosmic Web* (Ithaca, N.Y.: Cornell University Press, 1985).

14. Immanuel Kant, *Critique of Judgment*, trans. J. H. Bernard (New York: Macmillan, 1974), 210, par. 62.

15. Today, of course, medicine and a number of other "dubious" sciences operate within paradigms that are tied much more directly to the formalized sciences—in medicine's case, to chemistry and its offspring, biochemistry. This, along with continuing specialization, has made the dubious sciences increasingly less permeable to ordinary language. One nonetheless remains more likely to understand what a doctor is talking about than what a physicist is, not only because the very urgent reality dealt with by the doctor is also phenomenologically one's own, but also because the mass media in our morbid society continuously disseminate the new medical vocabulary through which medicine grasps and articulates that reality.

16. This encrustedness of the positive sciences, and their distinctiveness from formalized sciences, is evident at the level of individual practitioners as well as of fields: a "quack" doctor or economist is possible in a way that a "quack" mathematician is not.

17. Aristotle, *Politics* 8.7.41342a5–23.

18. Emile Zola, "The Experimental Novel," in *The Experimental Novel and Other Essays*, trans. Belle M. Sherman (New York: Haskell House, 1963), 3.

CHAPTER TWO

1. "Flaubert's Presuppositions," *Diacritics* 11, no. 4 (Winter 1981): 2–11.

2. Jonathan Culler, "Presupposition and Intertextuality," *Modern Language Notes* 91, no. 6 (1976): 1380–96.

3. Charles Baudelaire,"*Madame Bovary*, by Gustave Flaubert," excerpted in the fine English translation of *Madame Bovary* by Paul de Man (New York: Norton, 1965), 339. All future translated quotations from *Madame Bovary* in this chapter are from the Norton edition. All other translations are my own, except where noted.

4. Cf. Michel Riffaterre, *La Production du texte* (Paris: Seuil, 1979).

5. Cf. Foucault, *L'Archéologie du savoir* for Foucault's most extensive theoretical discussion of the concept of "discourse"; for Foucault's analysis of nineteenth-century medical discourse, cf. *Naissance de la clinique* and *Les machines à guérir* (Paris: Institut de l'Environment, 1976). I have also found the following works very useful for gaining an overview of the intellectual and institutional structure of nineteenth-century medicine: Ernest Ackerknecht, "Medical Education in Nineteenth-century France," *The Journal of Medical Education* 1 (1957): 15–18; Ackerknecht, *Medicine at the Paris Hospital, 1794–1848* (Balti-

more, Md.: Johns Hopkins University Press, 1967); Larson, *The Rise of Professionalism*, chap. 3; Peterson, *The Medical Profession in Mid-Victorian London*; Waddington, *The Medical Profession in the Industrial Revolution*; George Rosen, *Madness in Society* (London: Routledge and Kegan Paul, 1969); Andrew Scull, ed., *Madhouses, Mad-Doctors, and Madmen* (Philadelphia: University of Pennsylvania Press, 1981); Ivan Illich, *Medical Nemesis* (London: Trinity Press, 1975). For a comparable account of the medical profession in its American context, see Paul Starr, *The Social Transformation of American Medicine* (New York: Basic Books, 1982).

6. "Les tomes du *Dictionnaire des sciences médicales*, non coupés, mais dont la brochure avait souffert dans toutes les ventes successives par où ils avaient passé, garnissaient presque à eux seuls les six rayons d'une bibliothèque en bois de sapin." *Madame Bovary* (Paris: Club de l'Honnête Homme, 1971), 77. All future quotations in French from *Madame Bovary* cited in the footnotes are to this edition.

7. Terry Eagleton, *Literary Theory: An Introduction* (Minneapolis: University of Minnesota Press, 1983), 15.

8. On Cabanis, see Martin S. Staum, *Cabanis* (Princeton, N.J.: Princeton University Press, 1980). On the institutional transformation of medicine in France during the Revolutionary period, see Foucault, *Naissance*, chaps. 2–5.

9. Canivet's surgical background is evident even in his name, which puns *canif*, or penknife.

10. Foucault, *Birth of the Clinic*, 81.

11. "Il . . . entrait son bras dans des lits humides, reçevait au visage le jet tiède des saignées, écoutait des râles, examinait des cuvettes, retroussait bien du linge sale" (100).

12. See Eugenio Donato, "Flaubert and the Question of History," *Modern Language Notes* 91, no. 5 (1970): 864–65; Tony Tanner, *Adultery in the Novel* (Baltimore, Md.: Johns Hopkins University Press, 1979), especially 301–3.

13. For accounts of this competition, see Matthew Ramsey, "Medical Power and Popular Medicine: Illegal Healers in Nineteenth-Century France," *Journal of Social History*, 10, no. 4 (1977): 560–77, and Jacques Donzelot, *The Policing of Families*, trans. Robert Hurley (New York: Pantheon Books, 1979), especially the section on "The Priest and the Doctor," 171–87. For a comparative account that includes information on the conflict in France between the Church and the medical profession during the 1840s, see Ramsey, "The Politics of Professional Monopoly in Nineteenth-Century Medicine: The French Model and Its Rivals," in Gerald Geison, ed., *Professions and the French State, 1700–1900* (Philadelphia: University of Pennsylvania Press, 1984), 225–305.

14. Ramsey, "Medical Power," 579.

15. Donzelot, *Policing of Families*, 171.

16. As Foucault has pointed out, this new arrangement of duties between doctor and priest was connected with a broader discursive development in which sex ceased to be an object of religious control and came to be conceptualized as an object of scientific knowledge. Hysteria obviously participates in this transformation. But what was involved was less a displacement of terms than a shift in epistemological authority. The old connotations of hysteria as

demonic possession were subsumed by the medical perspective, adduced no longer as evidence of damnation but as symptoms of illness. A standard mid-nineteenth-century medical textbook, for example, claims that hysteria is characterized by "vociferation, singing, cursing, aimless wandering; occasionally by more formal delirium of a religious or demoniacal character; or there are attacks of all kinds of noisy and perverse, but still coherent actions" (Wilhelm Griesinger, *Mental Pathology and Therapeutics*, trans. C. L. Robertson et al. [London: New Sydenham Society, 1867], 179). For a detailed discussion of the changing religious and medical attitudes toward hysteria, see Ilza Veith, *Hysteria: The History of a Disease* (Chicago: University of Chicago Press, 1965).

17. Cf. Ramsey, "Medical Power," 570.

18. "Les circonstances qui prédisposent le plus à l'hystérie sont . . . une constitution nerveuse, le sexe feminin et l'âge de douze à vingt-cinq ou trente ans. . . . La plupart ont montré dès le bas âge des dispositions aux affections convulsives, un caractère mélancolique, colère, emporté, impatient. . . . Les causes excitants sont plus particulièrement des affections morales vives, . . . amour contrarié, . . . affections vives de l'âme, . . . un mouvement violent de jalousie, . . . chagrins violens, . . . contrariété vive. . . . La constitution nerveuse et l'état maladif qui précédent et facilitent le développement des attaques sont occasionés par les excès de la masturbation." *Dictionnaire de Médecine* (Paris: Béchet jeune, 1824), vol. 11, 532–33. It is interesting to note that Flaubert himself not only makes use of the medical dictionary, but also corrects it. Writing to Sainte-Beuve (23–24 December 1862), for example, he defends his description in *Salammbô* of bitches' milk as a remedy for leprosy, referring the critic (himself an ex-medical student!) to the *Dictionnaire des sciences médicales*. Flaubert then goes on to say that he has revised the article on leprosy, correcting some of the facts and adding others from his own first hand observation of the disease in Egypt. Cf. *Corréspondance*, in *Oeuvres Complètes* (Paris: Conard, 1933), vol. 5, 59.

19. "the prisoner of a sort of reciprocal causality that operates between the vital spirits and the mind, between passion and the body." Paul Hoffmann, *La femme dans la pensée des Lumières* (Paris: Editions Ophrys, n.d.), 179.

20. Denis Diderot, *Rameau's Nephew*, trans. Leonard Tancock (New York: Penguin, 1978), 114. On eighteenth-century neurological theories of hysteria, see Veith, *Hysteria*, and Hoffmann, *La femme*; John F. Sena, "The English Malady," Ph.D. diss., Princeton University, 1967. Two excellent collections of source material on early psychiatric theories of insanity are Richard Hunter and Ida Macalpine, eds., *300 Years of English Psychiatry, 1535–1860* (New York: Oxford University Press, 1963) and Vieda Skultans, *English Madness: Ideas on Insanity, 1580–1880* (Boston: Routledge and Kegan Paul, 1979). See also Foucault, *L'Histoire de la folie à l'âge classique* (Paris: Gallimard, 1972), especially 193–226.

21. P.-J.-G. Cabanis, *Rapports du physique et du moral de l'homme* (Paris, 1824), 27.

22. P.-J.-G. Cabanis, *Oeuvres philosophiques*, ed. Claude Lehec and Jean Cazeneuve (Paris, 1956), vol. 1, 364. See Staum, *Cabanis*, chaps. 7 and 8, for a detailed discussion of Cabanis's theories of sensitivity and temperament. For

a discussion of how the concepts of sensibility and reflex become tied to a notion of normality in the biological sciences of this period, see Georges Canguilhem, *Le normal et le pathologique* (Paris: Presses universitaires de France, 1966).

23. M.-F. Xavier Bichat, *Recherches physiologiques sur la vie et la mort* (Paris: Chez Brosson, Gabon, et Cie, 1800), 162. For a broader view of the conceptual transformation initiated by Bichat, see Foucault, *Birth*, chap. 8; P. Lain Entralgo, "Sensualism and Vitalism in Bichat's 'Anatomie Générale,'" *Journal of the History of Medicine* 3, no. 1 (1948): 47–55; and François Jacob, *La Logique du vivant* (Paris: Gallimard, 1970), chap. 2.

24. "one castrates men to change their voices." Bichat, *Recherches*, 100.

25. See in particular Steven Marcus, *The Other Victorians* (New York: Basic Books, 1966). Stephen Heath has traced the development of sexual rhetoric into a modern discourse on sexuality in *The Sexual Fix* (London: Macmillan, 1983).

26. François Lallemand, *Des pertes séminales involontaires* (Paris: Béchet, 1836).

27. Raymond de Vieussens, *Histoire des maladies internes suivis de la névrographie* (Toulouse: J. J. Robert, 1775–1776), quoted in Hoffmann, *La femme*, 178.

28. On Georget, see Jean Marie Bruttin, *Différentes théories sur l'hystérie dans la première moitié du XIXᵉ siècle* (Zurich: Jenris, 1969).

29. See Robert Brudenell Carter, *On the Pathology and Treatment of Hysteria* (London: J. Churchill, 1853). On Carter's position in the history of hysteria, see Skultans, *English Madness*, 21–30.

30. Henry James, *The Art of Fiction* (New York: Oxford University Press, 1948), 74.

31. "Julien's illness . . . was caused by a deadly breeze or an unfulfilled desire. But the young man, in response to all questions, shook his head." Gustave Flaubert, *Trois Contes* (Paris: Garnier Flammarion, 1965), 102.

32. For a discussion of Flaubert's relation to older theories of the relation between weather and emotional flux, see Terry Castle, "The Female Thermometer," *Representations* 17 (Winter 1987): 18–19. Castle correctly points out that Flaubert is "self-conscious, even sly" in invoking these earlier theories, but he does not recognize that Flaubert rejects the etiology purveyed by those theories, or that Flaubert promotes a different view of what Castle calls "modern man's unstable inner weather."

33. See Bruttin, *Différentes théories sur l'hystérie*, for a more detailed summary of these four steps.

34. Cf. Hayden White, "The Problem of Style in Realistic Representation: Marx and Flaubert," in Berel Lang, ed., *The Concept of Style* (Philadelphia: University of Pennsylvania Press, 1979), 213–32. For White, however, the movement through the four tropal modes is unconnected with medical logic or discursive structure. Instead, White places it within an Hegelian schema of cognitive development. Flaubert's novel, in this view, provides a classical example of bildungsroman, depicting the four-stage process whereby the Spirit, or Desire, comes to (ironic) self-consciousness. But Flaubert's term for what happens is "l'éducation sentimentale," not "l'éducation de l'esprit," and the

former term has a precise connotation, for Ideologues and clinicians, of "power of sensitivity" (*sentiment, sensitivité*, and *sensibilité* are roughly interchangable in Bichatian discourse). The education of Frédéric's sentiments, then, although occurring in four stages, results not in a German idealist *Bildung* of the *Geist* but in a medicalized formation of constitution.

35. Bruttin, *Différentes théories sur l'hystérie*, 31.

36. "Charles, de temps à autre, ouvrait les yeux; puis, son esprit se fatiguant et le sommeil revenant de soi-même, bientôt il entrait dans une sorte d'assoupissement où, ses sensations récentes se confondant avec des souvenirs, lui-même se percevait double, à la fois étudiant et marié, couché dans son lit comme tout à l'heure, traversant une salle d'opérés comme autrefois" (61).

37. Josef Breuer and Sigmund Freud, *Studies on Hysteria*, trans. and ed. James Strachey (New York: Basic Books, 1955), 7.

38. Flaubert to Hippolyte Taine, 1 December 1866. Cf. *Correspondance*, ed. Jean Bruneau (Paris: Gallimard, 1973–1980).

39. "Les ombres du soir déscendaient; le soleil horizontal, passant entre les branches, lui éblouissait les yeux. Ça et là, tout autour d'elle, dans les feuilles ou par terre, des taches lumineuses tremblaient, comme si des colibris, en volant, eussent éparpillé leurs plumes. Le silence était partout; quelque chose de doux semblait sortir des arbres; elle sentait son coeur, dont les battements recommençaient, et le sang circuler dans sa chair comme un fleuve de lait. Alors, elle entendit tout au loin, au delà du bois, sur les autres collines, un cri vague et prolongé, une voix qui se traînait, et elle l'écoutait silencieusement, se mêlant comme une musique aux dernières vibrations de ses nerfs émus" (193).

40. In *Littérature et sensation* (Paris: Editions de Seuil, 1954), Jean-Pierre Richard gives a brilliant phenomenological reading of this and other passages dealing with Emma's perception. The difference between Richard's phenomenological approach and my archaeological one is actually a matter of degree rather than of substance: Richard seeks to imitate the lived experience of the characters within Flaubert's literary universe, while my concern is to show how that experience is made sense of by means of encoded presuppositions that function as a phenomenological a priori.

41. "Aux fulgurations de l'heure présente, sa vie passée, si nette jusqu'alors, s'évanouissait tout entière, et elle doutait presque de l'avoir vécue. Elle était là; puis autour du bal, il n'y avait plus que de l'ombre, étalée sur tout le reste" (94).

42. "Le souvenir du vicomte revenait toujours dans ses lectures. Entre lui et les personnages inventés, elle établissait des rapprochements. Mais le cercle dont il était le centre peu à peu s'élargit autour de lui, et cette auréole qu'il avait, s'écartant de sa figure, s'étala plus au loin, pour illuminer d'autres rêves" (99).

43. Cf. Jonathan Culler, *Flaubert: The Uses of Uncertainty* (Ithaca, N.Y.: Cornell University Press, 1974), 91–108.

44. For a similar effort to account for a seemingly meaningless detail (in fact, the precise detail chosen by Barthes), see Castle, "The Female Thermometer," 26.

45. Cf. Bruttin, *Différentes théories sur l'hystérie*, 18: "Le seuil de la sensibilité, de l'excitabilité du cerveau malade étant ainsi de plus en plus abaissé, les plus petites stimulations suffiront à déclencher la crise. Une douleur, une petite contrariété, voire même un son ou une odeur désagréables, déchargeront le cerveau malade; la réaction hystérique est devenue inadéquate, totalement disproportionée et, tres souvent, il devient impossible de trouver la cause immédiate de ces accès répétés."

46. The case study has yet to be adequately defined as a literary genre, as G. S. Rousseau has pointed out in "Literature and Medicine: The State of the Field," *Isis* 72, no. 263 (1981): 406–24. Those critics who have dealt with case studies (most notably Steven Marcus and Peter Brooks) have focused almost exclusively on Freud's case histories, rather than examining Freud's work as a transformation of an already existing genre. Cf. Steven Marcus, "Freud and Dora: Story, History, Case History," in *Representations* (New York: Random House, 1975), 247–309; Peter Brooks, "Fictions of the Wolf Man: Freud and Narrative Understanding," in *Reading for the Plot* (New York: Knopf, 1984), 264–85. Foucault provides a brilliant but elliptical discussion of the change in medical hermeneutics in *Birth*, chap. 6, and offers a discussion of the role of a doctor's subjectivity within the process of writing case studies in "The Life of Infamous Men," in Morris and Patton, *Michel Foucault*, 76–91. Flaubert, of course, is not a physician but a literary artist, and the generic constraints of the realistic novel clearly are not identical with those of the case study. Nevertheless, in terms of the epistemological and hermeneutic imperatives that structure the two genres, a certain commonality does exist.

47. Bichat, *Recherches*, 218.

48. "—Sens donc: quelle odeur! fît-il en la lui passant sous le nez à plusieurs reprises.

—J'étouffe! s'écria-t-elle en se levant d'un bond.

Mais, par un effort de volonté, ce spasme disparut; puis:

—Ce n'est rien! dit-elle, ce n'est rien! c'est nerveux! Assieds-toi, mange!

Car elle rédoutait qu'on ne fût à la questionner, à la soigner, qu'on ne la quittât plus.

Charles, pour lui obéir, s'était rassis, et il crachait dans sa main les noyaux des abricots, qu'il déposait ensuite dans son assiette.

Tout à coup, un tilbury bleu passa au grand trot sur la place. Emma poussa un cri et tomba roide par terre, à la renverse" (233).

49. "Il y a des natures si impressionnables a l'encontre de certaines odeurs! et ce serait même une belle question à étudier, tant sous le rapport pathologique que sous le rapport physiologique" (234).

50. Quoted in Foucault, *The History of Sexuality*, trans. Robert Hurley (New York: Pantheon, 1978), 56, n. 1.

51. "Puis, ne pensez-vous pas qu'il faudrait peut-être frapper l'imagination?

—En quoi? comment? dit Bovary.

—Ah! c'est là la question! Telle est effectivement la question: 'That is the question!' comme je lisais dernièrement dans le journal.

Mais Emma, se réveillant, s'écria:

—Et la lettre? et la lettre?

On crût qu'elle avait le délire; elle l'eût à partir de minuit: une fièvre cérébrale s'était declarée" (235).

52. "In short, a young woman from a good social background, with a nervous constitution, not doing manual work and leading an idle life between attending concerts and reading novels, is the ideal subject predisposed to hysteria." Bruttin, *Différentes théories sur l'hystérie*, 17.

53. Girard, *Deceit, Desire, and the Novel*, 149.

54. For a summary of the various medical positions on this question, see Dr. Eduard Allain, *Le mal de Flaubert* (Paris: M. Lac, 1928). Cf. also René Dumesnil, *Flaubert et la médecine* (Geneva: Slatkine, 1969) and Maxime Du Camp's unreliable but still fascinating reminiscences, "La maladie de Flaubert," *La Chronique médicale* 3 (1896): 584–87.

55. Quoted in *The Letters of Gustave Flaubert, 1830–1857*, trans. and ed. Francis Steegmuller (Cambridge, Mass.: Belknap Press, 1980), 22. All further English quotations from Flaubert's correspondence are from this edition.

56. "Elle resta perdue de stupeur, et n'ayant plus conscience d'elle-même que par le battement de ses artères, qu'elle croyait entendre s'échapper comme une assourdissante musique qui emplissait la campagne. Le sol sous ses pieds était plus mou qu'une onde, et les sillons lui parurent d'immenses vagues brunes, qui déferlaient. Tout ce qu'il y avait dans sa tête de réminiscences, d'idées, s'échappait à la fois, d'un seul bond. comme les mille pièces d'un feu d'artifice. Elle vît son père, le cabinet de Lheureux, leur chambre là-bas, un autre paysage. La folie la prenait" (326).

57. Both Eugene F. Gray, in "The Clinical View of Life: Gustave Flaubert's *Madame Bovary*," in *Medicine and Literature*, ed. Edmund Pellegrino (New York: N. Watson, 1980), 60–84, and John C. Lapp, in "Art and Hallucination in Flaubert," *French Studies* 10, no. 4 (1956): 322–43, have discussed this passage and pointed out the similarity between Emma's hallucinations and those of Flaubert. Neither critic, however, has adequately described or explained the parallelism between Flaubert's description of his and Emma's experience and the medical description of the same kind of experience.

58. Thibaudet's comment about what he called Flaubert's "binocular vision" is developed at length by Barbara Smalley, who emphasizes Flaubert's "awareness of two worlds, the world of private experience and the world of scientific reality," as a fundamental characteristic of his realism. No stylistic analysis in itself, however, could grasp the constituting conditions of this double perspective. Cf. Smalley, *George Eliot and Flaubert* (Athens: Ohio University Press, 1974), and Thibaudet, *Gustave Flaubert* (Paris: Gallimard, 1935), 119.

59. Jean Starobinski, "The Style of Autobiography," in *Literary Style: A Symposium*, ed. Seymour Chatman (New York: Oxford University Press, 1971), 285–94. Benveniste's distinction is actually between "l'énonciation historique" and "discours," not between different subjects. See Emile Benveniste, *Problèmes de linguistique générale* (Paris: Gallimard, 1966), 242.

60. Jean-Paul Sartre, *The Family Idiot*, trans. Carol Cosman (Chicago: University of Chicago Press, 1981), vol. 1, 443.

61. This is Sartre's position, as well as that of Harry Levin in *The Gates of*

Horn, 219. The identification seems to have been made first by René Dumesnil in *Flaubert et la médecine*.

62. Sartre claims that Larivière's "calm consciousness of having great talent can only be the acceptance of mediocrity," and concludes that Flaubert is therefore opposing Larivière's/Achille-Cléophas's talent (read "mediocrity" by Sartre) to his own genius. But Sartre fails to point out that Flaubert nowhere opposes genius to talent and mediocrity. In fact, Flaubert often cited the following maxims of La Bruyère and Buffon as guides: "Un esprit médiocre croit écrire divinement, un bon esprit croit écrire raisonnablement," and "Le génie n'est qu'une plus grande aptitude à la patience" ["A mediocre writer believes he writes divinely; a good writer believes he writes reasonably," and "Genius is merely a great aptitude for patience"] (Steegmuller, *Letters of Gustave Flaubert*, 66 and 182). I would argue that for Flaubert, in many ways an antiromantic, the alternative to mediocrity is not genius, but professional competence.

63. Cf. Charles Augustin Sainte-Beuve, "De la littérature industrielle," in *Portraits Contemporaine* (Paris: Didier, 1846), vol. 1, 495–557. On the development of the professional writer during the 1820s and 1830s, as well as on the general phenomenon of professionalization during that period, see chapter 3.

64. See Honoré de Balzac, *Oeuvres Complètes* (Paris: Bibliophiles de l'Originales, 1968), vol. 19, 546, for Balzac's discussion of the "moral malady" of society that he proposes to solve in his writing.

65. On the formation of a self-conscious professional class, see Harold Perkin, *The Origins of Modern English Society, 1770–1880* (London: Routledge and Kegan Paul, 1969), 321–25. Perkin develops this argument at much greater length in *The Rise of Professional Society* (London and New York: Routledge, 1989).

66. Cf. Lukács, *The Historical Novel*, 182.

67. On the arguments within Marxism about whether or not professionals should be considered a class, see Barbara Ehrenreich and John Ehrenreich, eds., *Between Labor and Capital: The Professional-Managerial Class* (Boston: South End Press, 1979); Dietrich Rueschemeyer, *Power and the Division of Labor* (Cambridge, Mass.: Polity Press, 1986), 104–41.

CHAPTER THREE

1. Gustave Flaubert to Louise Colet, 27 December 1852; quoted in *The Letters of Gustave Flaubert*, 177–78.

2. All page references to quotations in the original French from this book are to the Garnier Frères edition (Paris, 1976). Page references to quotations in English are from the translation by Ellen Marriage, *The Country Doctor* (Philadelphia: Gebbie Publishers, 1899).

3. On the distinction between a sentence and a statement, see Foucault, *The Archaeology of Knowledge*, 106–9.

4. On the opposition between readerly classical texts and writerly modernist texts, see Roland Barthes, *S/Z*, trans. Richard Miller (New York: Hill and Wang, 1974), 3–16. See also Stephen Heath, *The Nouveau Roman* (Philadel-

phia: Temple University Press, 1972), 15–25. The distinction between critical realism and merely descriptive naturalism is developed by Georg Lukács in a number of works, the most accessible being *The Meaning of Contemporary Realism*, trans. John Mander and Necke Mander (London: Merlin Press, 1979).

5. Lukács's comments on Balzac are scattered throughout his later work, but can be found in their most developed form in *Balzac et le Réalisme Français* (Paris: François Maspéro, 1967). Auerbach's well-known discussion of Balzacian realism occurs in *Mimesis*, trans. Willard Trask (Princeton, N.J.: Princeton University Press, 1974), 468–82.

6. "... la reproduction rigoreuse de la réalité." *Oeuvres Complètes illustrées de Balzac* (Paris: Bibliophiles de l'originale, 1976), vol. 14, 819.

7. On the type as a literary phenomenon peculiar to realism, see Lukács, *The Historical Novel*, and René Wellek, "Realism in Literary Scholarship," in *Concepts of Criticism* (New Haven, Conn.: Yale University Press, 1963). Wellek traces the literary-historical provenance of the notion of type to Taine, in "Hyppolite Taine's Literary Theory and Criticism," *Criticism* 1, no. 1 (1959): 1–18, 123–38. On the scientific and cultural sources for Balzac's use of the term, see Robert Nisbet, "Herder, Goethe, and the Natural 'Type,'" *Publications of the English Goethe Society* 37 (1967): 83–119; Heinrich Hömel, "Type and Proto-Phenomenon in Goethe's Science," *PMLA* 71, no. 4 (September 1956): 651–58; and Peter Demetz, "Balzac and the Zoologists," in Demetz, ed., *The Disciplines of Criticism* (New Haven, Conn.: Yale University Press, 1968), 397–418.

8. Demetz, "Balzac and the Zoologists," 58.

9. Cf. Lukács, *The Historical Novel*, 126–27.

10. "the representative sign of a creation, of an idea." Quoted in Demetz, "Balzac and the Zoologists," 75.

11. Auerbach, *Mimesis*, 471.

12. Charles-Augustin Sainte-Beuve, *Selected Essays*, trans. Francis Steegmuller and Norbert Guterman (Garden City, N. J.: Doubleday, 1963), 255.

13. On the history of physiognomy and phrenology, see Gräeme Tytler, *Physiognomy in the European Novel* (Princeton, N.J.: Princeton University Press, 1982); Roger Cooter, "Phrenology and the British Alienists, ca. 1825–1845," and William Bynum, "Rationales for Therapy in British Psychiatry, 1780–1835," in *Madhouses*, Scull, ed., 35–105; Owsei Temkin, "Gall and the Phrenological Movement," *Bulletin of the History of Medicine* 21, no. 3 (1947): 275–321; Jason Hall, "Gall's Phrenology: A Romantic Psychology," *Studies in Romanticism*, 16, no. 3 (1977): 305–17; Roger Cooter, *The Cultural Meaning of Popular Science: Phrenology and the Organisation of Consent in Nineteenth-Century Britain* (Cambridge: Cambridge University Press, 1984). For an analysis of the ways phrenological analysis was enlisted in the stereotyping of women as inferior, see Cynthia Russett, *Sexual Science* (Cambridge, Mass.: Harvard University Press, 1989).

14. Lavater, quoted in Tytler, *Physiognomy*, 71.

15. Temkin, "Gall," 279.

16. On the professional stakes of the phrenology movement, see Cooter,

Cultural Meaning of Popular Science. On the popular confusion between phrenology and physiognomy, see Tytler, *Physiognomy*, 88–90.

17. ". . . a fait marcher les maximes de Larochefoucault [*sic*], qu'il a donné la vie aux observations de Lavater en les appliquant." Félix Davin, "Introduction" to *Etudes de Moeurs*, in Balzac, *Oeuvres Complètes* (Paris: Bibliophiles de l'Originales, 1968), vol. 19, 613. All references to Balzac's *Oeuvres* will be to this edition, except where otherwise noted.

18. ". . . la vie habituelle fait l'âme, et l'âme fait la physiognomie."

19. Quoted in Fernand Baldensperger, "Les théories de Lavater dans la littérature française," in *Etudes d'histoire littéraire* (Paris: La Hachette, 1910), 75.

20. I do not have space to deal with mesmerism in this book, but its relevance to the first stage of nineteenth-century realism is undeniably great. For a study of how mesmerism functions in the work of Balzac's British counterpart, Dickens, providing an "emphasis on will, energy, and the mind as intensified metaphors for his exploration of the condition of man" (234), see Fred Kaplan, *Dickens and Mesmerism* (Princeton, N.J.: Princeton University Press, 1975).

21. On the epistemological and political disputes between clinical medicine and marginal medical sciences, see Paul Starr, *The Social Transformation of American Medicine* (New York: Basic Books, 1982), 47–59. On the English context, see Ian Inkster, "Marginal Men," ed. John Woodward and David N. Richards, *Health Care and Popular Medicine in Nineteenth-Century England* (New York: Holmes and Meier, 1977), 128–63. On the local versions of these disputes within a specifically French context, see Ramsey, "Medical Power and Popular Medicine," 560–77.

22. The fullest discussion of the Cuvier versus Geoffroy St.-Hilaire controversy (including Balzac's role in it) is Toby Appel's *The Cuvier-Geoffroy Debate* (New York: Oxford University Press, 1987). For philosophically informed views of the controversy, see Cassirer in *The Problem of Knowledge*, 126–36; François Jacob in *The Logic of Life*, trans. Michael Spillman (New York: Vintage, 1976), 100–111; and Georges Canguilhem, *La connaissance de la vie* (Paris: Vrin, 1965), 174–84.

23. "Depuis ce jour, la béauté de mademoiselle Grandet prît un nouveau caractère. Les graves pensées d'amour par lesquelles son âme était lentement envahie, la dignité de la femme aimée, donnèrent à ses traits cette éspèce d'éclat que les peintres figuraient par l'auréole. Avant la venue de son cousin Eugénie pouvait être comparée à la Viérge avant la conception; quand il fût parti, elle ressemblait à la Viérge mère: elle avait conçu l'amour." Balzac, *Eugènie Grandet* (Oxford: Oxford University Press, 1967), 169–70.

24. "Jamais madame Bovary ne fût aussi belle qu'à cette époque; elle avait cette indéfinissable béauté qui résulte de la joie, de l'enthousiasme, du succès, et qui n'est que l'harmonie du tempérament avec les circonstances." *Madame Bovary*, 222.

25. In fact, Flaubert is *anti*physiognomic in ways that Tytler misses because he doggedly insists on identifying the presence of physiognomy in the novel. For Flaubert, what seems a physiognomical transformation under the influence of love—the lyricism Tytler identifies—is in fact nothing more than a

delusion. Tytler's misreading is most evident when he proffers the following passage as proof that Flaubert writes physiognomically: "Jamais elle n'avait eu les yeux si grands, si noirs, ni d'une telle profondeur. Quelque chose de subtil épandu sur sa personne la transfigurait" ["Never had she had eyes so large, so black, of such depth. Something subtle spreading over her transfigured her"] (194). This transfiguration, however, is not an objective fact recorded by Flaubert, but a subjective fact of Emma's self-perception. She is viewing herself in a mirror, and an earlier draft clarifies the narcissistic context of Emma's physiognomic perception: "Cependant elle s'aperçut dans la glace et elle eût presque de la stupéfaction en reconnaissant son visage. Comment n'exprimait-il rien de ce qui emplissait son âme? Comment faisait-il qu'elle pût paraitre la même? Alors, elle avança de plus près pour se considérer, et elle se trouva tout à coup extraordinairement belle. Elle n'avait jamais eu les yeux si grands . . . " ["However, she glanced at herself in the mirror and was almost stupefied in recognizing her face. How could it fail to express what filled her soul? How could it be that she appeared the same? Then she moved closer to consider herself, and she found herself suddenly extraordinarily beautiful. She had never had eyes so large . . ."] (195). That Flaubert suppresses this passage in his final version does not imply that he now thinks of Emma's transformation as a physiognomic fact, but that he expects his ideal reader—a medical man, as I have argued in the previous chapter—to negate the physiognomic perspective. Tytler's failure (despite the many virtues of his work) to specify the literary *situation* of his discourse is a telling one, betraying as it does a methodological lacuna within new historicism which this book attempts to address.

26. Robert Castel, *L'Ordre psychiatrique* (Paris: Editions de Minuit, 1976). A useful overview of Castel's work may be found in Peter Miller, "The Territory of Psychiatry," *Ideology and Consciousness* 8 (Spring 1981): 63–106.

27. On the medicalization of the notion of environmental determinism, see Leo Spitzer, "Milieu and Ambiance: An Essay in Historical Semantics," *Philosophy and Phenomenological Research* 3 (1942): 1–42, 169–218; reprinted in Spitzer, *Essays in Historical Semantics* (New York: S. F. Vanni, 1948), 179–316.

28. Philippe Esquirol, "Question médico-légale sur l'isolement des aliénés," *Mémoire présenté à l'Institut le premier octobre 1832* (Paris: Crochard, 1832), 31.

29. For a fascinating account of the pathology of shock in nineteenth-century medicine, see Wolfgang Schivelbusch, *The Railway Journey*, trans. Anselm Hollo (New York: Urizen, 1979).

30. "a été pendant ce temps la victime de tous les caprices des gens riches, lesquels, pour la plupart, n'ont rien de constant ni de suivi dans leur générosité, bienfaisants par accès ou par boutades, tantôt amis, tantôt maîtres. . . . Tour à tour demoiselle de compagnie et femme de chambre, on fît d'elle un être incomplète" (127).

31. As one group of psychiatrists put it, "political upsets bring with them real and powerful causes of madness." See Lucien Belhomme, *Influence des évènements et des commotions politique sur le développement de la folie* (Paris: Germer Bailliére, 1849), 23. The ideological position I am sketching out here is most fully worked through in the writings of Brierre de Boismont and, in an inter-

esting American variation, in Benjamin Rush's work. Bichat, Alibert, and a number of other clinicians who lived through the French Revolution also studied the effects of political turmoil on health. So far as I know, there is no exhaustive historical analysis of the various pathologizations of revolution. See Jan Goldstein, *Console and Classify* (Cambridge: Cambridge University Press, 1987).

32. "incessament dissoute, incessament recomposée, . . . sans liens, sans principes, sans homogénéité." *Oeuvres Complètes* (Paris: Le Prat, 1963), vol. 11, 230.

33. On this aspect of Balzacian narrative, see Christopher Prendergast, *Balzac: Fiction and Melodrama* (London: E. Arnold, 1978). Franco Moretti, in *Signs Taken for Wonders*, trans. Susan Fischer et al. (New York: Holmes and Meier, 1983), 109–30, offers a cultural analysis of Balzacian narrative that resonates in important ways with the one I am offering here, but that relies on what I would suggest is a view of social context that is discursively fuzzy.

34. "les lois de la conscience sociale, qui ne ressemble en rien à la conscience naturelle."

35. This two-sided aspect of Balzac's style has been recognized by Peter Brooks, who argues that in the *Comédie* "an inherited hierarchy disciplines the natural anarchy of social life in much the same way as Balzac's naïvely systematic narration contains and organizes his stylistic incoherence and exuberance." See *The Melodramatic Imagination* (New Haven, Conn.: Yale University Press, 1976), 56. Unfortunately, Brooks's formalism prevents him from exploring in any detail the actual historical context for the opposition he perceives between incoherence and system. The discipline in Balzac's novels derives from neither an inherited hierarchy nor a melodramatic systematization, but a quasi-scientific perspective on disorder.

36. In a strangely ahistorical moment for a critic whose motto is "Always historicize!" Fredric Jameson perceives the nature of what he brilliantly calls "appetency" in Balzac, but then immediately denies appetency's sociohistorical determinations in favor of purely literary ones: "The human existence is at all times motivated by appetency, that is, by a clear desire that always poses a precise object before itself. The proper cross-references are not psychology or psychoanalysis, but that vague welling dissatisfaction characteristic of desire in the novels of Flaubert; or the metaphysical value with which desire is invested by the surrealists: two wholly different formal conventions." Cf. "*Cousin Bette* and Allegorical Realism," *PMLA* 86, no. 2 (March 1971): 244. Flaubert's formal conventions concerning desire are wholly different from those of Balzac, but this difference needs to be explained by analyzing the discursive cross-references on which each novelist depends.

37. "L'état de société fait de nos besoins, de nos nécessités, de nos goûts, autant de plaies, autant de maladies, par les excès auxquels nous nous portons, poussés par le développement que leur imprime la pensée: il n'y a rien en nous par où elle ne se trahisse. De la ce titre [*Pathologie de la vie sociale*] pris à la science médicale. Là où il n'y a pas maladie physique, il y a maladie morale." *Oeuvres Complètes* (Paris: Bibliophiles de l'Originales, 1976), vol. 19, 546.

38. For a detailed description of the "monomania controversy," see Gold-

stein, *Console*, 152–96. Like phrenology and physiognomy, monomania was abruptly discredited in the 1850s. Cf. J.-P. Falret, *De la non-existence de la monomanie* (Paris: Rignoux, 1854).

39. Not that writers before Balzac did not represent characters whom one could appropriately describe as "monomaniacs." Sterne's Uncle Toby or even Don Quixote immediately come to mind. But in Balzac's case this kind of character is imagined by the writer himself through the category of monomania.

40. As Owsei Temkin has pointed out, Balzac's more balanced attitude toward the passions may be traceable to the physiological (rather than therapeutic) assumptions of such contemporaries as Magendie, who argues that "great poets, heroes, great criminals and conquerors are empassioned men." Cf. *The Double Face of Janus* (Baltimore, Md.: Johns Hopkins University Press, 1977), 341.

41. Esquirol, "Question médico-légale," 31.

42. See Goldstein, *Console*, 277–321, for this story in its French context. The most important study of this topic in an American context is David Rothman's *The Discovery of the Asylum* (Boston: Little, Brown, 1971).

43. "un village au delà duquel il n'y aurait plus eu de terre, qui semblait n'aboutir et ne tenir à rien; ses habitants paraissaient former une même famille en dehors du mouvement social, et ne s'y rattacher que par le collecteur d'impôts ou par d'imperceptibles ramifications" (15).

44. On the *traitement moral*, see Robert Castel, "Le Traitement moral: Thérapeutique Mentale et Contrôle Social au XIXème siècle," *Topique* 2 (February 1970): 109–29; Andrew Scull, "Moral Treatment Reconsidered: Some Sociological Comments on an Episode in the History of British Psychiatry," in Scull, *Madhouses*, 105–20.

45. Goldstein, *Console*, 35, quoting S. Pinel, "Traité du régime sanitaire des aliénés," 41.

46. On the distinction between patriarchy and paternalism, see Richard Sennett, *Authority* (New York: Knopf, 1980), 52–54.

47. Cf. *The History of Sexuality*, trans. Robert Hurley (New York: Pantheon, 1978), vol. 1, 81–91.

48. According to Louis Marin, utopian discourse always proceeds in this way, selecting certain qualities from a given reference-community and projecting their opposites onto the utopia. Cf. Louis Marin, *Utopiques: jeux d'éspaces* (Paris: Minuit, 1973). Eugene W. Holland discusses *Le Médecin de campagne* as a hybrid of utopian and romance genres in *MMLA* 17, no. 1 (Spring 1984): 54–69, but he argues that Balzac's utopia should be understood in narrowly political terms as an "electoral allegory" promoting Balzac as a potential candidate for office. *Le Médecin* very obviously does set out a political project, but the real question is how that overt politics can be connected with the project inherent in Balzacian realism.

49. Tanner, *Adultery in the Novel*, 15.

50. See Sennett, *Authority*, 50–83, for a brilliant discussion of the uses of paternalism by the bourgeoisie in the era of high capitalism.

51. On paternalism within the ideology of professionalism, see Larson, *The*

Rise of Professionalism 220–23. On paternalism as a nineteenth-century ideology powerfully expressed as well as challenged in the novel, see Edward Said, *Beginnings* (Baltimore, Md.: Johns Hopkins University Press, 1975), chap. 3.

52. Goldstein, *Console*, 224.

53. One index of this change is the presence of a phrenological head in Charles Bovary's examining room: phrenology has degenerated from a masterscience in Balzac to a form of bêtise. Eliot, too, may be said to have left phrenology behind in her mature work. Cf. N. N. Feltes, "Phrenology: From Lewes to George Eliot," *Studies in the Literary Imagination* 1, no. 1 (1968): 13–22.

54. Larson, *The Rise of Professionalism*, 49. My analysis in what follows bears some resemblance to the argument Pierre Bourdieu has advanced about what he calls the "literary field." Cf. "Intellectual Field and Creative Project," trans. Sian France, *Social Science Information* 8, no. 2 (April 1969): 89–119. Bourdieu, however, seems to take for granted that such a field exists, when what is most interesting about Balzac's and the early psychiatrist's enterprise is precisely its formational, emergent quality, which Larson's analytic registers more fluently.

55. Indeed, Eliot Freidson goes so far as to define profession itself as "organized autonomy." See Freidson, *Professional Dominance* (New York: Atherton Press, 1970), 133–35. See also Ernest Greenwood, "Attributes of a Profession," *Social Work* 2, no. 3 (1957): 45–55; Carlo Cipolla, "The Professions: The Long View," *Journal of European Economic History* 2, no. 1 (1973): 37–52.

56. On Balzac's participation in early efforts to secure copyright, see Louis de Royaumont, *Balzac et la Société des gens de lettres* (Paris: Dorbon-aîné, 1913). A brilliant but truncated discussion of Balzac as a seminal figure in the professionalizing of letters can be found in the preface of Régis Debray's *Le pouvoir intellectuel en France* (Paris: Editions Ramsay, 1979). See also Christopher Prendergast, *Balzac: Fiction and Melodrama* (London: E. Arnold, 1978). For an overview of the profession of letters, see Raymond Williams's innocuously entitled essay, "Notes on English Prose, 1780–1950," in *Writing in Society* (London: Verso, n.d.), 67–121, and Williams's longer discussion of the same issue in *The Long Revolution* (New York: Columbia University Press, 1961), 156–213.

57. See, for example, Jeffrey Berlant, *Profession and Monopoly* (Berkeley: University of California Press, 1975), where professional ethics are analyzed not as a nexus of deeply held personal beliefs but as an institutionalized set of tools aimed at establishing professional monopolies.

58. For a notable exception, see Bruce Robbins's valuable essay, "Telescopic Philanthropy: Professionalism and Responsibility in *Bleak House*," in Homi Bhabha, ed., *Nation and Narration* (London: Routledge, 1990), 213–30.

59. One result of this previous orientation was that many of the early proponents of moral treatment were not psychiatrists but religiously motivated reformers like the Tukes or members of charitable organizations.

60. As Larson puts it, "until almost the nineteenth century, we cannot speak of an internal stratification of the professions, for 'common' and 'learned' practitioners inhabited different social worlds." *The Rise of Professionalism*, 3.

61. As Williams points out, at the prices charged for books "book-buying

was obviously socially limited. . . . While this expansion [of the reading public during the eighteenth century] continued, there was surprisingly little change in the general output of books . . . [while] the demand for almanacs, chapbooks, ballads, broadsheets, and pamphlets seems not to have slackened." *Long Revolution*, 162–63.

62. As Peterson points out, in England, "while the old tripartite division of health care continued, it did so in attenuated form." See *The Medical Profession in Mid-Victorian London*, 29–30. For a more complete analysis of this uneven development within the English medical profession, see Ivan Waddington, "General Practitioners and Consultants in Early Nineteenth-Century England: The Sociology of an Intra-Professional Conflict," in Woodward and Richards, ed. *Health Care and Popular Medicine*, 164–88.

63. Kathleen Tillotson, *Novels of the Eighteen-Forties* (London: Oxford University Press, 1965), 15.

64. On Dicks, cf. Victor Neuberg, *Popular Literature* (New York: Penguin, 1977), 177. Neuberg's study provides an excellent overview of the rise of modern markets for literature, as does Gabriel Josipovici, *The World and the Book* (London: Macmillan, 1971).

65. *The National Magazine* 1 (December 1837): 446; quoted in Louis James, *Fiction for the Working Man, 1830–1850* (London: Oxford University Press, 1963), 47.

66. For details about Balzac's 1826 printing fiasco, see Noël Gerson, *The Prodigal Genius: The Life and Times of Honoré de Balzac* (Garden City, N.Y.: Doubleday, 1972), 75–85.

67. See "Politics as a Vocation," in *From Max Weber*, ed. H. H. Gerth and C. Wright Mills (New York: Oxford University Press, 1979), 78.

68. In American as well as European medicine, "the authority of the profession as gauged by the willingness of legislatures, philanthropists, physicians, and the general public to support and patronize medical institutions, was established long before the content of medical practice could justify it." Peter D. Hall, "The Social Foundations of Professional Credibility: Linking the Medical Profession to Higher Education in Connecticut and Massachusetts, 1700–1830," in Thomas Haskell, ed., *The Authority of Experts* (Bloomington: Indiana University Press, 1984), 107.

69. Weber, *From Max Weber*, 79. See also William Goode, "Community within a Community: The Professions," *American Sociological Review* 22, no. 2 (April 1957): 194–98.

70. "Pour qu'une littérature ait de la vie avec ensemble et consistance, il faut une certaine stabilité non stagnante; il faut, pour l'émulation, un cercle de juges compétents et d'élite, quelque chose ou quelqu'un qui organise, qui régularise, qui modère et qui contienne, que l'écrivain ait en vue et qu'il désire de satisfaire; sans quoi il s'émancipe outre mesure, il se disperse et s'abandonne. . . . Les grands siècles littéraires ont toujours eu ainsi un juge, un tribunal dispensateur, de qui l'écrivain se sentait dépendre, quelque balcon . . . duquel descendait la palme et la récompense." Charles-Augustin Sainte-Beuve, *Chateaubriand et son groupe littéraire* (Paris: Michel Levy, 1889), vol. 1, 52–53; my translation.

71. Richard Sennett and Jonathan Cobb, *The Hidden Injuries of Class* (New York: Vintage, 1972), 227.

72. Starr, *Social Transformation*, 19.

73. Waddington, *The Medical Profession in the Industrial Revolution*, 19.

74. "Ce mot d'exactitude veut une explication. L'auteur n'a pas entendu ainsi contracter l'obligation de donner les fait un à un, sèchement et de manière à montrer jusqu'à quel point on peut fair arriver l'histoire à la condition d'un squelette dont les os sont soigneuesement numérotés." "Introduction à *Les Chouans*," *Oeuvres Complètes*, vol. 19, 536.

75. "Les déterminations les plus importantes se prennent toujours en un moment; [Balzac] a voulu représenter les passions rapidement conçus, qui soumettent toute l'existence à quleque pensée d'un jour; mais pourquois tenterait-il d'expliquer par la logique ce qui doit être compris par le sentiment. . . . Quoique la vie sociale aît, aussi bien que la vie physique, des lois en apparence immuable, vous ne trouverez nulle part ni le corps ni le coeur réguliers comme la trigonométrie de Legendre." *Oeuvres Complètes* (Paris: Le Prat, 1963), vol. 19, 167; my translation.

76. This is in marked contrast to Flaubert, whose ideal physician, Larivière, must be an agent of knowledge, not only an icon of professional authority.

77. Stanley Fish calls this kind of involuted rhetorical practice, in which a speech act works contradictorily to further the interests of the profession even while claiming independence from it, "professional antiprofessionalism." Fish argues convincingly that "anti-professionalism is not a position at all, but a form of professional behavior," tied to a "slow and complex interplay of forces." Rather than describing this interplay of forces or the historical nuances of such professional behavior, Fish—more interested in rejecting antiprofessional rhetoric as another version of "ahistoricism, essentialism, and utopianism"—simply alludes to context. It is precisely these pragmatic aspects of professional antiprofessionalism, however, that are crucial to understanding the phenomenon. As I have been trying to show, professional antiprofessionalism not only exists, but tends to be invoked by professionals (whether medical or literary) during specific historical conjunctures that give rise to crises of professional legitimation, and in particular during the early stages of drives for professional autonomy. Cf. Stanley Fish, "Professional Anti-Professionalism," *Times Literary Supplement*, 10 December 1982, 1363.

78. On the myth of Napoleon in French culture during the nineteenth century, see Albert Guerard, *Reflections on the Napoleonic Legend* (New York: Charles Scribner's Sons, 1924). On Balzac's use of the Napoleonic image, see Maurice Bardèche, *Une lecture de Balzac* (Paris: Les Sept Couleurs, 1964), 27–30.

79. André Maurois, *Prométhée, ou la vie de Balzac* (Paris: Hachette, 1965), 227.

80. ". . . n'a rien d'humain; ce n'est pas celui de l'ouvrier, de l'*homo faber*, dont le mouvement tout usuel va jusqu'au bout de lui-même à la recherche de son propre effet; c'est un geste immobilisé dans le moment le moins stable de sa course; c'est l'idée de la puissance, non son épaisseur, qui est ainsi éternisée. La main qui se lève un peu, ou s'appuie mollement, la suspension même du

mouvement, produisent la fantasmagorie d'un pouvoir étranger à l'homme. Le geste crée, il n'accomplit pas. . . ." Roland Barthes, *Essais Critiques* (Paris: Editions de Seuil, 1964), 36–37; my translation.

81. In A.-J. Gros's *Napoleon in the Pest-house at Jaffa*, for instance, a coterie of doctors surrounds Napoleon, who assumes a Christ-the-healer pose, laying on hands to cure a patient. Another such example is Charles Meynier's *Return of Napoleon to the Isle of Loban*, in which several doctors mediate between the Emperor and patients, echoing Napoleon's posture. What is important for my argument about these paintings is not the distinction that art historian Robert Rosenblum perceives in them between the "realistic concern" of the doctors and the "spiritual first aid" supplied by Napoleon, but the attempt to tie that realistic concern to Napoleon's charismatic authority. When artworks are commissioned directly by physicians, as in the case of the famous painting depicting the psychiatrist Pinel freeing mental patients from their chains, the physician may end up being cast directly in the charismatic mold of Napoleon. Pinel's figure appears in the same stance taken by Napoleon in other paintings, the traditional pose of the *exemplum virtus*. Here, however, the *virtus* has been appropriated by professionalism. Cf. Robert Rosenblum, *Transformations in Late Eighteenth-Century Art* (Princeton, N.J.: Princeton University Press, 1970), 67–68.

82. See Max Weber, *The Protestant Ethic and the Spirit of Capitalism*, trans. Talcott Parsons, 2d ed. (New York: Charles Scribner's Sons, 1958), chap. 3.

83. Alan Mintz, *George Eliot and the Novel of Vocation* (Cambridge, Mass.: Harvard University Press, 1978). I have found Mintz's discussion extremely suggestive, although lacking in the kind of decade-by-decade historical specification of the dynamics connecting professionalism and vocationalism (and connecting both to literary realism) I wish to establish here.

84. As Larson puts it, "career is a pattern of organization of the self" that only emerges in the wake of the drive for professional power (*The Rise of Professionalism*, 229). The various literary permutations of this pattern before its definitive emergence in the 1860s (in Stendhal, Trollope, and Dickens as well as Balzac) would be well worth exploring.

85. On the confession as a protonovelistic form, see John Frecerro, "Dante's Novel of the Self," *The Christian Century*, 6 October 1965, 1216–17.

86. "Enfin, c'était un beau pays, c'était la France!"

87. Fredric Jameson, *The Political Unconscious* (Ithaca, N.Y.: Cornell University Press, 1981), 156.

CHAPTER FOUR

1. On Kant's discussion of the interests of reason in biological theory, see Cassirer, *The Problem of Knowledge*, 182–84.

2. One way to account for this shift would be to argue that through Lydgate, Eliot promotes a notion of the feminized physician, because his sympathetic qualities were precisely those being emphasized by female physicians trying to preserve a place for themselves in medicine during this period. The ideology of professionalization worked against women in the literary field just

as it did in the field of medicine. Eliot's own attacks upon "scribbling women" could be seen as part (along with the invention of a sympathetic male physician) of her own way of negotiating this ideology. See Regina Morantz-Sanchez, *Sympathy and Science* (New York: Oxford University Press, 1985), for a discussion of these tensions within the medical field. My own analysis stresses intraprofessional and epistemological rather than gender tensions, but clearly all three are involved.

3. On the notion of a secular calling in Eliot, see Alan Mintz, *George Eliot and the Novel of Vocation* (Cambridge, Mass.: Harvard University Press, 1978). Mintz argues that Eliot's characters embody a secularized vocational ethos in which "selfish ambitions for personal distinction and selfless aspirations toward general amelioration are parts of a single matrix of desire" (20). But he does not distinguish scientific and medical vocation in *Middlemarch*, nor does he try to explain in detail the interplay in Eliot's characterizations between the rhetoric of vocation and the epistemology of the different organic models through which Eliot works.

4. F. R. Leavis and Q. D. Leavis, *Dickens the Novelist* (London: Chatto and Windus, 1970), 180.

5. Jonathan Arac has argued that this reforming impulse in fact subtends and grounds the realism of these writers. Cf. *Commissioned Spirits* (New Brunswick, N.J.: Rutgers University Press, 1979).

6. Charles Dickens, *Little Dorrit* (Toronto: Macmillan of Canada, 1969), 662.

7. On Lydgate as a knowledgeable general practitioner, see Patrick J. McCarthy, "Lydgate, 'The New, Young Surgeon' of Middlemarch," *Studies in English Literature, 1500–1900*, 10, no. 4 (1970): 805–16; C. L. Cline, "Qualifications of the Medical Practitioners of *Middlemarch*," in *Nineteenth-Century Literary Perspectives: Essays in Honor of Lionel Stevenson* (Durham, N.C.: Duke University Press, 1974), 271–81.

8. George Eliot, *Middlemarch*, ed. Gordon Haight (Boston: Houghton Mifflin Co., 1956), 109. All references to this edition are cited hereafter in the text.

9. Cf. N. N. Feltes, "George Eliot's 'Pier-Glass': The Development of a Metaphor," *Modern Philology* 67, no. 1 (1969): 69–71.

10. J. Hillis Miller, "Optic and Semiotic in *Middlemarch*," in William Buckley, ed., *The Worlds of Victorian Fiction*, (Cambridge, Mass.: Harvard University Press, 1975), 139.

11. Cf. W. J. Harvey, "The Intellectual Background of the Novel," in Barbara Hardy, ed., *Critical Approaches to* Middlemarch (London: University of London, The Athelone Press, 1967), 25–38.

12. G. H. Lewes, *Problems of Life and Mind*, 3d ser. (Boston: Houghton, Osgood and Company, 1880), 10.

13. This Cyclopaedia's undisturbed condition resembles that of Charles Bovary's *Dictionnaire des sciences médicales*, with its uncut pages. That Lydgate opens *his* book symbolizes the different status of knowledge in Eliot's realism: it has become accessible to the characters themselves—but as such, it can no longer function as a *principium stilisationis*, as it does in Flaubert's realism.

14. Augustine, *Confessions*, trans. R. S. Pine-Coffin (New York: Signet, 1978), book 8, para. 2.

15. On the discursive implications of Augustine's moment of conversion, see Lawrence Rothfield, "Autobiography and Perspective in the *Confessions* of St. Augustine," *Comparative Literature* 33, no. 3 (Summer 1981): 209–23.

16. Eliot's phrase, "for anything he knew his brains lay in small bags at his temples, and he had no more thought of representing to himself how his blood circulated than how paper served instead of gold," reflects this process of discovery-through-metonymy: the idea of having brains kept in small bags may have evoked the idea of gold (also kept in bags) and the associated analogy between knowledge and paper money.

17. As Gaston Bachelard, the most profound analyst of metaphor in scientific thought, puts it: "Like it or not, metaphors seduce our reason" (*La Formation de l'Esprit Scientifique* [Paris: J. Vrin, 1938], 78). On Bachelard and the "continuity between metaphor and concept" in philosophy as well as in science, cf. Jacques Derrida, "White Mythology: Metaphor in the Text of Philosophy," *New Literary History* 6, no. 1 (August 1974): 5–74.

18. See Michael Mason, "*Middlemarch* and Science: Problems of Life and Mind," *Review of English Studies* 22, no. 86 (1971): 151–69. On the impact of epistemological problems in the natural sciences upon the style of Victorian novelists, see George Levine, *The Realistic Imagination* (Chicago: University of Chicago Press, 1981), and Gillian Beer, *Darwin's Plots* (Boston: Routledge and Kegan Paul, 1983).

19. Lewes, *Problems*, 191, 106.

20. Ibid., 101.

21. Lorenz Oken, *Die Zeugung* (Bamburg uber Wirzburg: J. A. Goebhardt, 1805), quoted in William Coleman, *Biology in the Nineteenth Century* (Cambridge: Cambridge University Press, 1977), 25. George Rosen argues that "the Romantic medicine created on the basis of Schelling's philosophy of nature . . . represented the German approach to the problem of medical reconstruction . . . in a period of revolution." Cf. "Romantic Medicine," *Bulletin of the History of Medicine* 25, no. 2 (1951): 149–59. On the impact of *naturphilosophie* on English romanticism, see M. H. Abrams, *The Mirror and the Lamp* (Oxford: Oxford University Press, 1953).

22. François Jacob, *The Logic of Life* (New York: Vintage, 1976), 118.

23. On the English reception of Virchow's work, see W. H. McMenemey, "Cellular Pathology, with Special Reference to the Influence of Virchow's Teachings on Medical Thought and Practice," in F.N.L. Poynter, ed., *Medicine and Science in the 1860s* (London: Wellcome Institute of the History of Medicine, 1968), 13–43, 49–50.

24. *Problems* (London, 1874–1879), vol. 2, 122–23.

25. Within the field of mental medicine, which borrowed so much of its cognitive apparatus from pathological anatomy, the more basic sciences of the body would by the end of the century have attained enough intellectual predominance to be used by Freud to justify psychoanalysis as an avant-garde mental science as far in advance of psychiatry as cell-based medicine was in advance of clinical, anatomically based medicine: "Psychoanalysis is related to

psychiatry approximately as histology is to anatomy: the one studies the external forms of the organs, the other studies their construction out of tissues and cells. It is not easy to imagine a contradiction between these two species of study, of which one is a continuation of the other. Today, as you know, anatomy is regarded by us as the foundation of scientific medicine. But there was a time when it was as much forbidden to dissect the human cadaver in order to discover the internal structure of the body as it now seems to be to practice psychoanalysis in order to learn about the internal mechanism of the mind." *Introductory Lectures on Psychoanalysis*, trans. James Strachey (New York: Norton, 1966), 255.

26. See Harry Elmer Barnes, "Representative Biological Theories of Society," *Sociological Review* 7, nos. 2, 3 (1925): 120–30, 182–94 for a succinct overview of the organic model in nineteenth-century social thought.

27. Cf. Thomas Henry Huxley, *Science and Culture and Other Essays* (London: Macmillan, 1881).

28. Eliot's and Lewes's medical friendships mark them as committed to a medical culture different from the misogynistic one exemplified by names like Acton and Maudsley. For a discussion of Eliot's relationship to one such physician, see M. Jeanne Peterson, "Dr. Acton's Enemy: Medicine, Sex, and Society in Victorian England," *Victorian Studies* 29 (1986): 4.

29. Lewes, *Physiology of Common Life*, 2 vols. (Edinburgh: Blackwood, 1859–1860), vol. 2, 453.

30. Quoted in *Letters*, ed. G. S. Haight (New Haven, Conn.: Yale University Press, 1955), vol. 6, 98–99.

31. Letter of 25 May 1870, quoted in Haight, *Letters*, vol. 5, 100.

32. See Bernard J. Paris, "Science and Art in George Eliot's Quest for Values," *The Humanist* 20 (1960): 52.

33. On Eliot's psychology of composition, see Quentin Anderson's illuminating discussion in "George Eliot in *Middlemarch*," in Boris Ford, ed., *From Dickens to Hardy* (Baltimore, Md.: Penguin Books, 1958), 274–76; cf. also Mintz, *George Eliot and the Novel of Vocation*, 145–48.

34. Letter of 8 May 1869.

35. On "organic form" in Eliot, see Terry Eagleton, *Criticism and Ideology* (London: Verso, 1978), chap. 5; for the Marxist view that organicism is sought but never found due to ideological contradictions; for the deconstructive view of Eliot's organic form, see Cynthia Chase, "The Decomposition of the Elephants: Double-Reading in *Daniel Deronda*," *PMLA* 93 (March 1978): 215–27.

36. Mark Schorer has distinguished five stories, held together by what he has called a "matrix of analogy." Cf. "The Structure of the Novel: Method, Metaphor, and Mind," in Barbara Hardy, ed., *Middlemarch: Critical Approaches to the Novel* (New York: Oxford University Press, 1967), 12–24.

37. *Adam Bede* (New York: Signet, 1961), 179.

38. For a discussion of these two fictional functions of disease, see Sontag, *Illness as Metaphor*, 36.

39. On Eliot's changing attitude toward organicism, see Sally Shuttleworth, *George Eliot and Nineteenth-Century Science* (Cambridge: Cambridge University Press, 1984).

40. The mind-body analogy is also the basis of Lewes's physiological psychology: "The mind is built up out of assimilated experiences, its perceptions being shaped by its pre-perceptions, its conceptions by its pre-conceptions. Like the body, the mind is shaped through its history" (*Problems* [Boston: Houghton, Osgood and Company, 1879–1880], vol. 1, 202). It is worth noting that in support of this assertion, Lewes footnotes Eliot's *The Spanish Gypsy*.

41. Lewes, *Problems* (1880), 203.

42. George Eliot, "Notes on Form in Art" (1868), in *Essays*, ed. Thomas Pinney (New York: Columbia University Press, 1963), 433.

43. Eliot's concept of form in this essay thus is temporal. That temporal orientation, I would argue, stems from Eliot's adherence to a model of bodily form that is medical. The medical model, on the other hand, is less useful in clarifying spatial forms such as those offered by sculpture and what Flaubert would call received ideas: "The old phrases should not give way to scientific explanation, for speech is to a great extent like sculpture, expressing observed phenomena & remaining true in spite of Harvey & Bichat" ("Notes on Form in Art," 436).

44. Eliot clearly objects to Lydgate's classificatory impulse as prescientific, and in the context of my argument, which assumes a valorization of the scientific perspective by Eliot, her antagonism to Lydgate's attitude toward women on these grounds makes sense. But there may also be a more personal kind of antagonism at play in Eliot's condemnation of Lydgate—who is for the most part, after all, scientific enough—to Rosamond's company. As Lewes's wife, Eliot must have felt at least a twinge of jealousy at the avidity with which Lewes pursued his specimen gathering. In particular, Lewes's fascination with the beauty of his sponges, snails, and other seaside creatures must have aroused some feeling, at times, that her own, more intellectual beauties were being slighted by him. Lewes himself drew the analogy and candidly acknowledged the advantages of beauty over intelligence, in a tongue-in-cheek passage of *Sea-side Studies* (Edinburgh: Blackwood, 1860), writing of the experiences of a trip that Lewes and Eliot took together to the English coast in 1856 and 1857:

> The Anemone has little more than beauty to recommend it; the indications of intelligence being of by no means a powerful order. What then? Is beauty nothing? Beauty is the subtle charm which draws us from the side of the enlightened Miss Crosser to that of the lovely though "quite unintellectual" Caroline, whose conversation is not of a novel or brilliant kind; whereas Miss Crosser has read a whole Encyclopaedia, and is so obliging as to retail many pages of it freely in her conversation. (139)

Is it not likely that Eliot inwardly fumed at this admission? But she gained her revenge by drawing out the implications of Lewes's implicit comparison of a beautiful woman and an anemone. The anemone image is not applied directly to Rosamond (although it will be to Rosamond's successor, Gwendolen Harleth in *Daniel Deronda*), but Lewes's comments occur in the context of his discussion of the stinging or stunning power of anemones, and Eliot transfers this power to Rosamond, whose "torpedo shock" paralyzes Lydgate. Lydgate's fate, then, might be a kind of object lesson to Lewes by Eliot, exemplifying the dangers of not attending to his enlightened partner's needs for companionship as well as to his own scientific pleasures.

45. Foucault, *Birth of the Clinic*, 186–87. On Broussais's presence in *Middlemarch*, see Robert A. Greenberg, "Plexuses and Ganglia: Scientific Allusion in *Middlemarch*," *Nineteenth-Century Fiction* 30 (1976): 33–52.

46. On the impact of Darwinism on literary form in the work of Eliot and other Victorian novelists, see Gillian Beer, "Plot and the Analogy with Science in Later Nineteenth-Century Novelists," in E. S. Shaffer, ed., *Comparative Criticism: A Yearbook*, 2 (Cambridge and New York: Cambridge University Press, 1980), 131–49; Stanley Hyman, *The Tangled Bank* (New York: Atheneum, 1962).

47. Cf. Georges Canguilhem, "A New Concept in Pathology: Error," in *On the Normal and the Pathological* (Dordrecht, Holland: D. Reidel, 1978), 171–79.

48. Gustave Flaubert, *Madame Bovary*, trans. Paul de Man (New York: Norton, 1965), 148.

49. Ibid.

CHAPTER FIVE

1. Georg Lukács, *Studies in European Realism* (New York: Grosset and Dunlap, 1964), 6, 8.

2. Jameson, *The Political Unconscious*, 104.

3. On the spread of reification, see Georg Lukács, *History and Class Consciousness*, trans. Rodney Livingstone (Cambridge, Mass.: MIT Press, 1971), 132.

4. D. A. Miller, *The Novel and the Police* (Berkeley and Los Angeles: University of California Press, 1988); Mark Seltzer, *Henry James and the Art of Power* (Ithaca, N.Y.: Cornell University Press, 1984).

5. For a more detailed analysis of Miller's reduction of discursive relations to a single relation of power, see Lawrence Rothfield, "Allegories of Policing," *Critical Texts* 5, no. 3 (Fall 1988): 30–36.

6. Lukács, *History and Class Consciousness*, 110.

7. In reality, of course, Bernard's relationship to clinical medicine, and to Magendie, is far more complicated than Zola makes it out to be. As Georges Canguilhem points out, "Magendie was a man of the laboratory as well a hospital physician." See Canguilhem, *Ideology and Rationality in the History of the Life Sciences*, trans. Arthur Goldhammer (Cambridge, Mass.: MIT Press, 1988), 58. For a nuanced discussion of Bernard's debt to clinical medicine, see John Lesch, *Science and Medicine in Modern France: The Emergence of Experimental Physiology, 1790–1855* (Cambridge, Mass.: Harvard University Press, 1984).

8. Cabanis argues that physicians could arrive only at "practical certainties," "more or less precise approximations" rather than a deductive grasp of absolute causes and effects. See *Oeuvres philosophiques de Cabanis*, ed. Claude Lehec and Jean Cazeneuve (Paris: Presses universitaires de France, 1956), vol. 2, 91.

9. Sir James Paget, *Lectures on Surgical Pathology*, 3d ed. (Philadelphia: Lindsay and Blakiston, 1870), 359.

10. On Magendie's emphasis on observing, see Owsei Temkin, "The Philosophical Basis of Magendie's Physiology," in *The Double Face of Janus* (Baltimore, Md.: Johns Hopkins University Press, 1977), 317–39.

11. Naomi Schor, *Zola's Crowds* (Baltimore, Md.: Johns Hopkins University Press, 1978).

12. On Zola's relation to theories of degeneration, see Sander Gilman, ed., *Degeneration* (New York: Columbia University Press, 1985). To my knowledge, the synergy between Zola and the hygienics movement of the last part of the century in France has not been dealt with adequately. For a fascinating social history of this movement, see Bruno Latour, *The Pasteurization of France*, trans. Alan Sheridan and John Law (Cambridge, Mass.: Harvard University Press, 1988).

13. *An Introduction to the Study of Experimental Medicine*, trans. H. C. Greene (New York: Dover, 1957), 103.

14. In a tantalizing, brilliant essay, Denis Hollier has suggested that Zola's adamancy is something like a defense mechanism mounted not against accusations of taking pleasure in the painful, but of taking pleasure in the sexual. Although Hollier is getting at something powerful in Zola, I think he somewhat prematurely reduces Zola's bodies to sexual bodies, when there is as much digestion and destruction as sex in these bodies. See Denis Hollier, "How Not to Take Pleasure in Talking about Sex," trans. Jean Andrews, *Enclitic* 8, no. 1–2 (Spring–Fall 1984): 84–93.

CHAPTER SIX

1. Jameson, "On Raymond Chandler," in Glenn Most and William Stowe, ed., *The Poetics of Murder* (San Diego, Cal.: Harcourt Brace Jovanovich, 1983), 124.

2. See Lacan's essay in J. Muller and W. Richardson, ed., *The Purloined Poe* (Baltimore, Md.: Johns Hopkins University Press, 1988). On Lacan's allegorizing tendency, see Barbara Johnson, "The Frame of Reference," in the same volume.

3. Peter Brooks, *Reading for the Plot* (New York: Vintage, 1984), 26, 28.

4. Bertrand Russell, "Descriptions," in A. P. Martinich, ed., *The Philosophy of Language* (New York: Oxford University Press, 1985), 218.

5. For the contributions by Eco, Sebeok, and Hintikka, see Umberto Eco and Thomas Sebeok, ed., *The Sign of Three* (Bloomington: Indiana University Press, 1983).

6. *The Complete Sherlock Holmes* (Garden City, N.Y.: Doubleday, 1930), 785. All references to Conan Doyle's Holmes stories are to this edition, except where otherwise indicated.

7. *Complete Holmes*, 261.

8. Readers are quite as fully historically determined as the text they enjoy, and the meshing of reader and text is itself an historically determinate phenomenon that requires a certain intellectual receptivity or compliance on the part of the reader. Because every text consists of more than one discourse, and because different readers may respond to different aspects of the same discourse, there is also more than one implied reader for every text (as in the case

of detective fiction, which interpolates both logicians and a mass audience). It is possible to read detective fiction without being excited in the way the reader I identify is; but what then needs to be analyzed is the correlation of discourses that makes the detective story readable in two such disparate ways. For Miller's discussion of sensation, see *The Novel and the Police* (Berkeley and Los Angeles: University of California Press, 1988), 146–91.

9. Roland Barthes, *The Pleasure of the Text*, trans. Richard Miller (New York: Hill and Wang, 1975), 62.

10. As the various literary histories of detective fiction show, the origins of the genre can be pushed back to Collins or Poe, or even further to Voltaire's *Zadig*, or to stories from the Old Testament or *A Thousand and One Nights*. But Conan Doyle's work marks a point when the genre consolidates itself to the extent that it becomes a cultural phenomenon, both produced and consumed in far greater quantities and with far more regularity than was previously the case.

11. Russell, "Descriptions," 218.

12. See Scarry, "Work and the Body in Hardy and Other Nineteenth-Century Novelists," *Representations* 3 (Summer 1983): 90–123.

13. *The Annotated Sherlock Holmes*, ed. W. Baring-Gould (New York: Potter, 1967) vol. 1, 639.

14. On the links between the Freudian case study and the detective story, see Steven Marcus, "Freud and Dora: Story, History, Case History," in Charles Bernheimer and Claire Kahane, ed., *In Dora's Case* (New York: Columbia University Press, 1985), 56–91; Geraldine Pederson-Krag, "Detective Stories and the Primal Scene," in *The Poetics of Murder*, 13–20.

15. Barthes, *Pleasure*, 62.

16. Stephen Knight, *Form and Ideology in Crime Fiction* (Bloomington: Indiana University Press, 1980). For similar assessments of the social function of Holmes's detective work, see Julian Symons, *Mortal Consequences* (New York: Schocken, 1973), 10–12, and Christopher Clausen, "Sherlock Holmes, Order, and the Late-Victorian Mind," *Georgia Review* 38 (Spring 1984): 104–23.

17. Cf. Michel Foucault, "About the Concept of the 'Dangerous Individual' in 19th-Century Legal Psychiatry," *International Journal of Law and Psychiatry* 1, no. 1 (1978): 1–18.

18. As one historian of medicine puts it: "The position of the general practitioner within the medical profession became clear during the second half of the nineteenth century when physicians and surgeons were increasingly perceived as consultants and specialists, and the general practitioners were clearly relegated to the 'subordinate grade.'" Irvine Loudon, *Medical Care and the General Practitioner, 1750–1850* (Oxford: Clarendon Press, 1986), 189.

19. On the symptom/sign distinction, see Foucault, *Birth of the Clinic*, 159–72; Roland Barthes, "Semiology and Medicine," in *The Semiotic Challenge*, trans. Richard Howard (New York: Hill and Wang, 1988), 203–13. The history of semiotics remains to be written; for an outline of the possible directions such a history might take, see Jerzy Pelc, "On the Prospects of Research in the History of Semiotics," *Semiotic Scene* 1, no. 3 (1977): 1–12.

20. *Round the Red Lamp* (New York: D. Appleton, 1899), 50.

21. *The Complete Sherlock Holmes* (Garden City, N.Y.: Doubleday, 1930), 22.

22. *Memories and Adventures* (Boston: Little, Brown, 1924), 69.

23. Joseph Bell, review of Conan Doyle's work in *The Bookman* (December 1892), 80. All further in-text references are to this edition.

24. As Carlo Ginzburg puts it, "In police work the aim is to get back from a particular event to its particular cause whereas in scientific work the aim is to find a fundamental theoretical law of general application or (more often) to fit an anomalous fact into the applicability of a fundamental law by rearranging the 'intermediate' laws" (*Sign of Three*, 126).

25. Cf. Alphonse Bertillon, *Signalements anthropométrique* (Paris: Masson, 1886), 22.

26. Galton, *Finger Prints* (London, 1897), 14. For Galton's discussion of the "utility of a sure means of identification" for the purposes of colonial and criminal administration, see "Identification by Finger-Tips," *The Nineteenth Century* (August 1891): 303–6.

27. Miller, *The Novel and the Police*, 35.

28. Foucault, *The History of Sexuality*, vol. 1, 45.

29. *Annotated Holmes*, vol. 2, 115.

30. *Annotated Holmes*, vol. 1, 611.

31. Bell, *Bookman*, 80.

32. *Annotated Holmes*, vol. 2, 226.

33. Irene short-circuits Holmes's logic of identification, leaving him with a "dubious and questionable memory" of her. One sign of this short-circuiting is Holmes's recurrent reference to her as "*the* woman"—a definite description without predicates. Some of the more avid Holmesians have found such a statement intolerable, and have suggested that Watson's pen slipped at these points, where he should have written that Irene Adler is the woman in the case of the purloined photograph.

34. This disavowal differs in essence from the naturalist excuse offered by Zola and Bernard. As Denis Hollier has argued, Zola actively "claims to prefer that which doesn't please, . . . that which normally repels." Holmes, in contrast, can find pleasure with less vocal professional protestation in using his detection to degrade people who are normally neutral or nondescript. Cf. Denis Hollier, "How to Not Take Pleasure in Talking about Sex," 87.

35. It is difficult to think of two men more opposed in temperament than Conan Doyle and Oscar Wilde, and yet Conan Doyle admired Wilde as a writer and was one of the few to defend him after Wilde's fall. But I am less interested in biographical than in textual connections between figures of decadence. It is worth noting that Conan Doyle and Wilde moved in some of the same circles. Doyle in fact was commissioned to write what became *The Sign of Four* at the same luncheon at which Wilde was commissioned by the same publisher to write what became *The Picture of Dorian Gray*.

36. On the late nineteenth-century history of the concept of the homosexual, see Jeffrey Weeks, "Movements of Affirmation: Sexual Meanings and Homosexual Identities," *Radical History Review* 5, no. 20 (1980): 164–79; Georges Lanteri-Laura, *Lecture des Perversions* (Paris: Masson, 1979); and Ed. Cohen, "Legislating the Norm: From Sodomy to Gross Indecency," *South Atlantic Quarterly* 88 (Winter 1989): 181–217.

CHAPTER SEVEN

1. Edmond Duranty, *La Cause du Beau Guillaume* (Paris: Aux Editions de la Sirène, 1920), vol. 2, 8; quoted in Levin, *The Gates of Horn*, 69.

2. Lukács, *The Meaning of Contemporary Realism*, 43.

3. On the political possibilities inherent in the professional class, see Dietrich Rueschemeyer, *Power and the Division of Labor*.

4. Cf. Larson, *The Rise of Professionalism*, chaps. 9 and 10, for a sociological discussion of this process of consolidation and incorporation of professionals within the new class system. On the consolidation of medicine as a profession during the latter half of the nineteenth century, see Peterson, *The Medical Profession in Mid-Victorian London*, 110–15, and Waddington, *The Medical Profession in the Industrial Revolution*, 151–53.

5. Cf. Virginia Woolf, "Mr. Bennett and Mrs. Brown," pamphlet, 30 October 1924 (London: Hogarth Press, 1924).

6. Thomas Mann, *The Magic Mountain*, trans. H. T. Lowe-Porter (New York: Vintage Books, 1969), 285.

7. See Kermode's "Introduction" to *Riceyman Steps* (New York: Oxford University Press, 1983).

8. Kermode, "Introduction," ix. All following page references to Bennett's novel are to this edition.

9. See Lukács, *The Meaning of Contemporary Realism*, 18.

10. On this shift in the beginning conditions of writing in modernism, see Edward Said, *Beginnings*, chap. 4.

11. In *The Innocent Eye* (New York: Farrar, Straus and Giroux, 1984), Roger Shattuck has argued that modernism is closely allied to the new modes of perception being developed at the turn of the century in "hard" sciences such as physics and mathematics. Shattuck's analysis supports my claim that the grounding discourses of modernism are not individualizing, as was medicine in realism. The status of medicine in the work of one particularly important figure in Shattuck's book, Paul Valéry, would be worth examining: Valéry, while exploring arcane issues in physics and mathematics, also was intensely interested in medicine, using physicians as figures in several of his "Dialogues." Valéry's use of medicine in a poetic context lies beyond the scope of this book, but we can say that one of its defining characteristics is that as a form of knowledge it is opposed to philosophical knowledge as, more generally, the body is opposed to the mind in Valéry's writings.

12. Georg Lukács, *The Theory of the Novel*, trans. Anna Bostock (Cambridge, Mass.: MIT Press, 1971), 124.

13. I should stress that this dissolution of the empirical in modernism does not—or at least need not—imply a cutting-off of subjectivity from objective reality, a fall into solipsistic relativism. Philosophical critiques of modernism that define it as a literary form of solipsism confuse the empirical with the objective, opposing subjectivity to both. But the empirical is simply one starting point from and with which knowing can begin. If realism implies that knowledge stems from embodiment, modernism grounds its knowing subject in a different, although equally "objective," domain: that which Said, in *Begin-*

nings, stipulates as "text." As Said points out, in "giving up the immediacy of objects" (246) modernist fiction abandons the individual human life as a locus for significance: in a number of ways, "a text is disjunctive with the human lifetime" (202), and writing itself has become "a transhuman work" (242). But human lifetimes and the immediacy of objects can be defined in any number of ways, and only by tracing this terminology back to its discursive sources in nineteenth-century medical fiction can one make clear the stakes of the disjunction.

14. Bakhtin has pointed out the importance of death in what he calls the realistic "finalization" of character; Tolstoy, he says, "presents death as a stage of life, as a stage illuminating that life, as the optimal point for understanding and evaluating that life in its entirety." Bakhtin's analysis of the hermeneutic functions of finalization, unfortunately, is somewhat crippled by his polemical dismissal of realism as a "monological" mode of writing. Cf. Mikhail Bakhtin, *Problems of Dostoevsky's Poetics*, ed. and trans. Caryl Emerson (Minneapolis: University of Minnesota Press, 1984), 69.

15. Wilde's *Dorian Gray*, with its simultaneous seduction into and condemnation of morbid sensualism, is a crucial transitional work in this tradition. Certain of Lord Henry's dicta reflect a clinical view of the self, from the claim that "life is a question of nerves, and fibres, and slowly built-up cells in which thought hides itself and passion has its dreams" (255–56), to the notion that at least some individuals "have more than one life. They become more highly organized" (174). Like Bichat and Flaubert, Wilde is interested in poison, and even recognizes poison as poison. But the tendency to invert the entire pathological framework is evidenced by Lord Henry's highly ambiguous claim that "there were poisons so subtle that to know their properties one had to sicken of them. There were maladies so strange that one had to pass through them if one sought to understand their nature" (82). Quoted from *The Portable Oscar Wilde* (New York: Penguin, 1946).

16. Franz Kafka, "A Country Doctor," trans. Willa Muir and Edwin Muir in *The Complete Short Stories and Parables*, ed. Nahum Glatzer (New York: Schocken, 1983).

17. Peter Hohendahl, "The Loss of Reality: Gottfried Benn's Early Prose," in A. Huyssens and David Bathrick, eds., *Modernity and the Text* (New York: Columbia University Press, 1989), 81–94.

18. Joseph Conrad, *Heart of Darkness* (New York: Penguin, 1987), 32.

19. On this issue, see James E. Miller, Jr., "Henry James in Reality," *Critical Inquiry* 2 (Spring 1976): 585–604, for the realist side of the argument, and J. Hillis Miller, "The Figure in the Carpet," *Poetics Today* 1, no. 3 (1980): 107–18 for the modernist side.

20. Henry James, *The Wings of the Dove*, eds. J. Donald Crowley and Richard A. Hocks (New York: Norton, 1978). All page references cited are to this edition.

21. See Virginia C. Fowler, "Milly Theale's Malady of Self," *Novel* 14, no. 1 (1980): 57–74.

22. Paul Valéry, *Leonardo-Poe-Mallarmé*, trans. Malcolm Cowley and James R. Lawler (Princeton, N.J.: Princeton University Press, 1972), 348.

23. Quoted in William James, *Partial Portraits* (1888; reprint, Ann Arbor: University of Michigan Press, 1970), 389. On Henry James's indebtedness to his brother's phenomenological insights, see Paul B. Armstrong, "Knowing in James: A Phenomenological View," *Novel* 12, no. 1 (1978): 5–20.

24. Edmund Wilson, "The Ambiguity of Henry James," in F. W. Dupee, ed., *The Question of Henry James* (London: Allan Wingate, n.d.), 195.

25. George Eliot, *Middlemarch*, ed. Gordon S. Haight (Boston: Houghton Mifflin Company, 1956), 578.

26. Joseph Conrad, "Henry James: An Appreciation," *North American Review* 180, no. 578 (1905): 107. Conrad's interpretation has become the generally accepted one, but I would argue that despite the balance of his assessment, it is overly optimistic about Milly's ability to free herself.

EPILOGUE

1. Donald Fanger, *Dostoevsky and Romantic Realism* (Chicago: University of Chicago Press, 1965), 31.

2. On degeneration, see Sander Gilman, ed., *Degeneration* (New York: Columbia University Press, 1985); on the chloroform controversy, see Mary Poovey, *Uneven Developments* (Chicago: University of Chicago Press, 1988); on hysteria, see D. English and B. Ehrenreich, *Complaints and Disorders* (Old Westbury, N.Y.: Feminist Press, 1973). Among the many recent feminist exposures of the misogyny inherent in the medical treatment of women, the most effective are Elaine Showalter, *The Female Malady* (New York: Pantheon, 1985); Ludmilla Jordanova, *Sexual Visions* (London: Harvester Wheatsheaf, 1989); and Cynthia Eagle Russett, *Sexual Science* (Cambridge, Mass.: Harvard University Press, 1989).

3. Thus, for example, Londa Schiebinger frames her excellent discussion of the history of medical anatomies of the female body with the thesis that medicine generated a "biology of incommensurability" to defend "otherwise indefensible social practices" that subordinated women: "wherever boundaries were threatened," Schiebinger writes, anatomical "arguments for fundamental sexual differences were shoved into the breach." See "Skeletons in the Closet: The First Illustrations of the Female Skeleton in Nineteenth-Century Anatomy," *Representations* 14 (Spring 1986): 18–19. As Russett points out, the view that biological theories of gender difference were a "weapon" invented in response to the threat posed by educated women does not adequately account for the intensity with which difference is pounced on in Victorian science, which must stem to some extent from the scientific method prevalent at that time. See Russett, *Sexual Science* 191. Russett's analysis of this method, although probably accurate in describing the methods employed by biological scientists when speaking about women, does not begin adequately to characterize the complexity of either the methods of clinical medicine (which flourishes in the period just before the one Russett treats) or the methods of Victorian biologists in their nonmisogynistic work. More generally, focusing on the ways in which science contributes to the sustaining of an already constituted difference runs the risk of blinding one to the ways in which science may be

articulating not differences but plural differentiations—not only between women and men but among a constellation of pathologized subjects: hypochondriacs, male hysterics, lust murderers, sadists, homosexuals, lesbians, and so on. For a spirited defense of the importance of difference, see Sander Gilman, *Difference and Pathology* (Ithaca, N.Y.: Cornell University Press, 1985).

4. The Althusserian notion of relative autonomy might serve to identify the relation between medicine as discourse and medicine as ideology, if that notion were not so deeply contaminated by totalizing tendencies among those who invoke it. A discursive system is neither homologous with, nor a superstructural "transcoding" of, either ideologemes or an economic system. As I shall go on to explain, however, this is not to say that discursive systems are unsituated either ideologically or materially, but only to argue for the importance of recognizing that medicine is situated discursively as well (and therefore exerts a power in that discursive situation that is distinctive from the power of ideology or of material expropriation).

5. Cf. Jan Goldstein, "The Uses of Male Hysteria," *Representations* 34 (Spring 1991): 134–65 for a broader interpretation of the gender complexities involved in the self-appropriation of hysteria by male writers and the medical collusion in this phenomenon.

6. Cf. M. Jeanne Peterson, "Dr. Acton's Enemy: Medicine, Sex, and Society in Victorian England," *Victorian Studies* 29, no. 4 (1986): 569–90.

7. Sir James Paget, *Lectures on Surgical Pathology* (Philadelphia: Lindsay and Blakiston, 1860; 2d American edition).

8. Even where a terminology is massively invoked, of course, there is no guarantee that it is discursively functional. In the mouth of a character like Homais in *Madame Bovary*, for instance, medical language's discursive authority is disqualified.

9. Cf. Annette Kolodny, *The Lay of the Land* (Chapel Hill: University of North Carolina Press, 1975); Eve Kosofsky Sedgwick, "Across Gender, Across Sexuality: Willa Cather and Others," *South Atlantic Quarterly* 88, no. 1 (Winter 1989): 55. Sedgwick correctly warns that "to fail to analyze such nominally ungendered constructs in gender terms can itself be a gravely tendentious move in the gender politics of reading" (55). But what is true of gender and sexuality also holds for pathology. To fail to analyze nominally unmedicalized constructs in medical terms—for instance, defining George Eliot's organicism as a political ideology without noting that it institutes a distinction between normal and pathological that is irreducible to class distinctions—is an equally tendentious and grave move in the (epistemic) politics of reading.

10. For the classic formulation of the politics of knowledge inherent in the imposition of a concept of the norm, see Georges Canguilhem, *On the Normal and the Pathological*, trans. Carolyn Fawcett (Boston, Mass.: D. Reidel, 1978).

11. Gustave Flaubert, *Oeuvres*, ed. Maurice Nadeau (Lausanne: Editions Rencontres, 1965), vol. 6, 260.

12. Nietzsche's work, in which the normal/pathological distinction becomes the basis for reevaluating all morals in physiological terms, marks the ultimate generalization of the medical view of man as "*the* sick animal." (Friedrich Nietzsche, *On the Genealogy of Morals*, ed. Walter Kaufmann [New York: Vin-

tage, 1967], 121.) Nietzsche in fact argues that philosophy itself should accept the medical viewpoint as at least as true as philosophy's own: "it is equally necessary to engage the interest of physiologists and doctors in these problems (of the value of existing valuations); it may be left to academic philosophers to act as advocates and mediators in this matter too, after they have on the whole succeeded in the past [*sic*] in transforming the originally so reserved and mistrustful relations between philosophy, physiology, and medicine into the most amicable and fruitful exchange" (55).

13. Said, *Beginnings*, 143–44.

14. Larson, *The Rise of Professionalism*. Larson's emphasis on the ideological features of what she calls "the professional model" makes her analysis of professionalism particularly valuable for my purposes. For more traditional sociological views of professionalism's ideology from an internalist and a culturalist perspective respectively, cf. W. J. Reader, *Professional Men* (London: Weidenfeld and Nicolson, 1966), and Burton Bledstein, *The Culture of Professionalism* (New York: Norton, 1976). For alternatives to Larson's professionalization hypothesis that expose different facets of the ideology of professionalism, see Andrew Abbott, *The System of Professions* (Chicago: University of Chicago Press, 1988), and Jeffrey Berlant, *Profession and Monopoly* (Berkeley and Los Angeles: University of California Press, 1975).

15. Cf. Andrew Abbott, *The System of Professions* (Chicago: University of Chicago Press, 1988).

16. Eliot, *Daniel Deronda*, 225. One way of drawing a preliminary distinction between the realistic novel and the novel of manners is by noting the difference in the urgency and range of claims for truth made by the writer in each genre. For instance, Dickens feels the need to assert his mastery of legal knowledge ("anything set forth in these pages concerning the Court of Chancery is substantially true, and within the truth"), and must appear willing to defend aggressively his assertion, as well as the even more hyperbolic assertion that spontaneous combustion is a fact. His own authority as a writer of fiction depends, it seems, upon that of the "authorities" he can adduce in support of these particular truth claims. Contrast Dickens's attitude toward the need for legitimating his truth claims with the attitude implied by Austen's allusion to "truth universally acknowledged." For Austen, the truth at stake is grounded not in scientificity but in communal consensus. Austen's confidence in the truth inherent in manners (even bad manners) has as its dark counterpart the timorousness of Trollope, a later novelist of manners for whom "important" questions are, as with Austen, matters of social codes rather than of facts, but who typically abandons the quest for mannered truth in favor of maintaining an avowedly insincere propriety: "I will not describe the ceremony [of Dr. Proudie's installation], as I do not precisely understand its nature. I am ignorant whether a bishop be chaired like a member of parliament, or carried in a gilt coach like a lord mayor, or sworn in like a justice of peace, or introduced like a peer to the upper house, or led between two brethren like a knight of the garter; but I do know that every thing was properly done, and that nothing fit or becoming to a young bishop was omitted on the occasion" (*Barchester Towers* [New York: Doubleday, 1945], 18). Trollope's authority rests on what he

knows, but what he knows has no particular epistemic reference, only a cultural one, and even his cultural knowledge is debased—his is an "ignorant" expertise. Trollope's capacity to convert an acknowledged epistemic deficit into a form of literary authority is an extraordinary phenomenon that has not been adequately analyzed. To undertake such an analysis is beyond the scope of this book, but one can hypothesize that Trollope's authority must depend on the emergence of a readership for whom questions of manners constitute a sort of refuge from the demands of a world where questions of truth increasingly dominate cultural discussion.

17. On the oppositional structure of social types, see Lukács, *The Historical Novel*; on the ideologeme as the fundamental semiotic element of narrative, see Jameson, *The Political Unconscious*, 87.

18. On the affiliation of early realism with the authority of the legal apparatus to represent criminality, see Michel Foucault, "The Life of Infamous Men," in *Michel Foucault: Power, Truth, Strategy*, 76–91. On the contract/transgression model, see Tanner, *Adultery in the Novel*, 3–18. On the novel's affiliation, at its inception, with journalistic authority, see Lennard Davis, *Factual Fictions* (New York: Columbia University Press, 1983).

19. On the concept of constituent models for the various human sciences, see Michel Foucault, *The Order of Things* (New York: Vintage, 1970), 358.

20. The fact that these narrative principles are theoretically distinct does not preclude the possibility that one narrative structure may be mistaken for another as one reads. For example, *Madame Bovary* has been interpreted insistently—and as I have tried to show, mistakenly—as a novel of adultery whose authority derives from the interpretative model provided by contract and transgression.

21. For Bakhtin's views of realism as a "finalizing" literary mode, see *Problems of Dostoevsky's Poetics*, 57; on the various ways in which discourse may be stratified in the novel, see "Discourse in the Novel," in *The Dialogic Imagination: Four Essays*, trans. Caryl Emerson, ed. and trans. Michael Holquist, (Austin and London: University of Texas Press, 1981), 259–422.

22. The most suggestive theoretical work on this general problematic has been done by Marxists, who have drawn on Marx's own conceptualization of the distinction between Balzac's overtly represented reactionary politics and the putatively more progressive ideological outlook his realism forges. See Fredric Jameson, "The Ideology of the Text," *Salmagundi* 31, no. 2 (Fall 1975–Winter 1976): 204–46. Unfortunately, the axiomatic categories of Marxist analysis (class and ideology) cannot be straightforwardly transposed into the categories of archaeological analysis (discourse and authority). For a structuralist attempt to begin theorizing the issues involved, see Philippe Hamon, "Du savoir dans le texte," *Revue des Sciences Humaines* 40, no. 160 (October–December 1975): 489–99.

23. On the function of homology within new historicism, see Fredric Jameson, *Postmodernism* (Durham, N.C.: Duke University Press, 1991), 181–216. Stephen Greenblatt describes his historicizing method as "swerving" in his influential *Shakespearean Negotiations* (Berkeley and Los Angeles: University of California Press, 1988), 72–73.

24. That need not have been the case. Medicine—or another discourse we picked—might well have turned out to be relatively peripheral to the formal, epistemological, or ideological concerns of the realist novel. But even then these concerns could be clarified by an analysis of how it is that they manage to make a given discourse peripheral.

INDEX

Abbott, Andrew, 183
Acton, William, 175, 177, 178
Adam Bede (Eliot), 103–4
Althusser, Louis, 223n. 4
anatomy
—microscopic anatomy, 142–43
—pathological anatomy, xvi, 52, 61, 151; concept of sensitivity in, 25–28; diagnostic implications of, 33–35; double life of self in, 26, 106–8; quest for primitive tissue in, 87–89, 95–99; status of truth in 41–43. *See also* Bichat
anti-professionalism, 77. *See also* professionalism
Arac, Jonathan, xi
archaeological analysis, distinguished from ideological analysis, 18–19, 44–45, 137–42, 175–77. *See also* discourse; literary history
archive, delimitation of, xv-xvii; scientific, 9
Aristotle, 13
asylum, utopian space of, 64. *See also* psychiatry
Auerbach, Erich, xii, 48, 51, 134, 190
Augustine, *Confessions*, 93–94
Austen, Jane, 84, 224n.16
author, physician as figure of, xvi-xvii, 14, 39–43, 77, 88, 156, 160–61, 185, 189
authority, xiii-xiv, xvii
—literary authority, xiv, xvii, 150, 164, 183–89; in James, 165
—medical authority, xiii, xvii; bases of, 180–82; challenges to, 21–23, 98–102, 141–43, 149, 181–83, 186; as literary theme, 184; as structuring principle of narrative, 185–86; professional features of, 67, 78
—professional authority, 85; charismatic element of 69–78; strategies for legitimating, 73–78
autobiography, disarticulated, 41
autonomy, professional: economic basis of, 70; of medicine, 89; writers' and psychiatrists' desire for, 69–77. *See also* professionalism
"Avant-Propos" (Balzac), 49–50, 67

Bakhtin, Mikhail, xi, 190, 221n.14
Balzac, Honoré de, xi, xiii-xiv, xvii, 6, 8, 10, 14, 20, 33, 43, 46–83, 103, 120–23, 129, 134, 146, 148, 150, 153–54, 159–67, 175, 179, 183, 188–90, 193n. 3; compared with Flaubert, 46–47, 84–87; etiology of passions in, 61–63; medical paternalism in, 65–68; professional project of, 72–78; professional vocation in, 78–83; realism of, 48–49; representation in, 75–76, 120–23; social totality in, 57–60; typification in, 49–47; utopia in, 63–65. Works: "Avant-Propos," 49–50, 67; *La Cousine Bette*, 60; *The Curé of Tours*, 53; *Eugènie Grandet*, 46, 56–57, 68; *Illusions perdues*, 46, 72, 127, 184, 187; "L'Interdiction," 62; *Louis Lambert*, 46, 62; *Le médecin de campagne*, 46–47, 55, 58, 64, 77–82, 86–87, 145, 155–56, 185, 151; *La messe de l'athée*, 55; *Monograph on the Paris Press*, 44; *La peau de chagrin*, 62; *Le Père Goriot*, 46, 54, 57, 81; *La recherche de l'absolu*, 62; *Une ténébreuse affaire*, 54; *Ursule Mirouet*, 54–55
Barchester Towers (Trollope), 224n.16
Barth, John, 11
Barthes, Roland, 15, 33, 48, 78–79, 131–32, 145
Baudelaire, Charles, 16, 18, 24
Bell, Joseph, 142
Benjamin, Walter, 78
Benn, Gottfried, *Gehirne*, 161
Bennett, Arnold, 150, 188; *Clayhanger*, 152; *Old Wives' Tale*, 152; *Riceyman Steps*, xv, 152–57
Bentham, Jeremy, 41
Benveniste, Emile, 41, 201n.59
Bernard, Claude, xiv, 14, 97, 123–29, 140
bêtise, 19–23, 90
Bichat, Xavier, xvi, 10, 19, 190; compared with Claude Bernard, 124, 127; concept of sensitivity in, 25–28, 61, 169; contribution to phrenology of, 52; diagnostic implications of, 33–35; double life of self in, 26, 106–8, 159; in *Madame Bovary*, 37–38, 41–43; in *Middlemarch*,